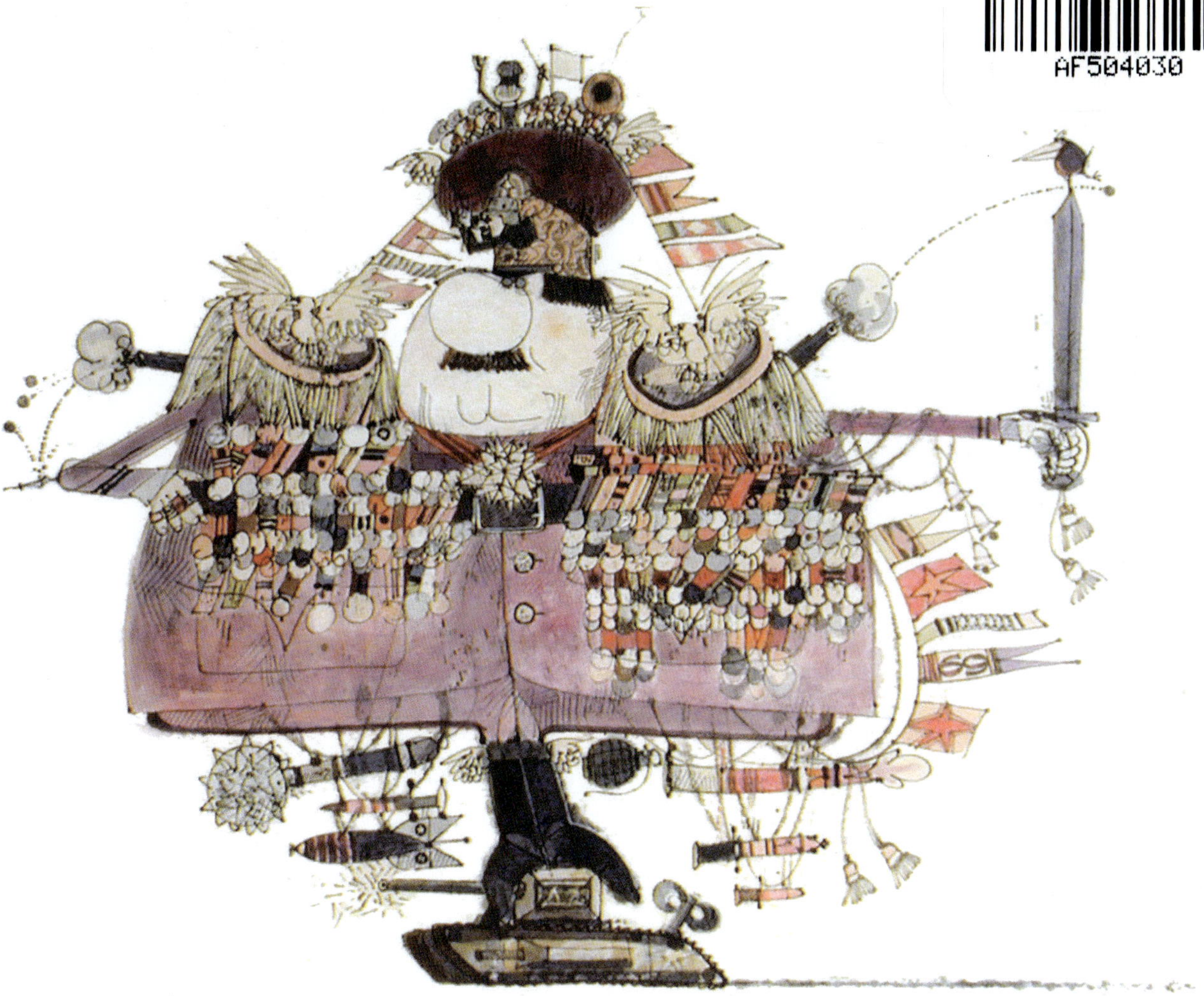

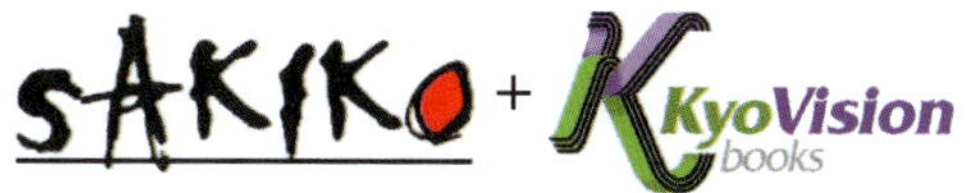

DONALD SILVERSTEIN

... a satirical illustrator

SAKIKO + KyoVision books

Compiled by Sakiko Silverstein / Composed by Kyo Takahashi

"DONALD SILVERSTEIN ... *a Satirical Illustrator*"
Copyright@2005 Sakiko Silverstein:
Published by Sakiko Silverstein+KyoVision Books, 155 W. 68th Street, New York, NY 10023

This book is composed by Kyo Takahashi, KyoVision. Original art were digitized, optimized, and color corrected by KyoVision, Roscommon, Michigan.

For more information regarding Don Silverstein's art and illustrations, please contact:
Sakiko@gallerySakiko.com and visit www.DonSilverstein.com

Library of Congress catalog number: 2013948548
ISBN 978-0-9816598-6-2 • 0-9816598-6-1
First Edition, 2013

• illustrator – illustration – art – artist – Donald Silverstein – Don Silverstein

This book of
Donald Silverstein's illustrations
is dedicated to
his family, friends, art lovers, publishers, and whoever loves his art
without knowing who the heck the artist was.

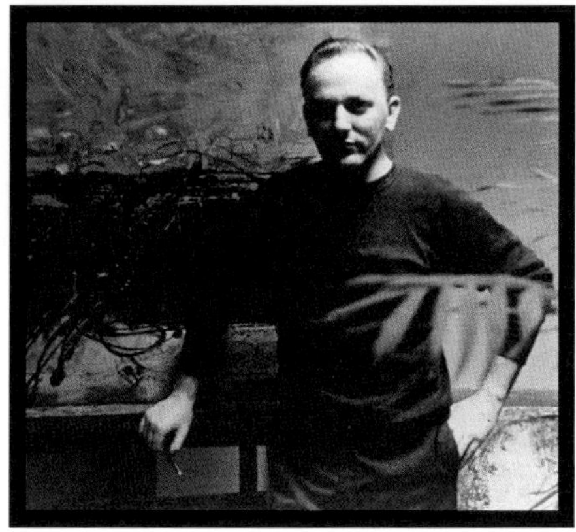

Donald Silverstein: circa 1960

CONTENTS

I

Who the heck is
Donald Silverstein?

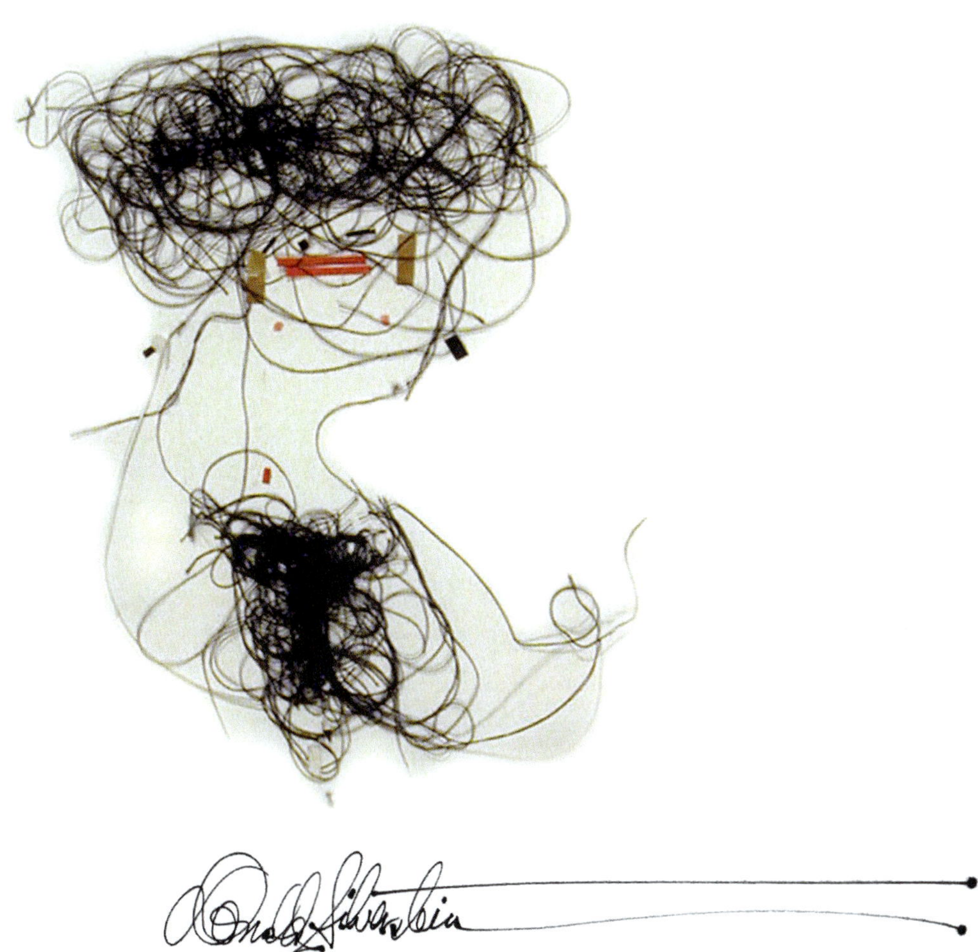

Donald Silverstein
...a satirical illustrator

"**I** was born in a Wilkes-Barre coal mine, in Pennsylvania in 1932. My great childhood joy was getting rescued every year by the Coast Guard during the annual spring floods," recalls artist Donald Silverstein of his early years.

In 1949, while attending The Society of Arts and Crafts in Detroit *(presently, the College for Creative Studies),* Donald worked for an art studio, Allied Artists. Here Donald acquired and developed his professional skills. After finishing two years service for the US Army in Alaska, he worked for art studios — New Center Stuudios, and MDM Studios for two more years. *(For details of his activities during these period, see Harry Borgman's "Remembering Donald Silverstein" on page 76.)*

He then moved to London where he freelanced for advertising agencies and book publishers. Donald moved to New York where he illustrated for advertising agencies, and publishing companies *(TV*

Guide, Pan American magazine, and children's books for McMillan). He won awards for advertising illustrations, and book illustrations, including a prestigious award from the Society of Illustrators, New York *(page 58~59).*

Subsequently, Donald Silverstein concentrated on creating fine art. Both his illustrations and fine art combine gesture and geometry to produce a dynamic effect. Stream lines and geometrical lines are intertwined creating a unique characteristic effect.

Donald traveled and exhibited widely, living ten years in Japan. His life in Japan strengthened the calligraphic aspects of his work. As shown in his "fine art" book, Donald's works were exhibited at the Detroit Institute of Art, the Museum, in Michigan.

Donald Silverstein's art is exhibited at galleries in Tokyo, New York, and Paris. Donald was a prolific artist in both art and illustrations.

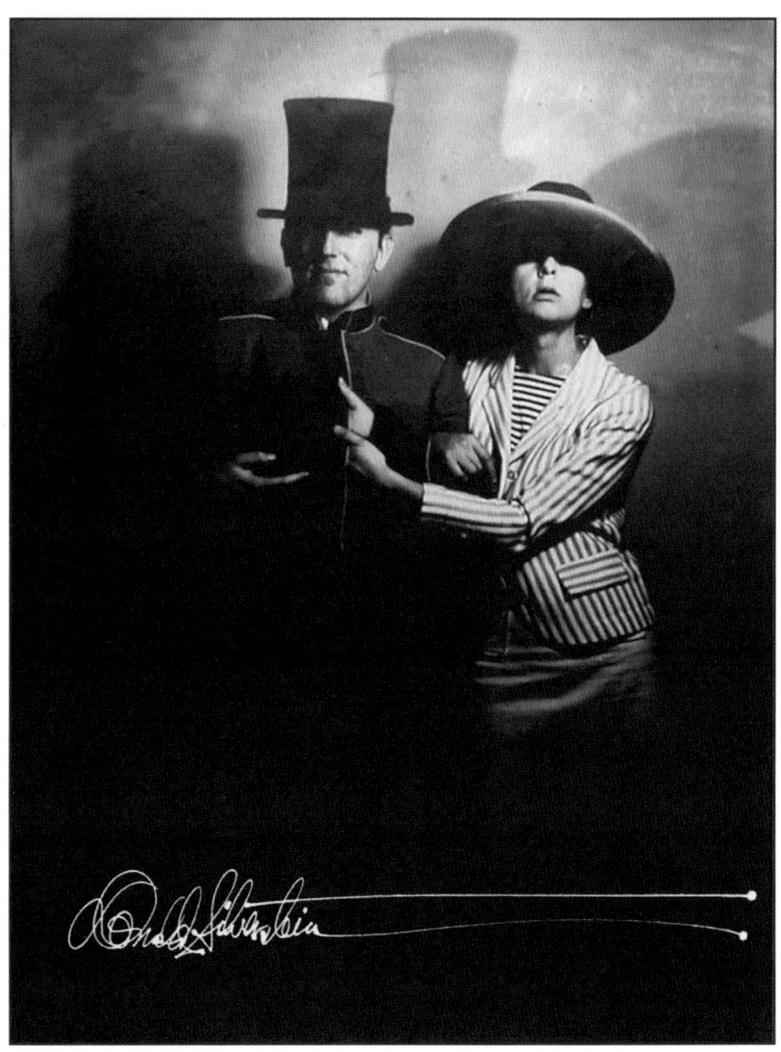

P.S. I

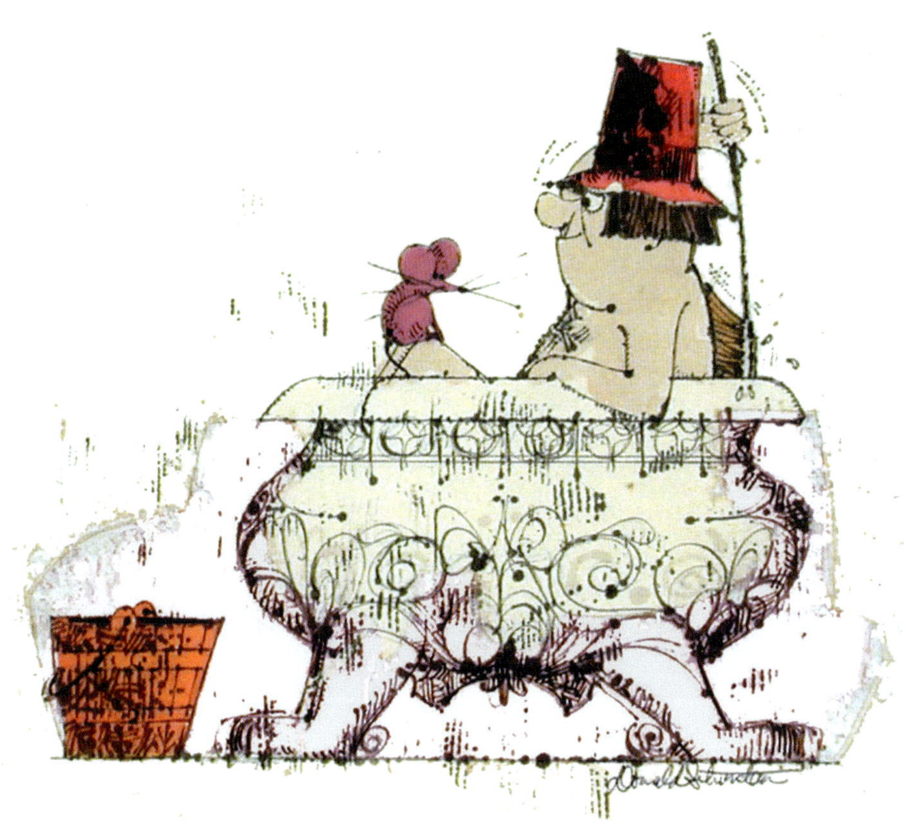

It's nice to have company, whoever it might be.

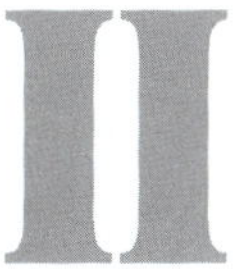

II

Donald,
the Flying Ace

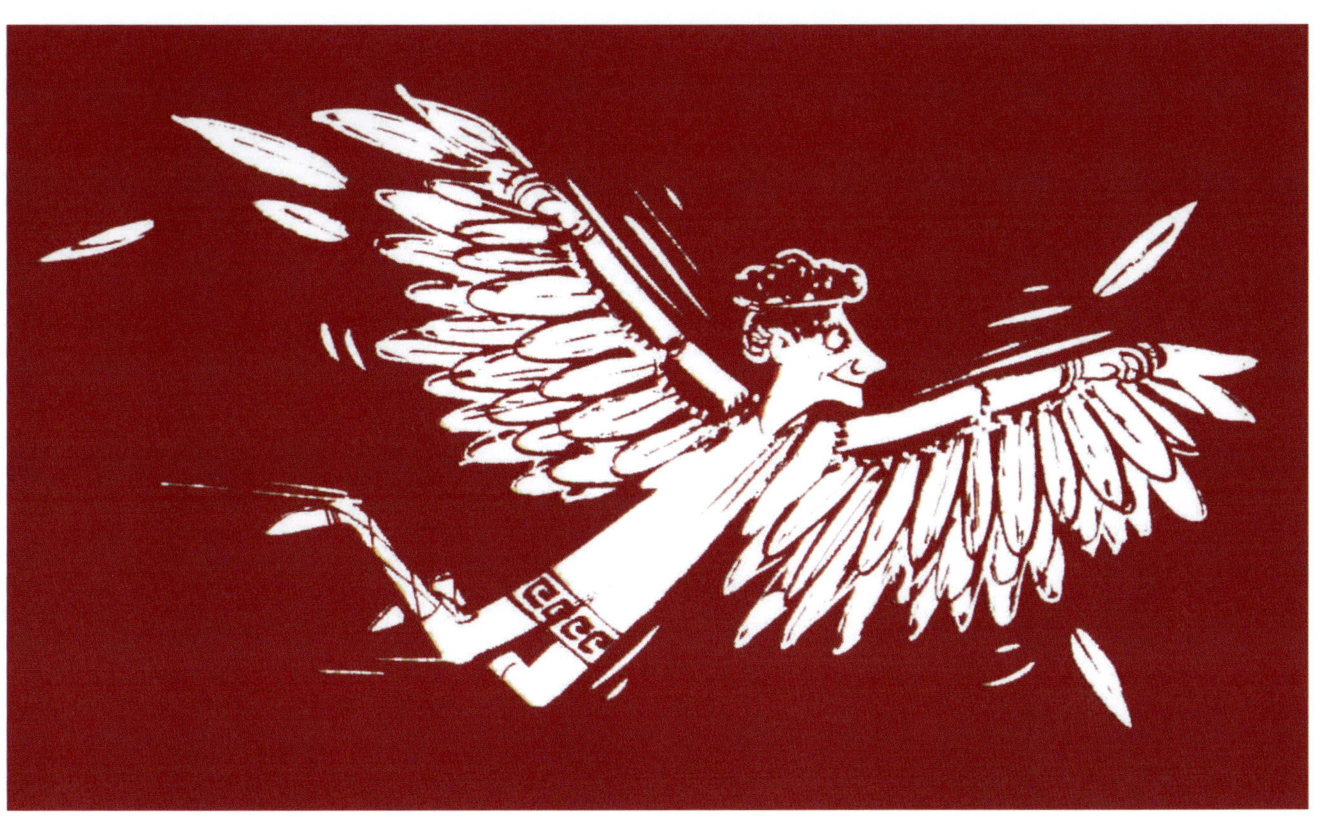

You remember Icarus.* He had a great scheme, a real break-
through in the state of the art. He figured he and his father
could fly by slapping together a few feathers and flapping away.

Only trouble was, he got hold of a bad batch of wax and
ended up inventing the backward four-and-a-half somersault with
a triple twist. If only he'd devoted his time to developing epoxy
glue, he'd have made the Wright Brothers look like buggy whip
manufacturers in the horseless carriage age.

*Icarus: A character in the Greek mythology.

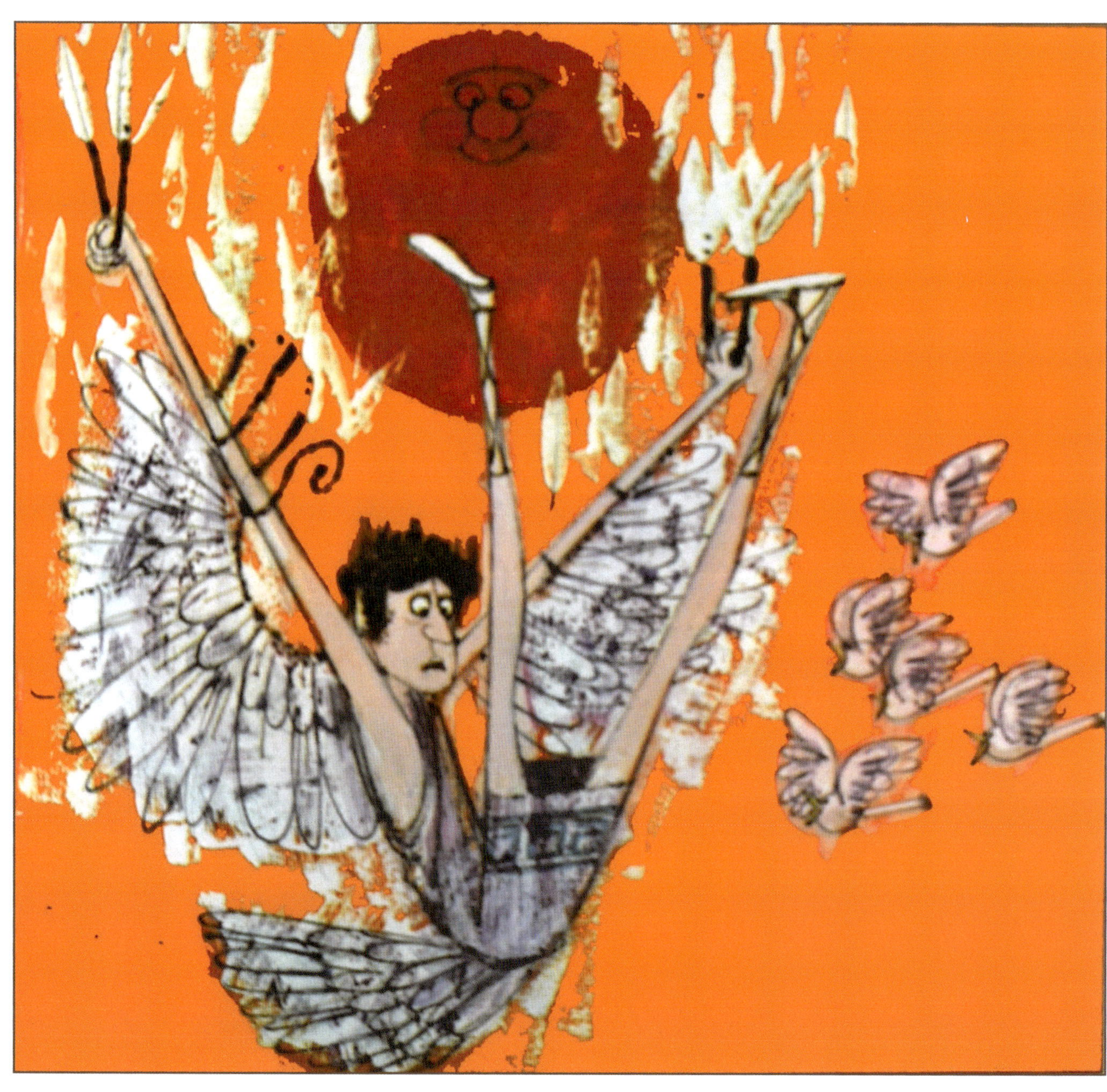

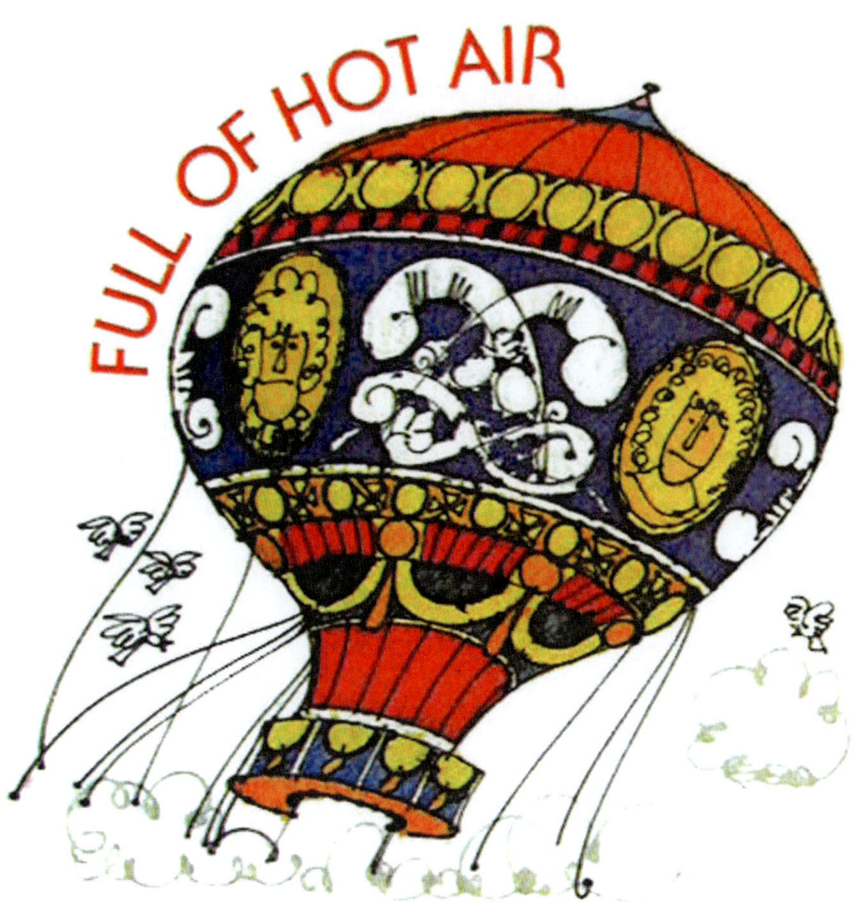

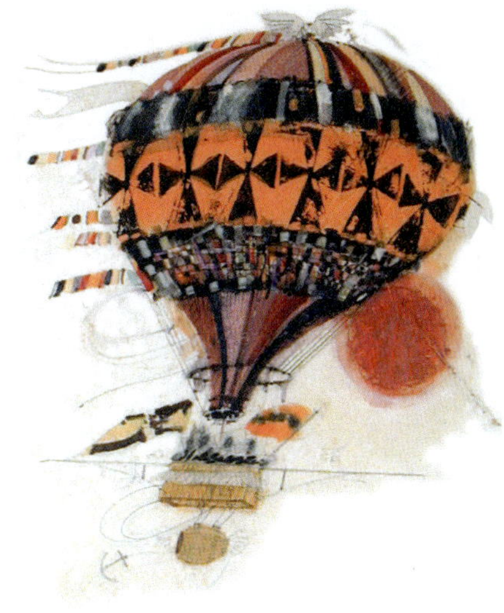

From Feather to Balloon

Floating through the air on a basket seems like a peaceful way to pass some time. But if you're counting on hot air to keep you up, you may not find it so peaceful. The first people to fly balloons had a tough time keeping the flights safe and comfortable.

A balloon is an airtight bag that is filled with gas. If the gas is lighter than the surrounding air, the balloon rises. It was this simple principle that enabled us at last to fulfill an age-old dream and fly through the air.

A French paper manufacture, Joseph Montgolfier, invented the balloon. One day in 1782, as he sat by his fireplace and watched the smoke, he mused on the possibility of an air assault for his country lifting their troops by the same force that was lifting the smoke from the fire. On December 14, assisted by his brother, the balloon was lifted so fast that they lost control of their craft on its very first flight. It was destroyed after landing by the "indiscretion" of passerby.

But new balloons were made and finally, on December 1, 1783, Charles and one of the Robert brothers rose in a hydrogen balloon. They rode in a basket hung from the bottom and in about two hours they traveled twenty-five miles.

— From "The Look-It-Up Book of Transportation" by Bernice Kohn —

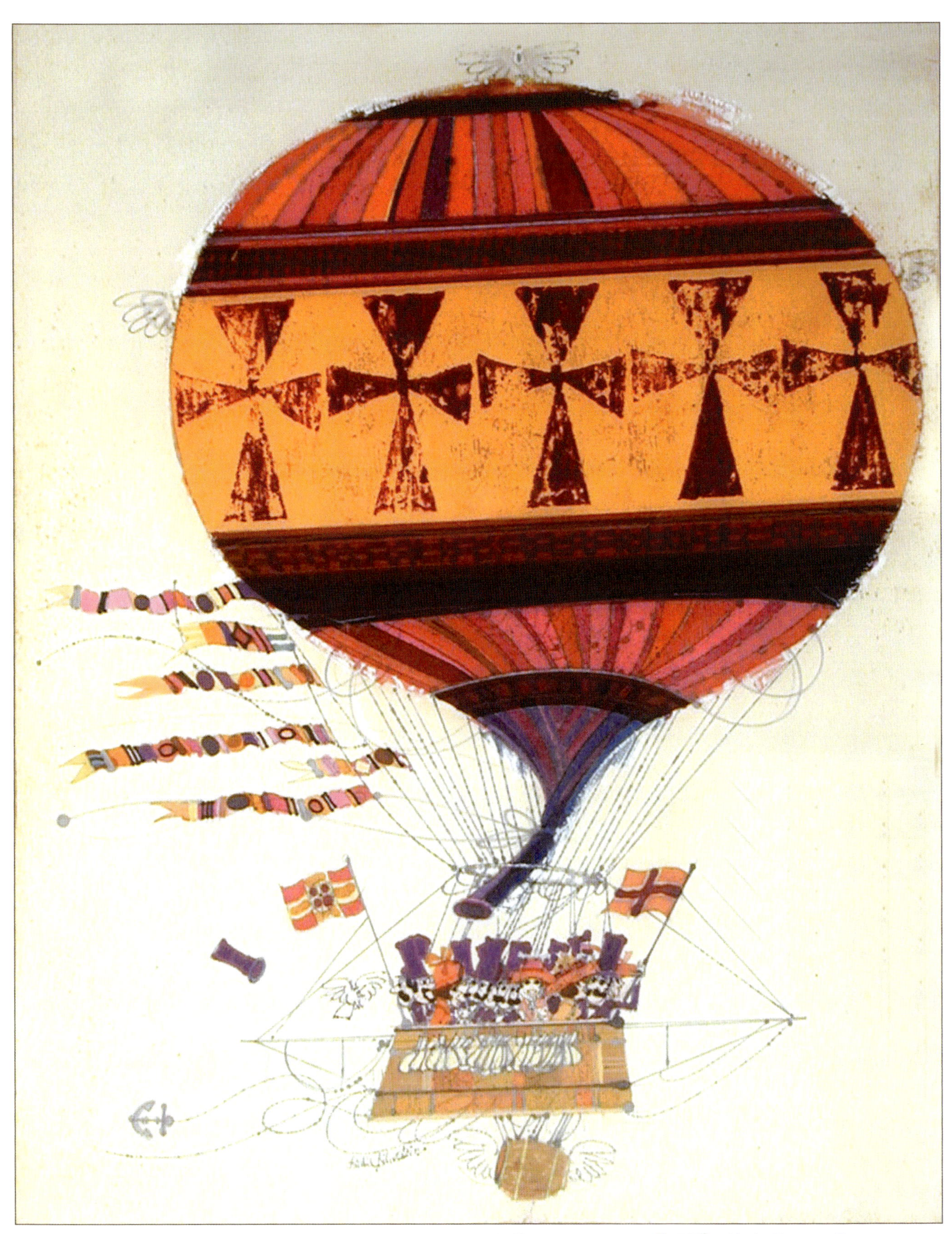

The Age of Flight has begun.

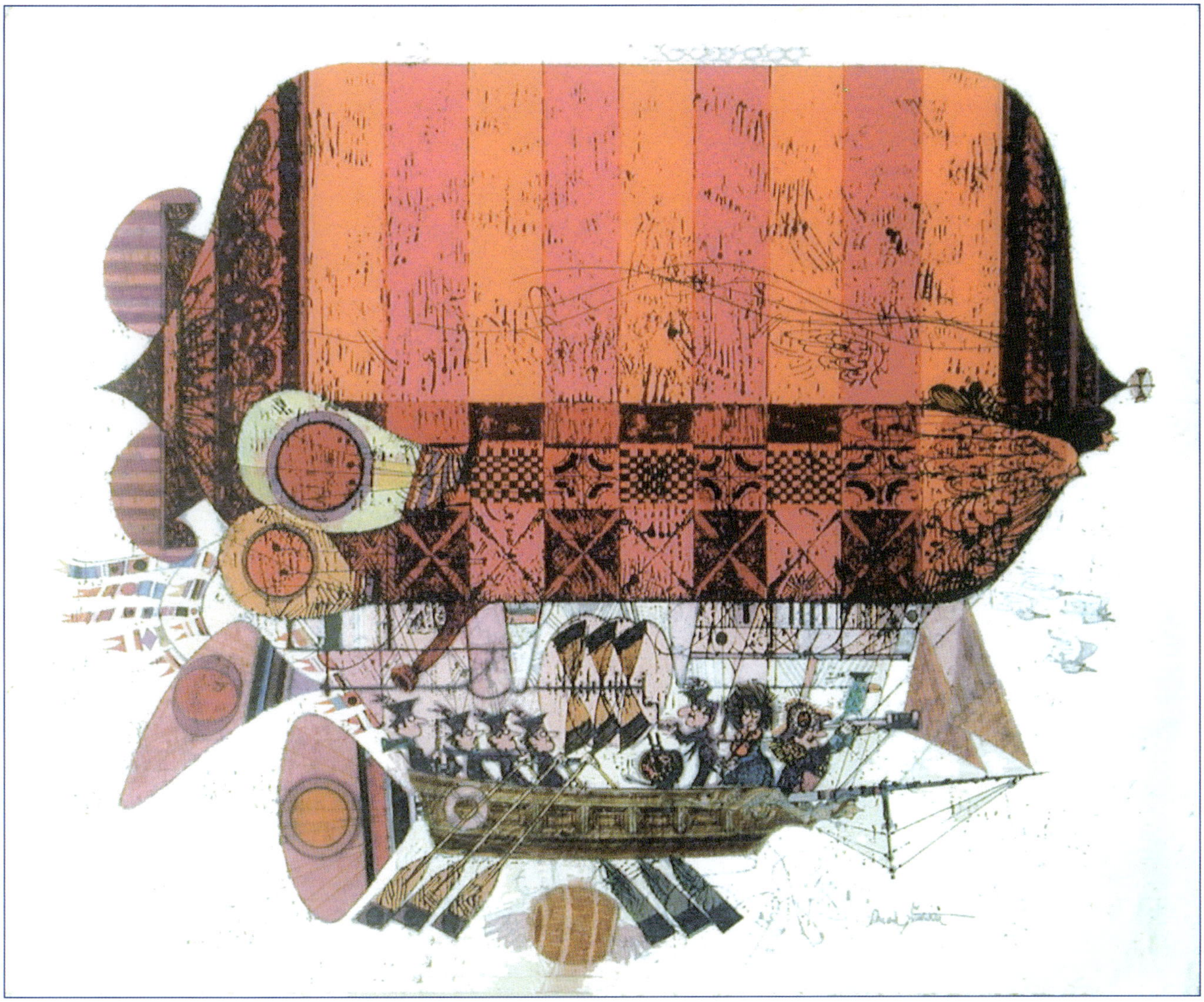

As more people wanted to float, the balloon grew larger.
However, the popularity of balloons diminished when the airplane was invented.

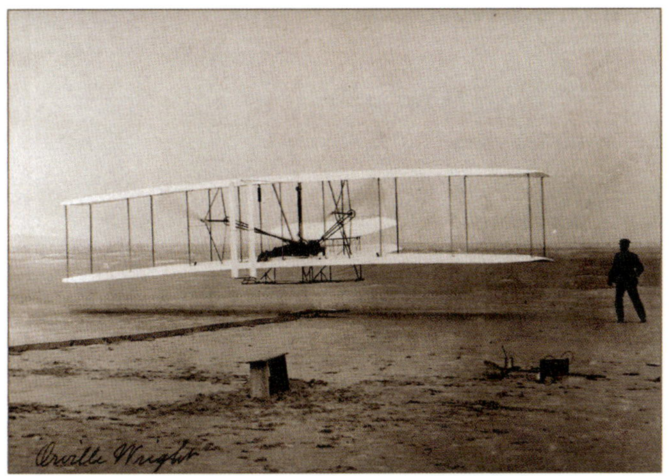

Orville and Wilber Wright realized their dream to fly.
December 17, 1903 in Kitty Hawk, North Carolina.

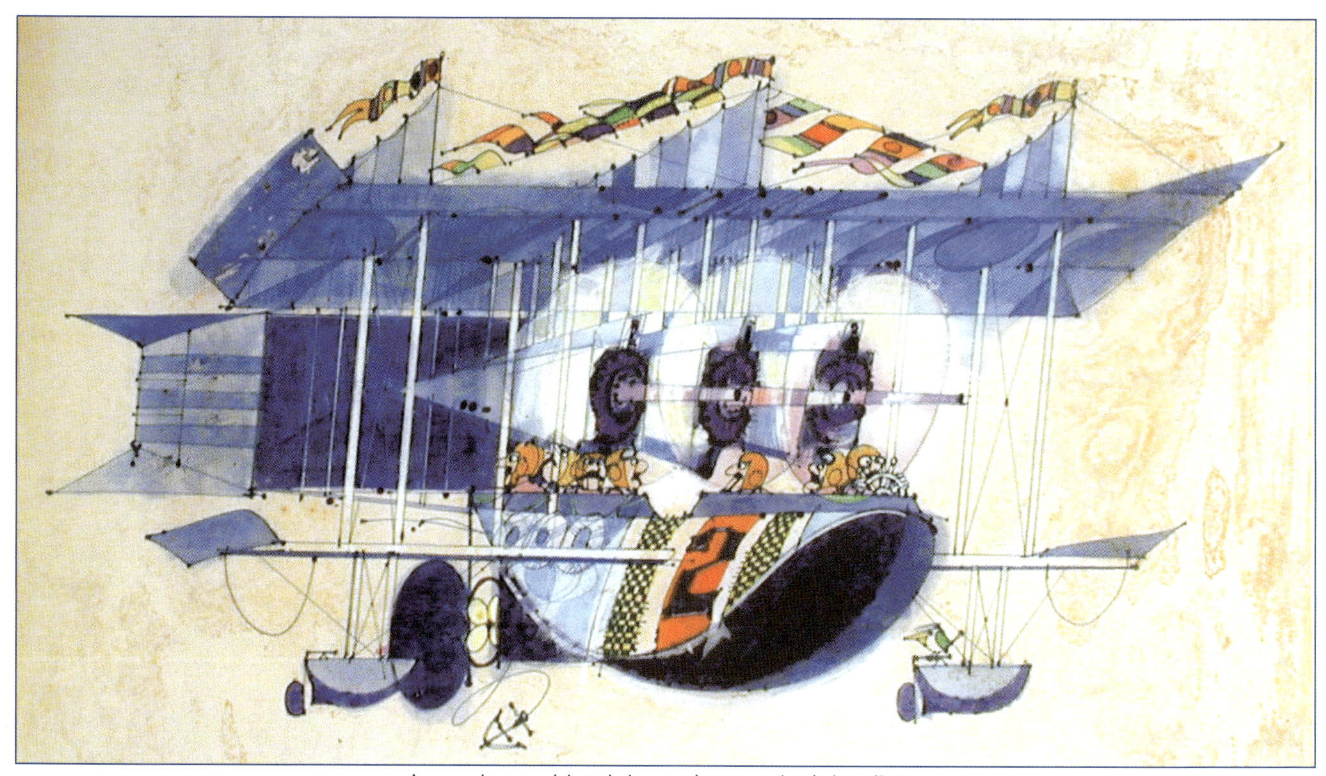

A seaplane with triple engines and triple pilots.

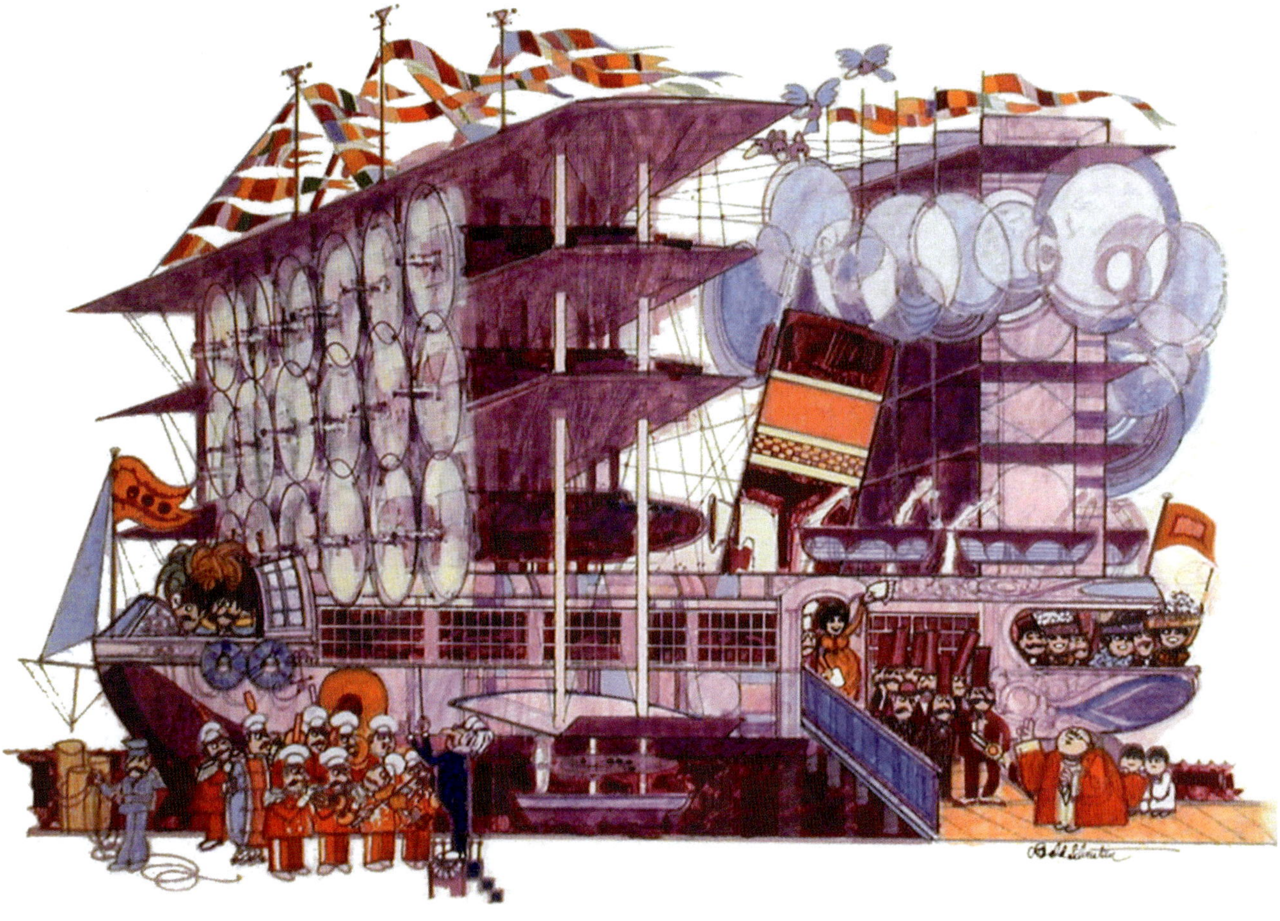

The bigger, the better.

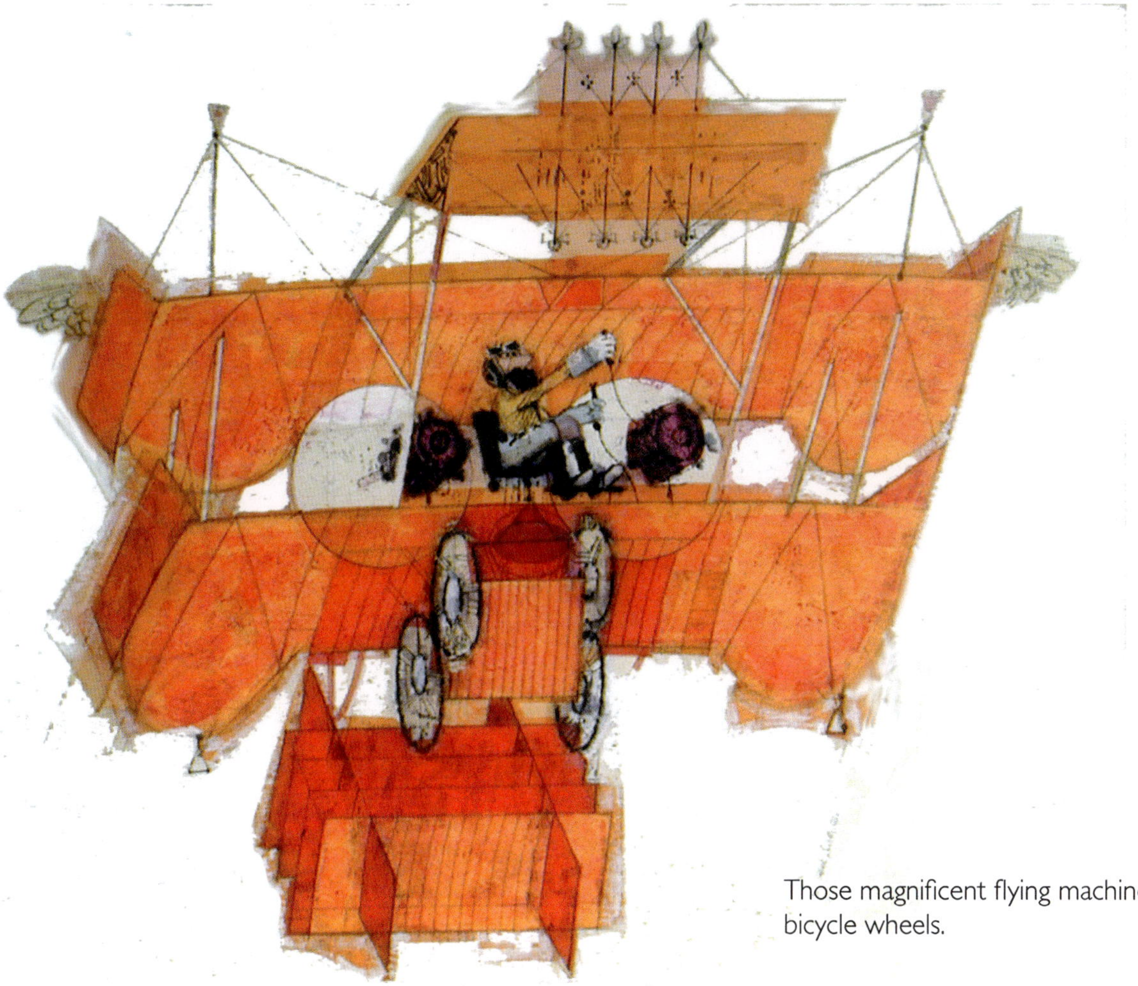

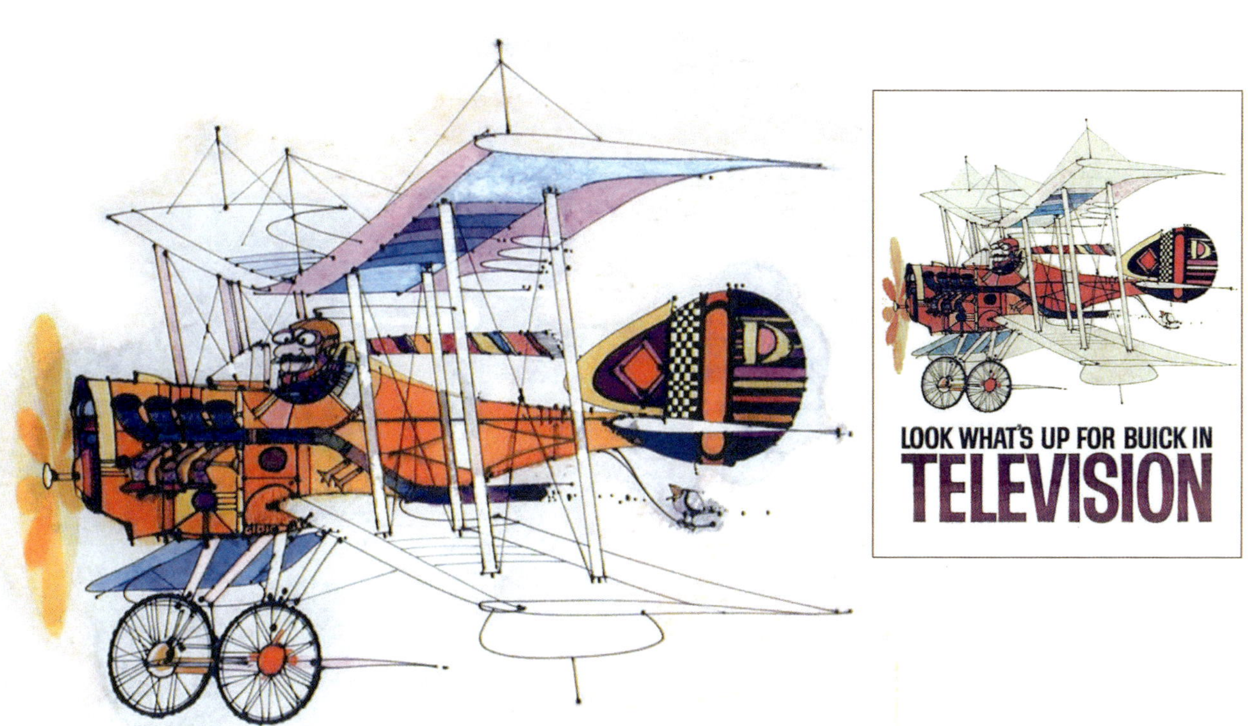

Those magnificent flying machines with bicycle wheels.

From Balloon to Wings

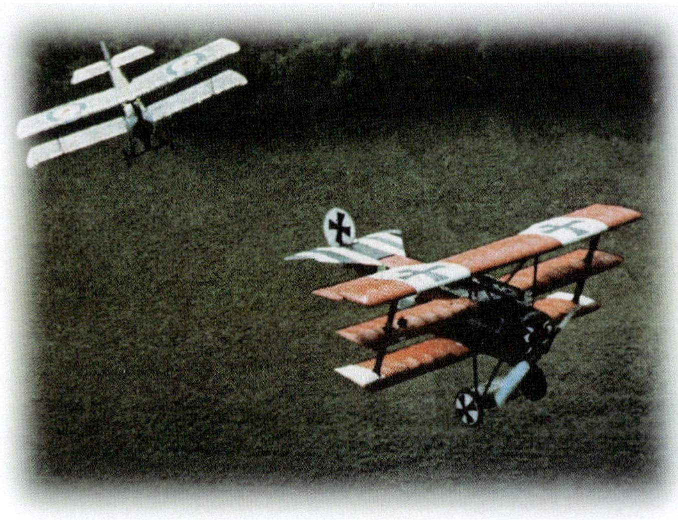

Cole Palen, an ex-flight mechanic assembled one of the world's largest private collection of antique planes. Spads, Sopwiths, Fokkers, and Nieuports, were all sheltered at his Old Rhinebeck Aerodrome, 100 miles north of New York City.

There, every Sunday afternoon between May and October, Palen and his pilot friends took whichever of the World War I planes that are in shape to fly, in a mock-combat air show that drew thousands of nostalgic and enthusiastic spectators.

In the show, Cole Palen was *"The Black Baron"* at the controls of the triple-winged Fokker D-7. At the finale of the show, the Baron gets shot down by the British Sopwiths, ending behind a veil of thick black smoke far out in the woods.

One day, Donald Silverstein was watching the show with breathless amazement and fascination.

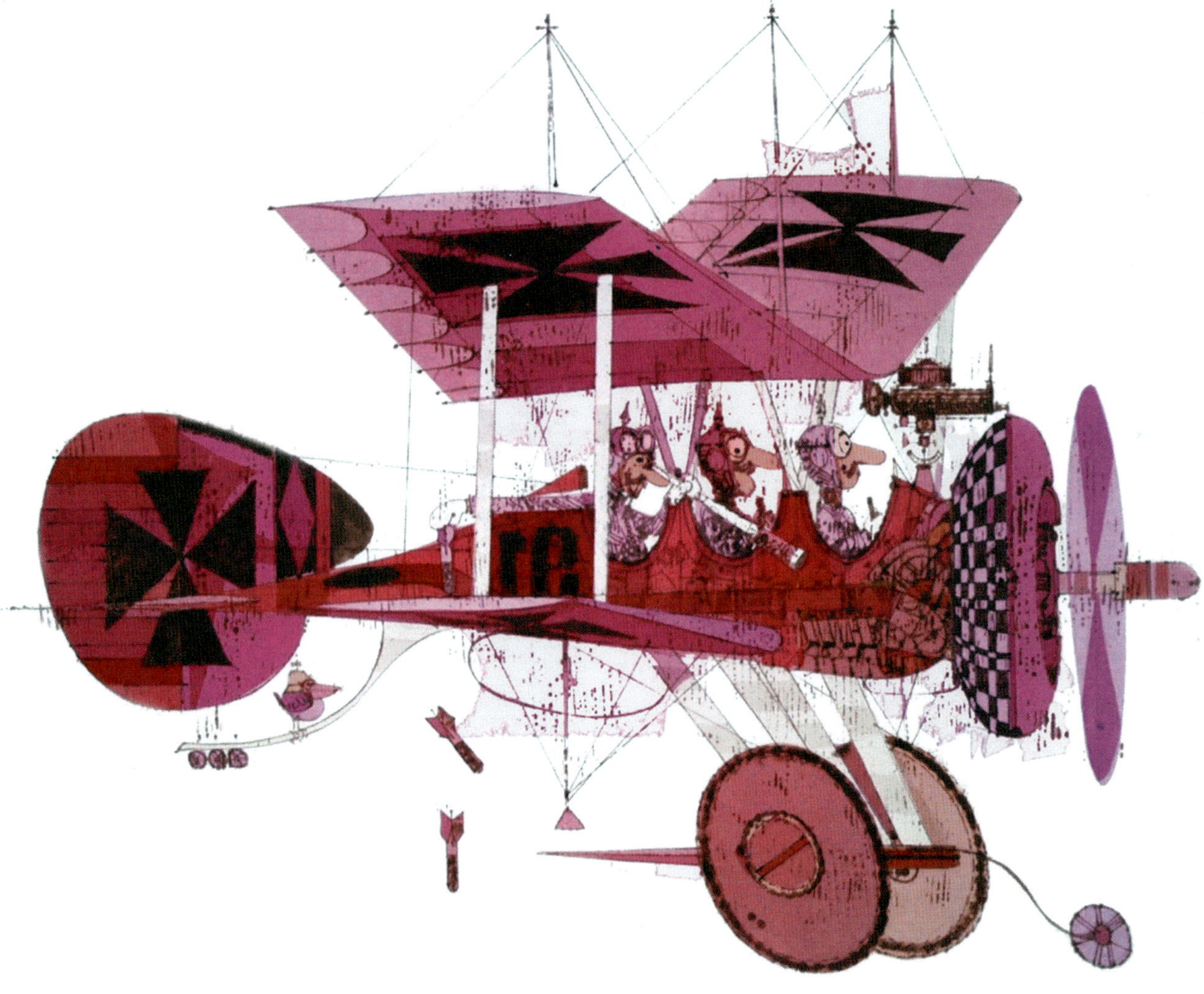

The War Up in the Air

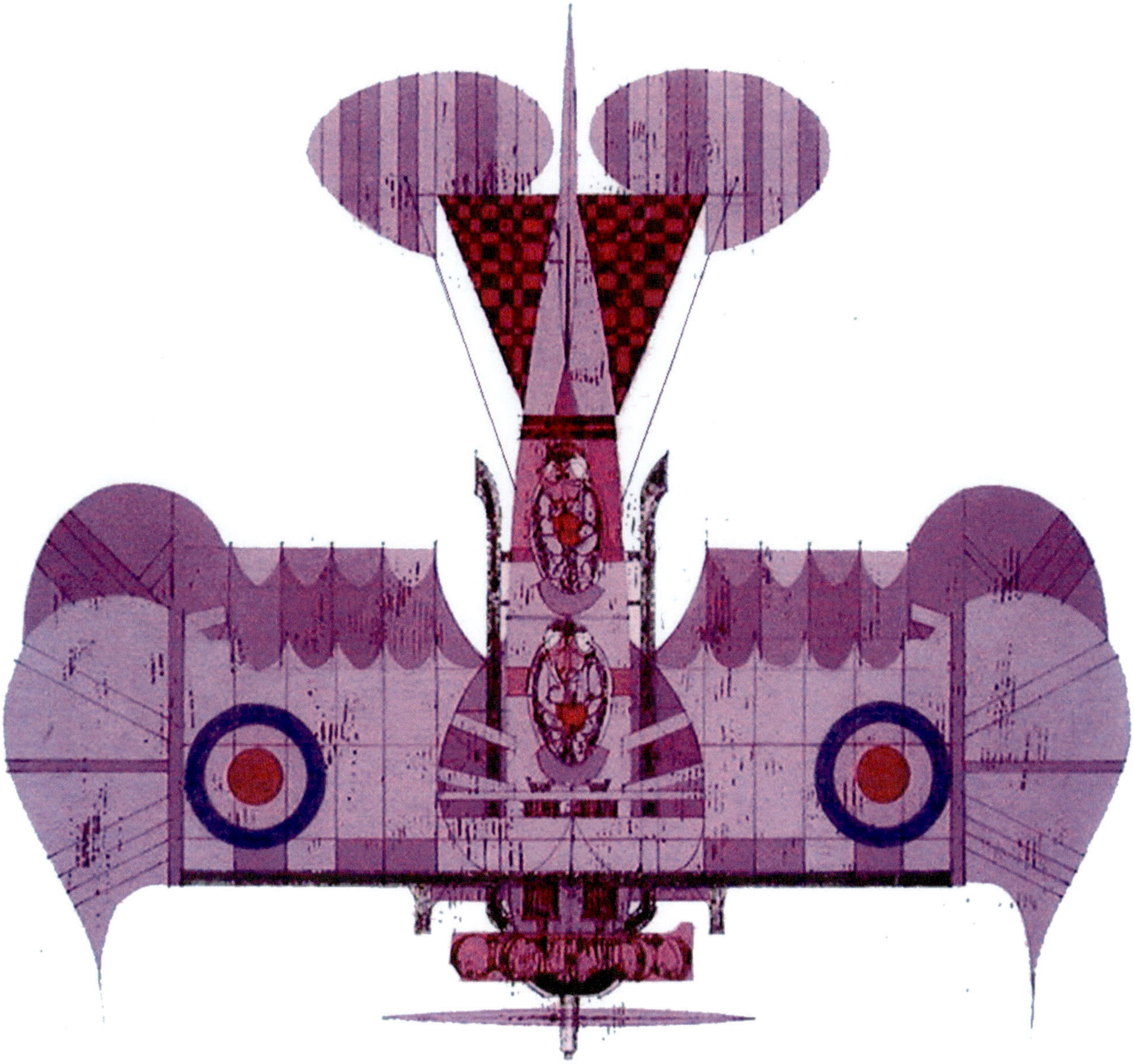

After the show, Donald bought more than a dozen postcards at the gift shop — all the same glossy print of the proudly posed *"Black Baron"* portrait. As soon as he was back to his studio, he began fund-raising, ***"Send me money, or I'll shoot you down…,"*** the same message on all the cards and mailed them out to everyone he could think of.

Responses to the cards were varied, many were his close friends. Nobody knows whether Donald found any success in his escapade.

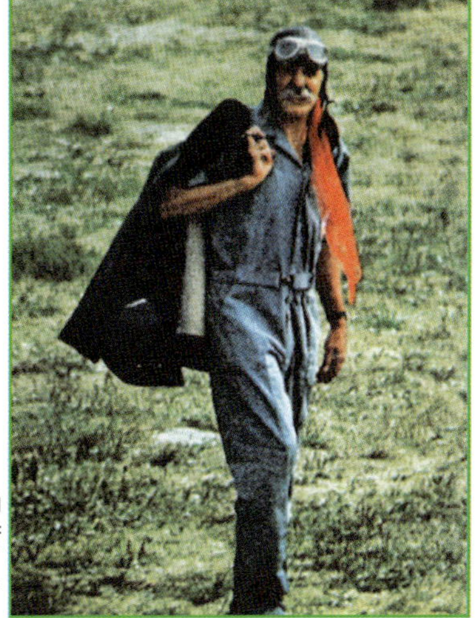

(*Photo on the right*) Dave Fox, the image of World War I "derring-do," is an IBM engineer who spent his Sundays with Cole Palen, demonstrating the incredible maneuverability of the Fokker D-7. Which he said was "the best plane of World War I." Fox was *not* on the postcard Donald mailed, but Cole Palen was .

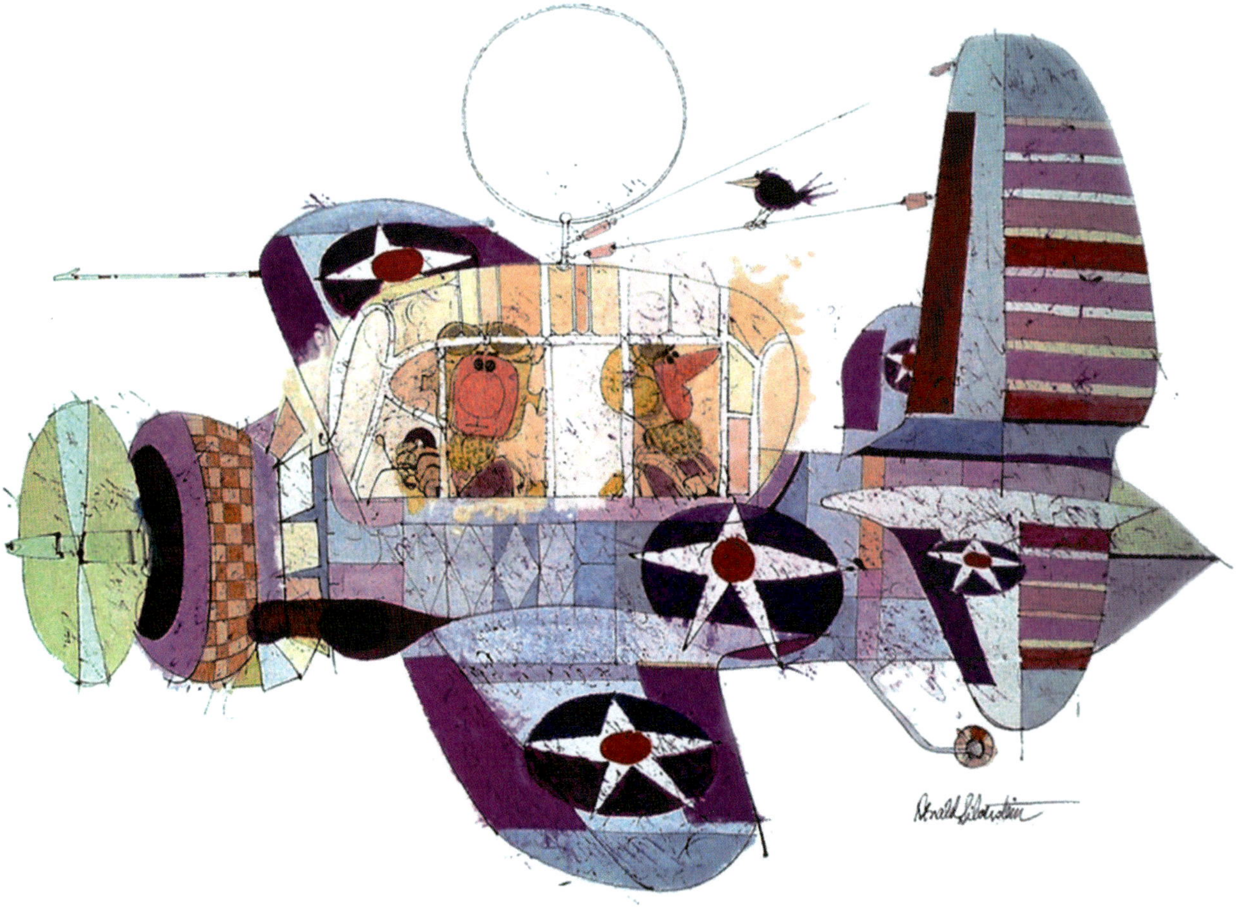

P.S. II

In the late 1960's, Donald drew an advanced jet plane *(below)*. His technique was strongly influenced by master illustrators, such as Bernie Fuchs, Ken Dallison, and Mark English.

However, it didn't last long, Donald quickly established his own style.

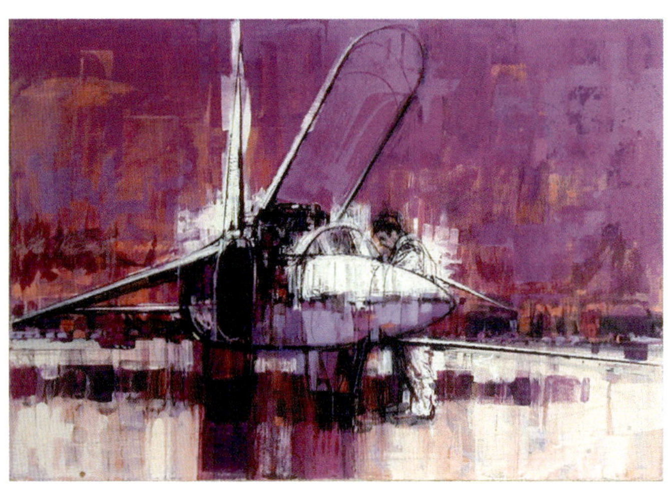

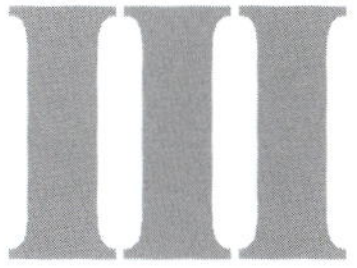

III

Around the World in Unlimited Days

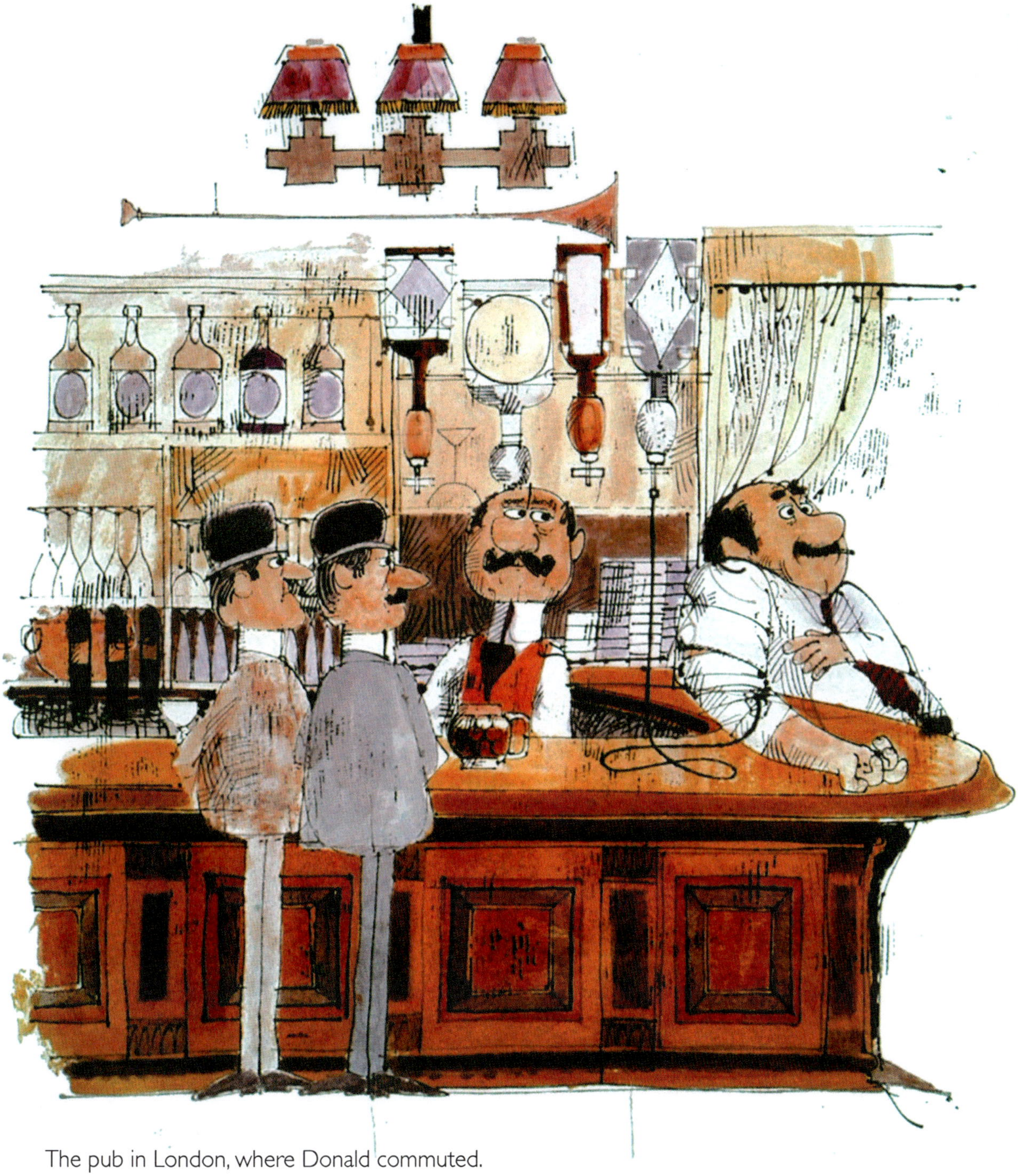

The pub in London, where Donald commuted.

Before I met Don, he was already a friend of my future husband, Laurence. They'd met in the Flask Pub in Flask Walk, London, where we now live, and where Don was living and working, during the "Swinging Sixties." Don had a Porsche flown in from America, which impressed everyone, as they were made just across the English Channel.

When I met Laurence, Don had returned to New York, but they had continued to correspond with each other. Don's letters were amazing, filled with drawings, asides, and attacks on the establishment; an incredible social comment on the America of the Sixties.

There was a lot of anger in them, which I found unsettling, I wasn't sure whether I liked Don or not. Little did I know that Laurence and I would end up as newly weds in New York, and that the first person I would meet there would be Don.

I fell in love with him immediately.

I was seriously moved by his work, and we shared a passion for music, both classical and jazz. *(He had a massive collection of Classical LPs and had actually seen Billy Holiday perform in the flesh!)*

His cartoons were unique in style, and his humor was rebellious, but his serious work was as serious as his cartoons were funny.

I recognized in his paintings that same spirit, the dry humor and the comment that I'd seen in his letters to Laurence, and in his cartoons.

Nothing demonstrates this more than his ability to take the components of the latest technology and force them into his paintings, forcing them to submit to Art... The Superior Form.

As mentor and teacher, Don has been one of the biggest artistic influences in my life.

(signed)

Pat Hutchins, *author*

    London

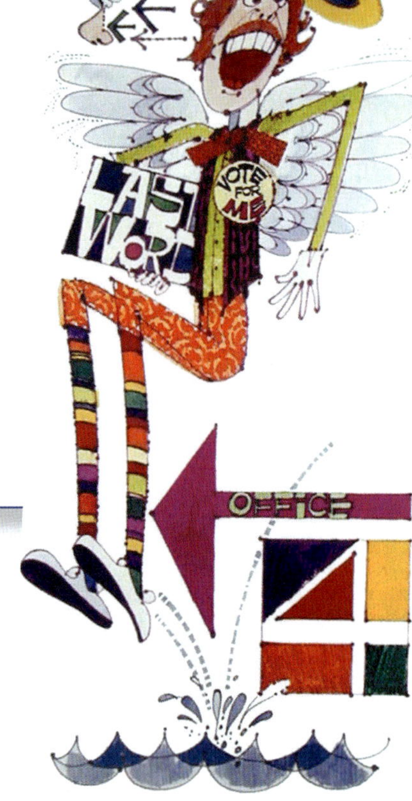

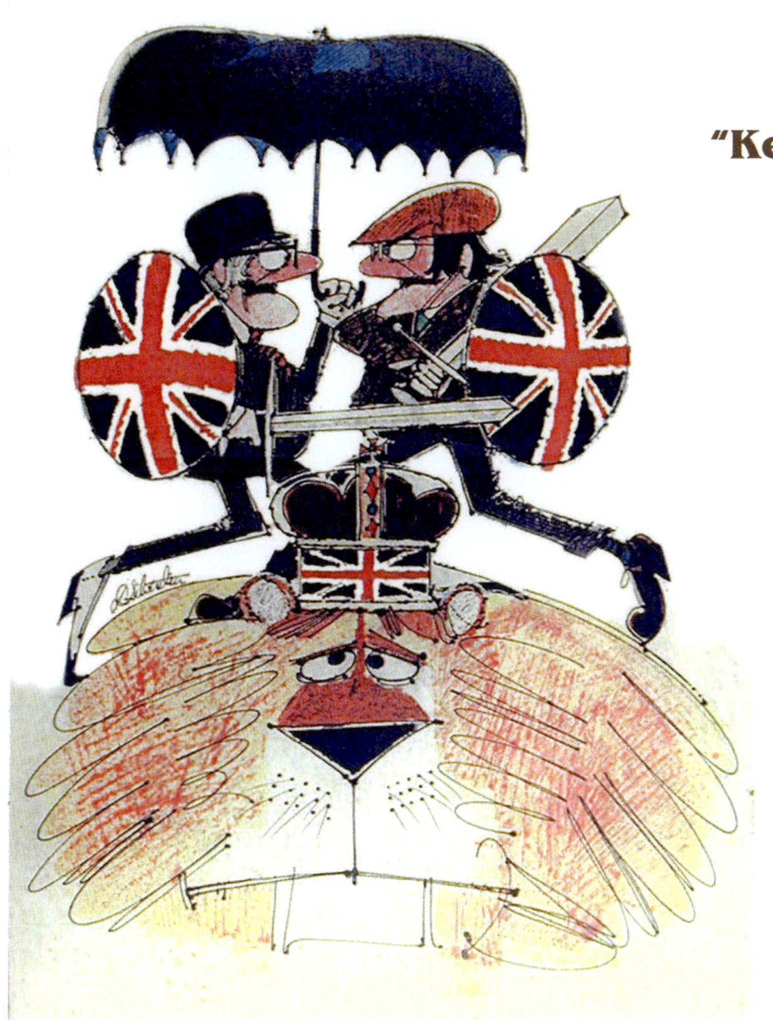

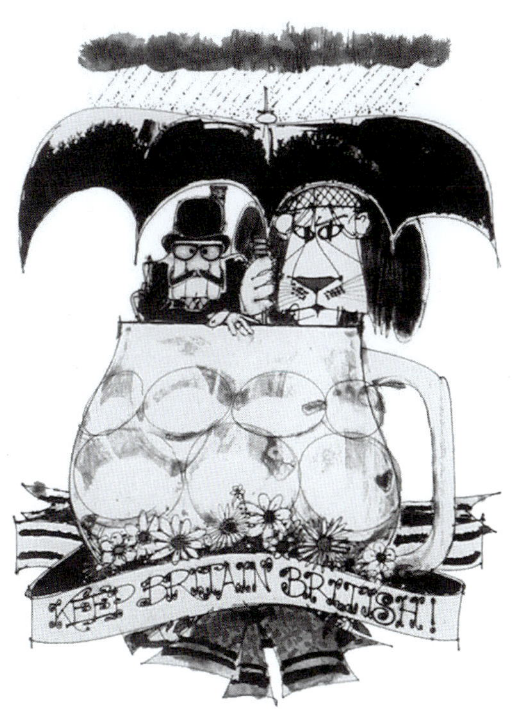

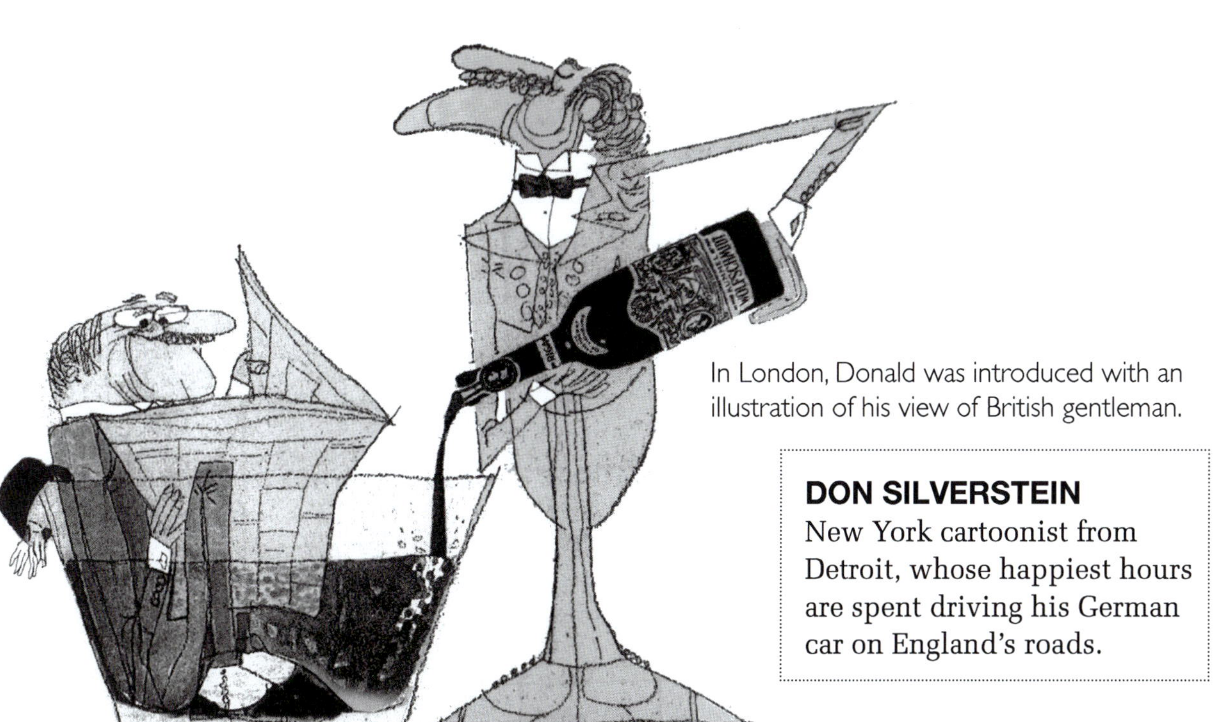

In London, Donald was introduced with an illustration of his view of British gentleman.

DON SILVERSTEIN
New York cartoonist from Detroit, whose happiest hours are spent driving his German car on England's roads.

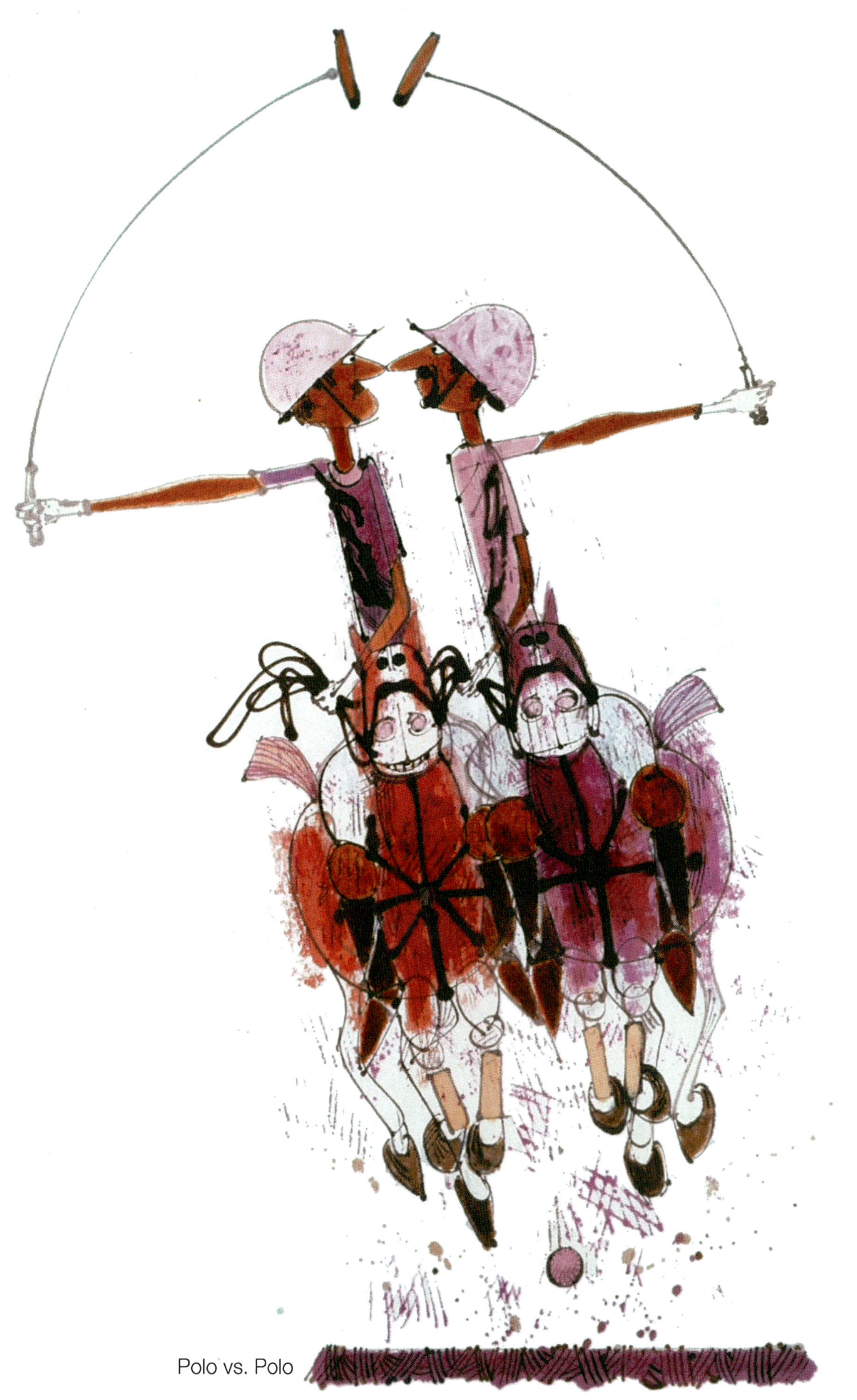

Polo vs. Polo

"Keep Polo British!"

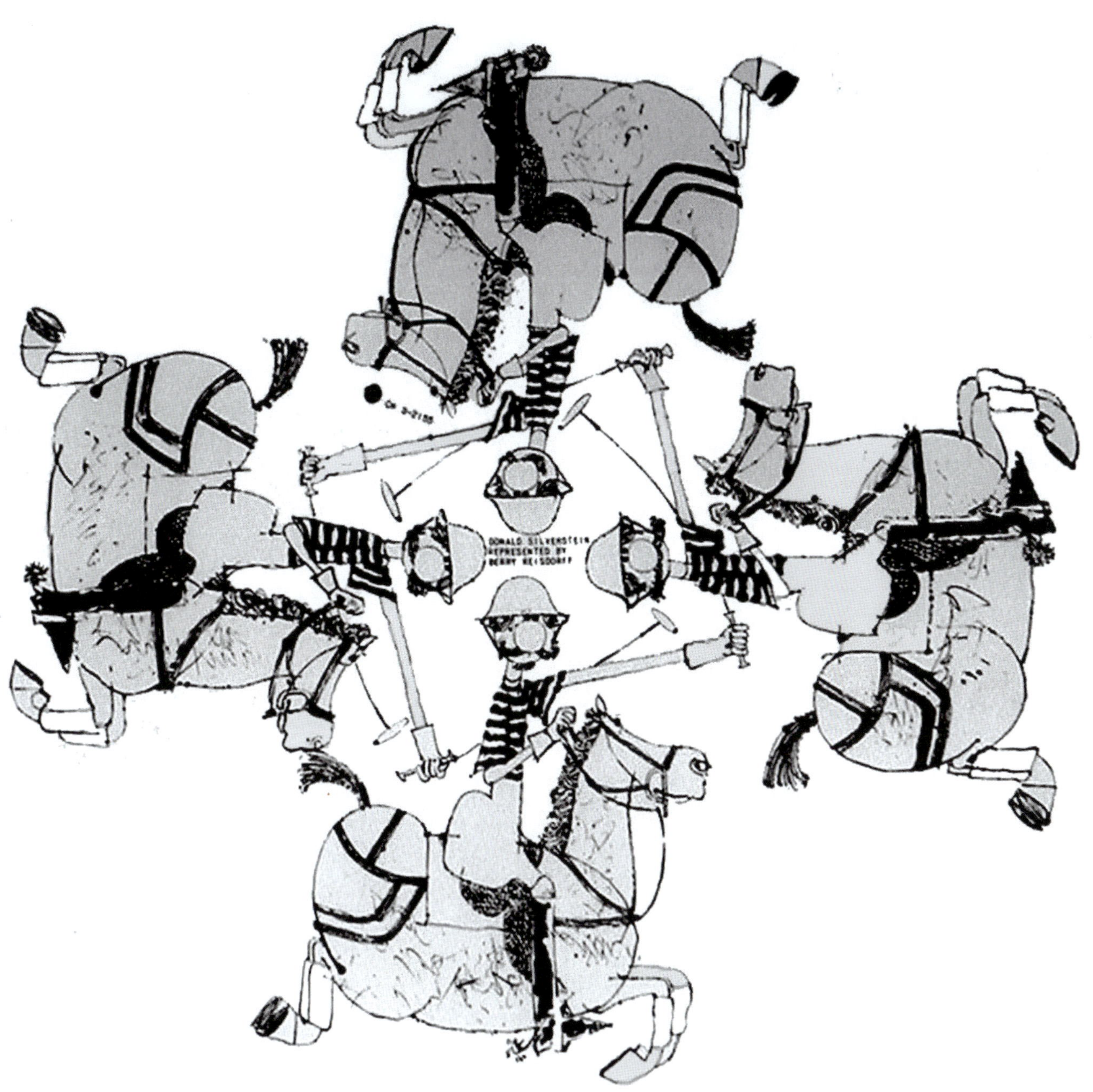

Polo, Polo, Polo, and Polo

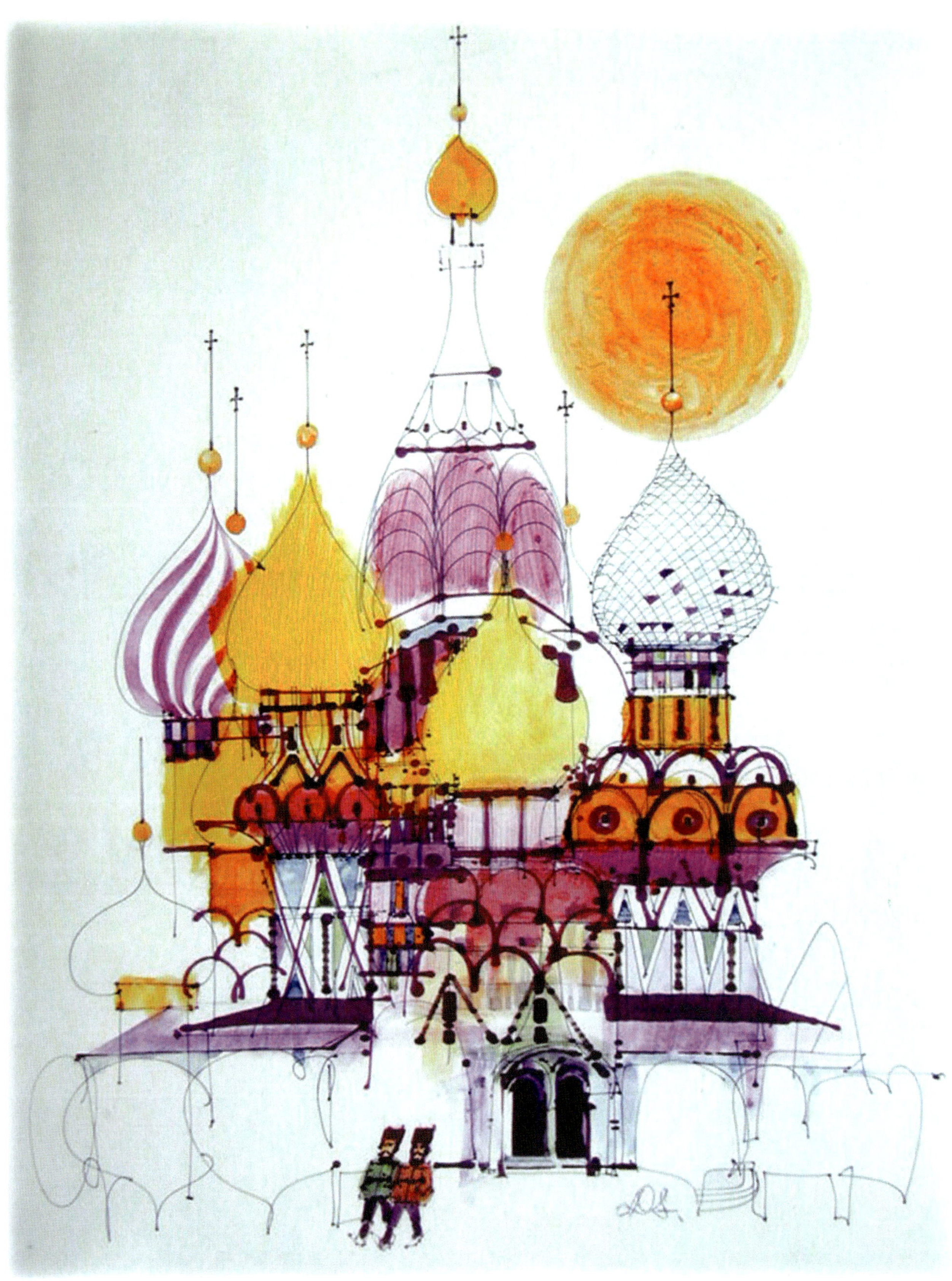

From Russia with Vodka

Russia, Switzerland, Middle East, and...

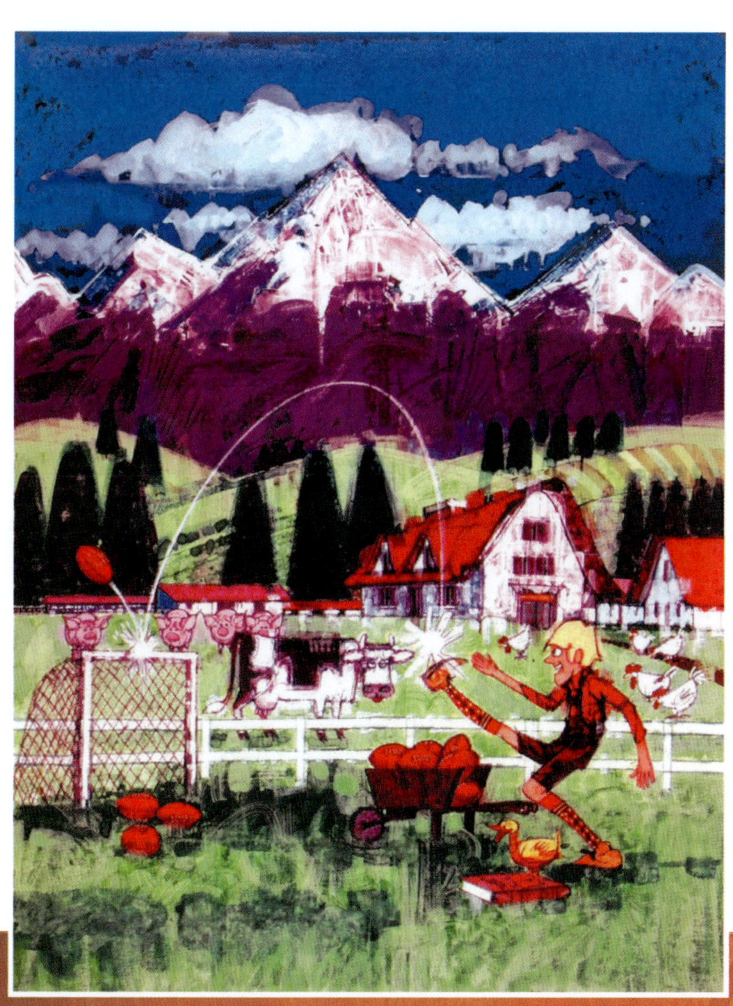

Switzerland:
the Alps as a background.

Flying Genie, Middle East.

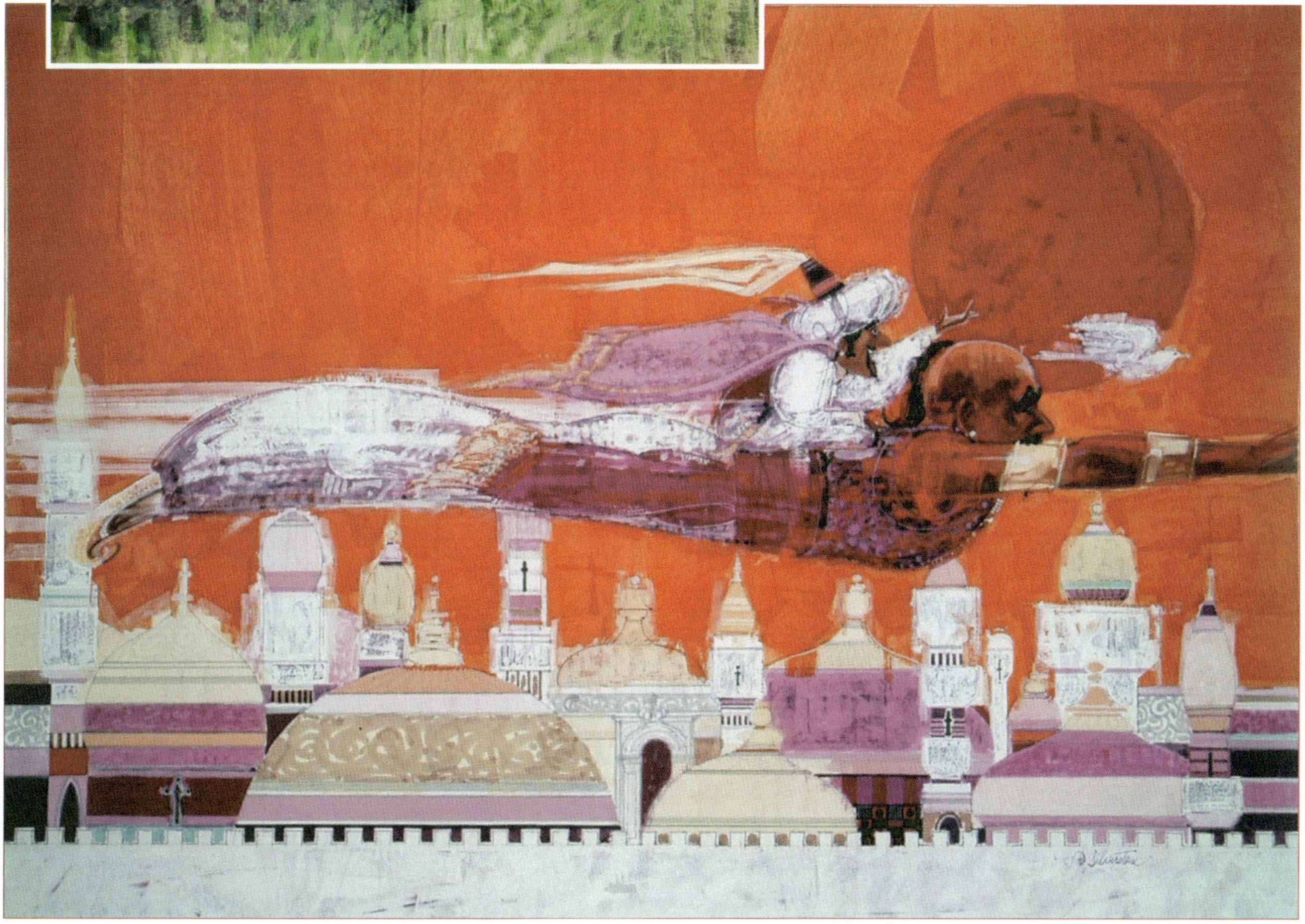

...Greece,
Egypt,
India,
and...

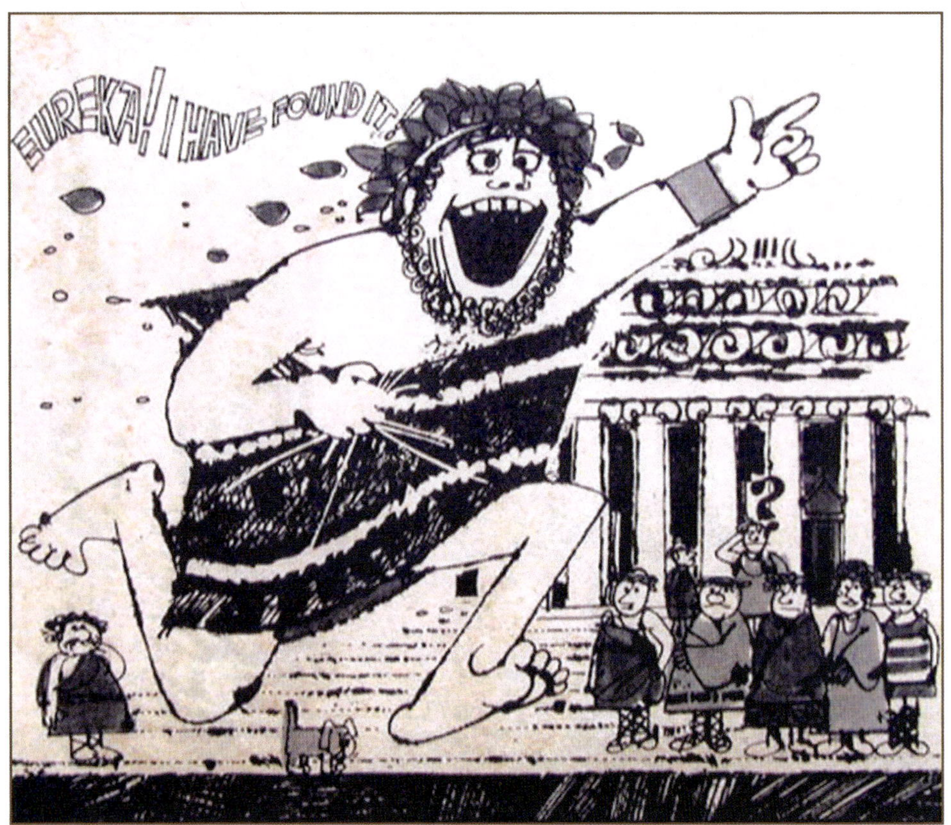

The Marathon runner, Greece.

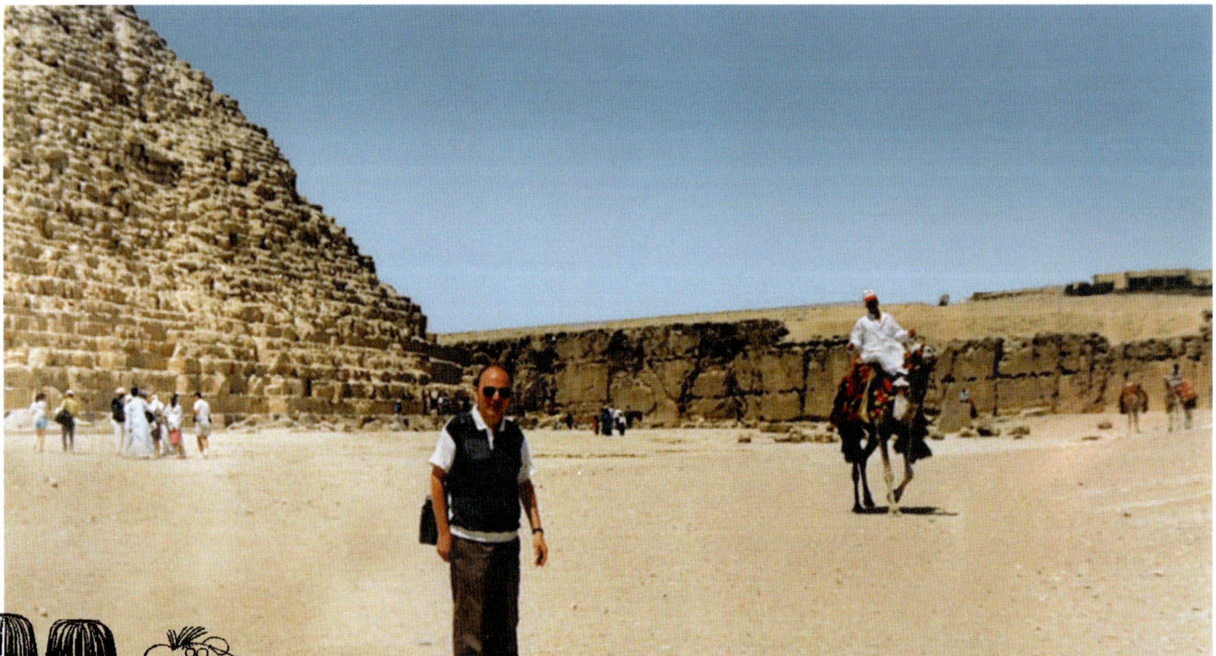

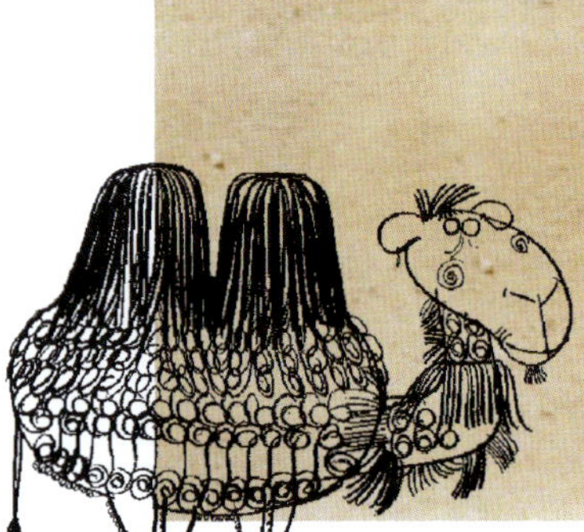

Donald in Egypt, 1992 (photo by Sakiko Silverstein)

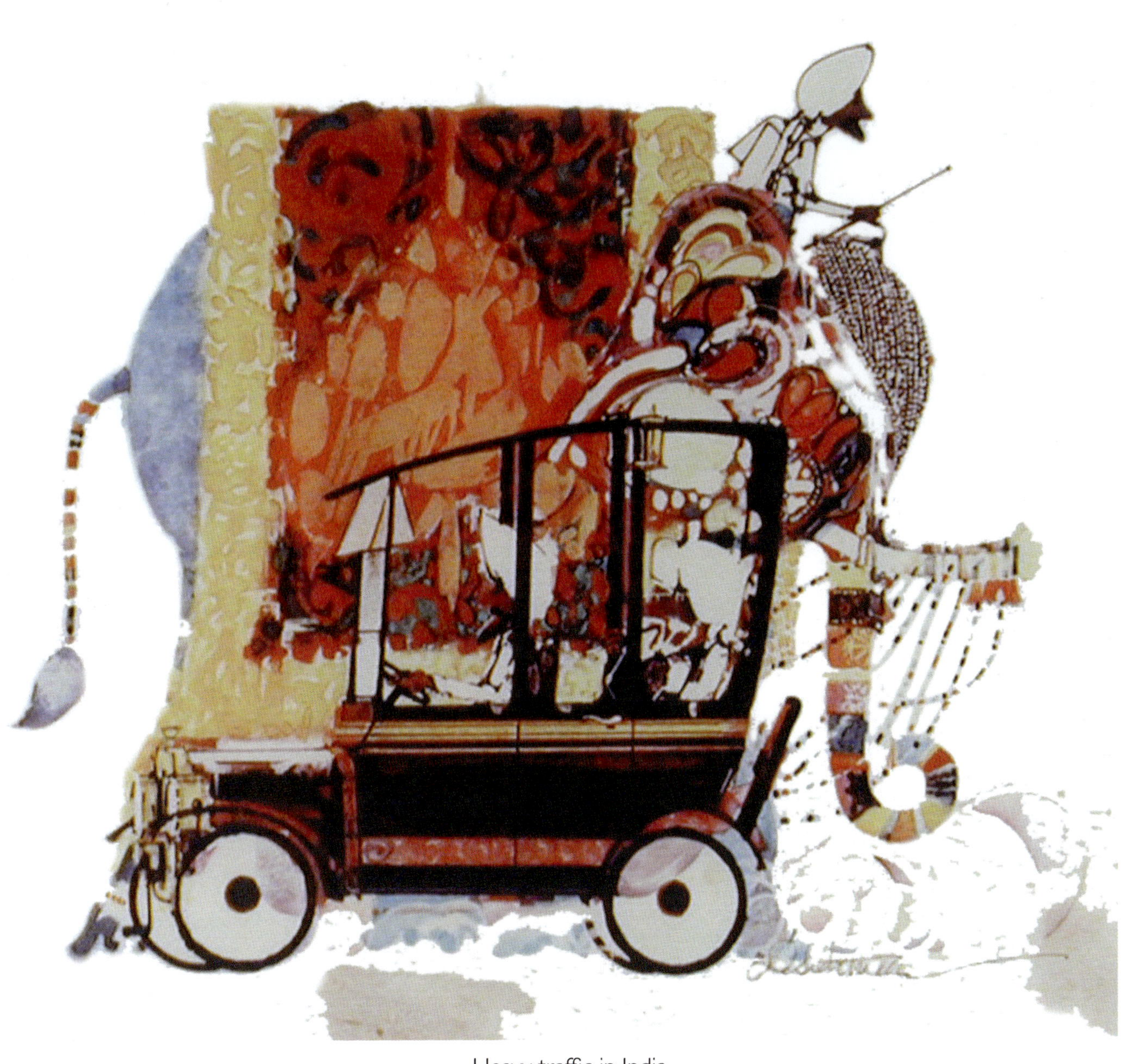

Heavy traffic in India.

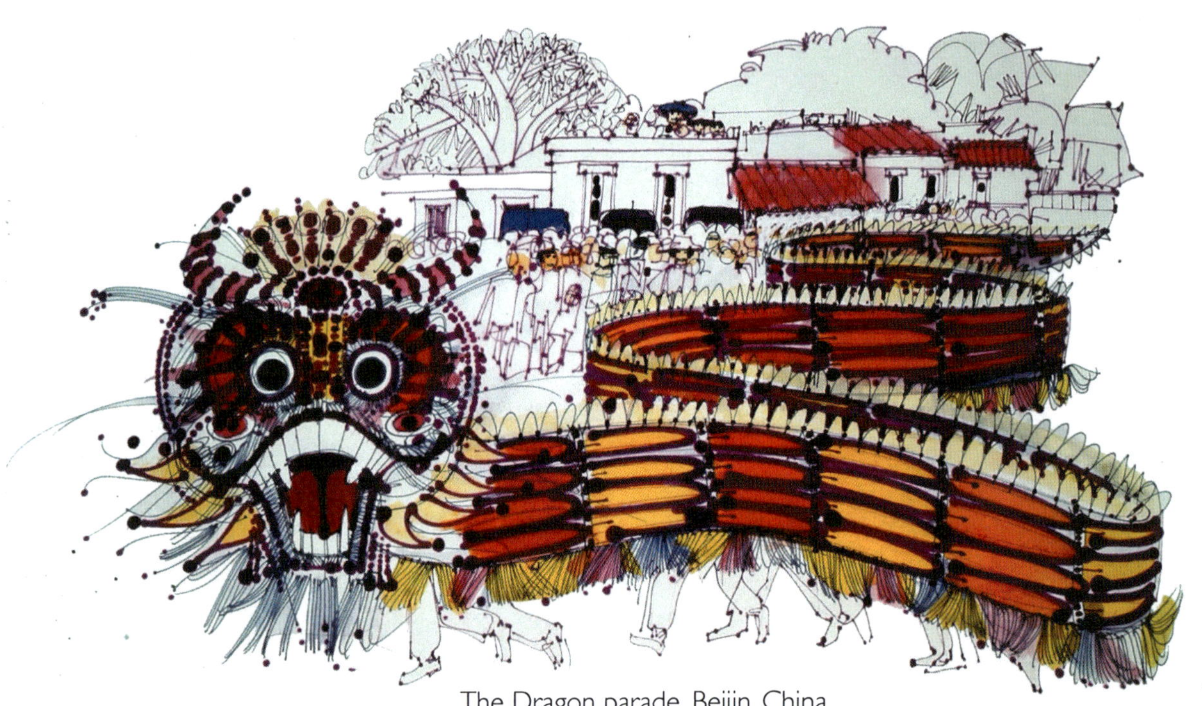

The Dragon parade, Beijin, China.

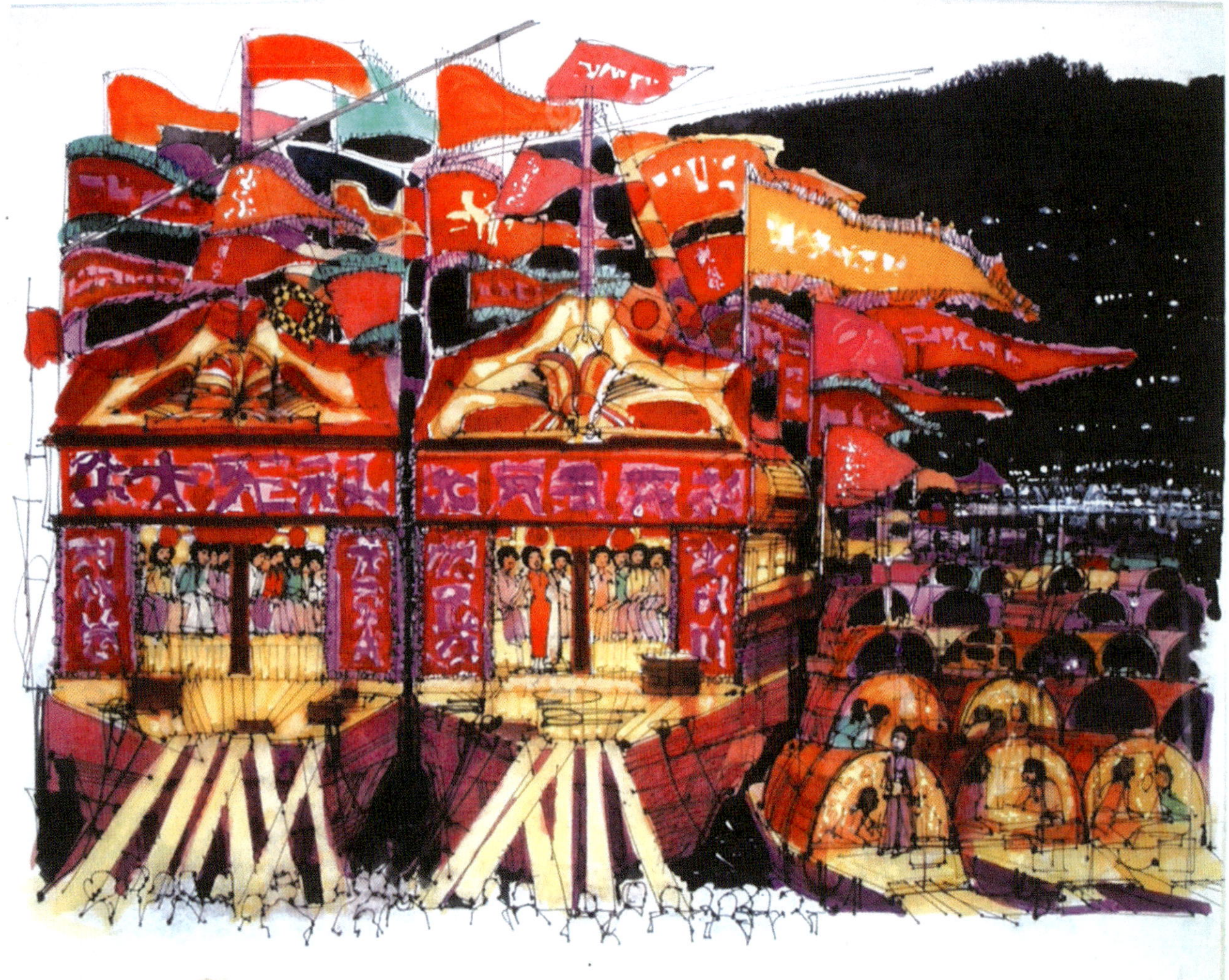

Hong Kong Harbor

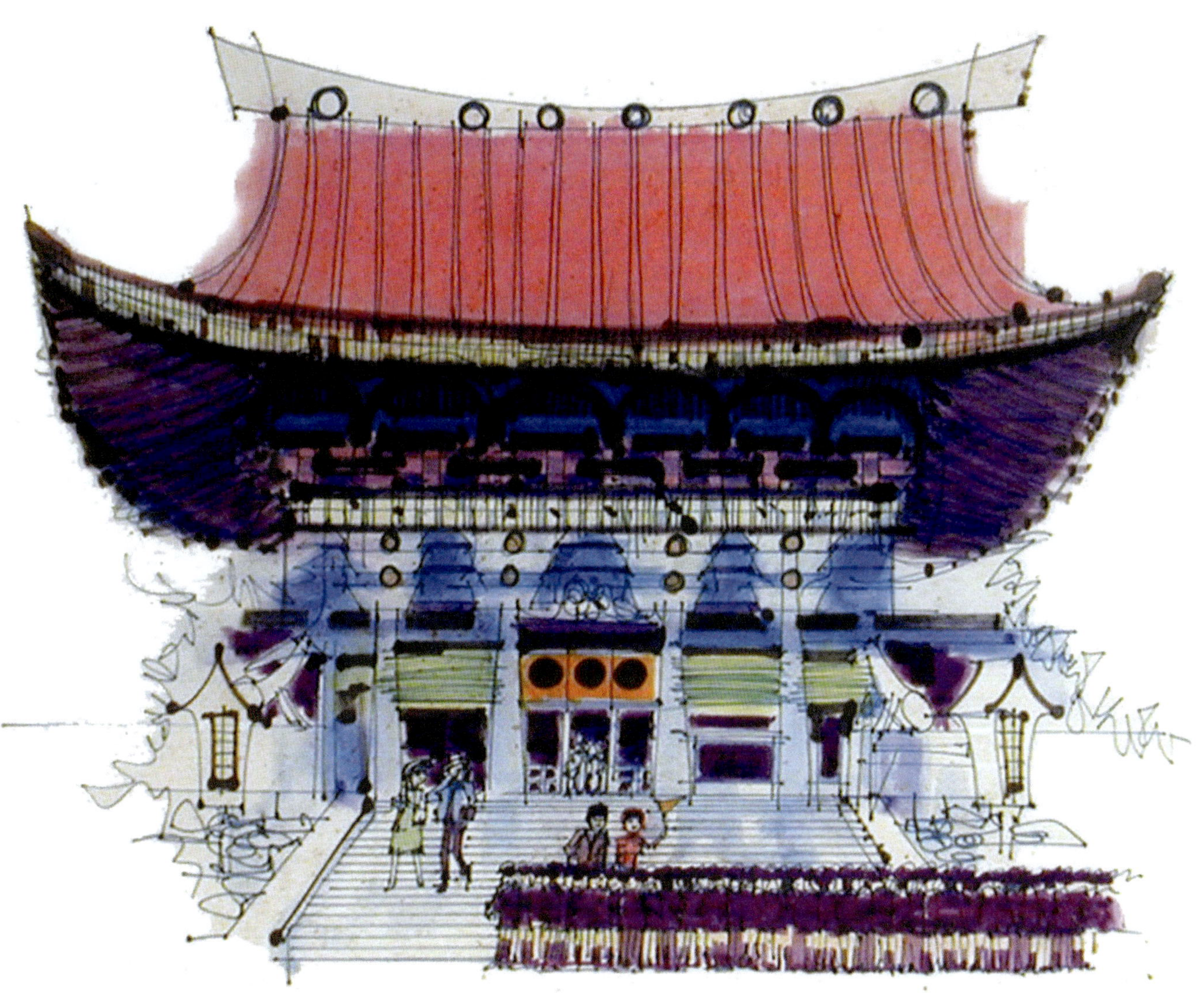

Tohsho-gu Shrine, Nikko, Japan.

**...China,
Japan,
and...**

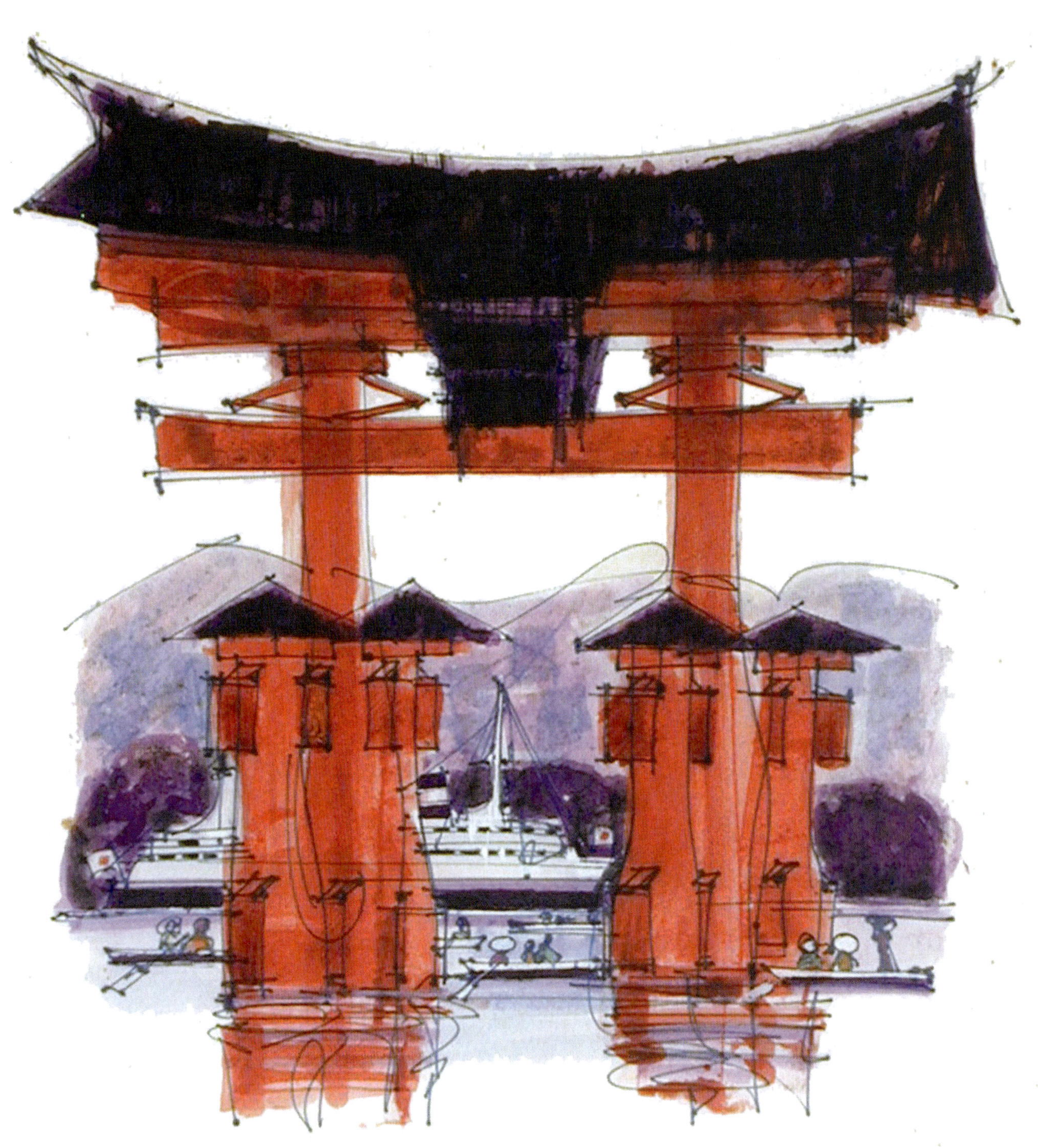

The Itsuku-shima Jinjya *(Shrine)*, Hiroshima, Japan.

... more Japan.

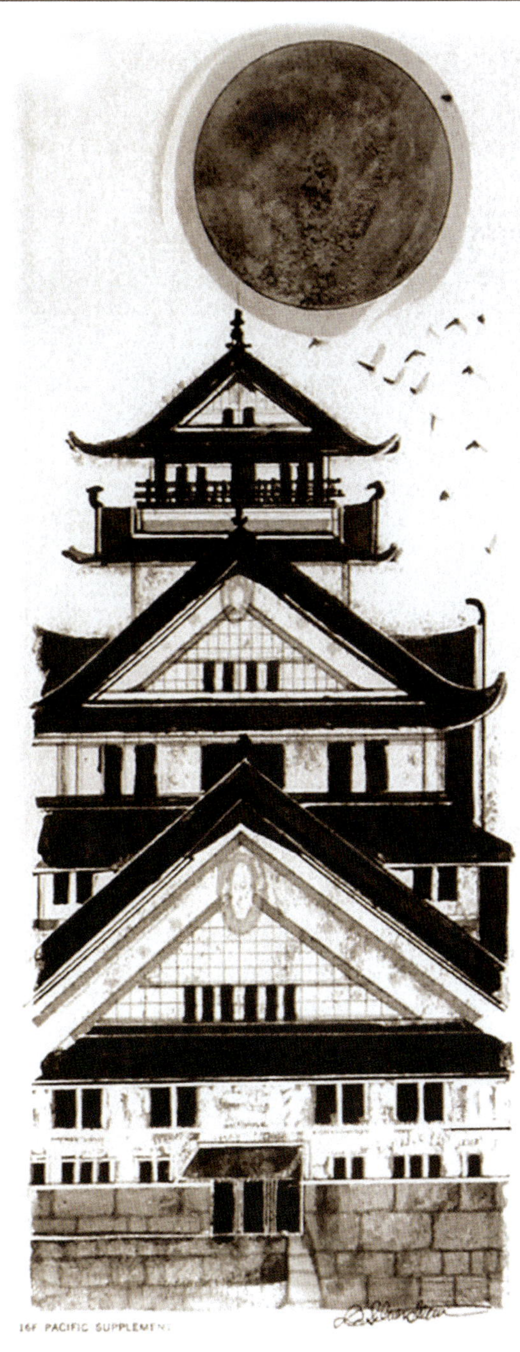

Osaka, Kyoto, Kobe:

Where Old Japan Joins the New

By Peter Lee

Three hundred and fifty miles south of Tokyo, but stretching into a culture gap, is Kansai, or Japan before television, the Bullet train and the Meishin-Tomei Expressway. Kansai is the ancient capital of Kyoto, the bustling commercial center of Osaka and the port of Kobe; all three connected by excellent networks of railroads and highways. In a continuous line, they aren't more than 40 minutes apart by commuter train.

Identifiab[...]
is even mor[...]
spirit, custo[...]
ple. An Osa[...]
confident [...]
("How's eve[...]
a profit?"), [...]
"Maama, M[...]
too bad"). [...]
who consid[...]
a *bunka-jin*[...]
at the mere[...]
thing as m[...]

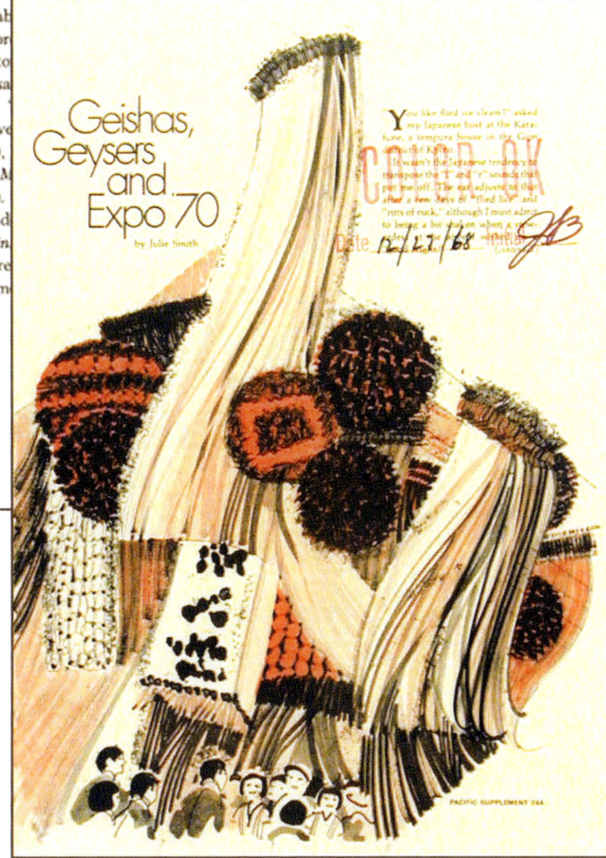

"Osaka, Kyoto, Kobe (Japan):
Where old Japan joins the new,"
by Peter Lee.

"Geisha, Geysers and Expo '70"
by Julie Smith

P.S. III

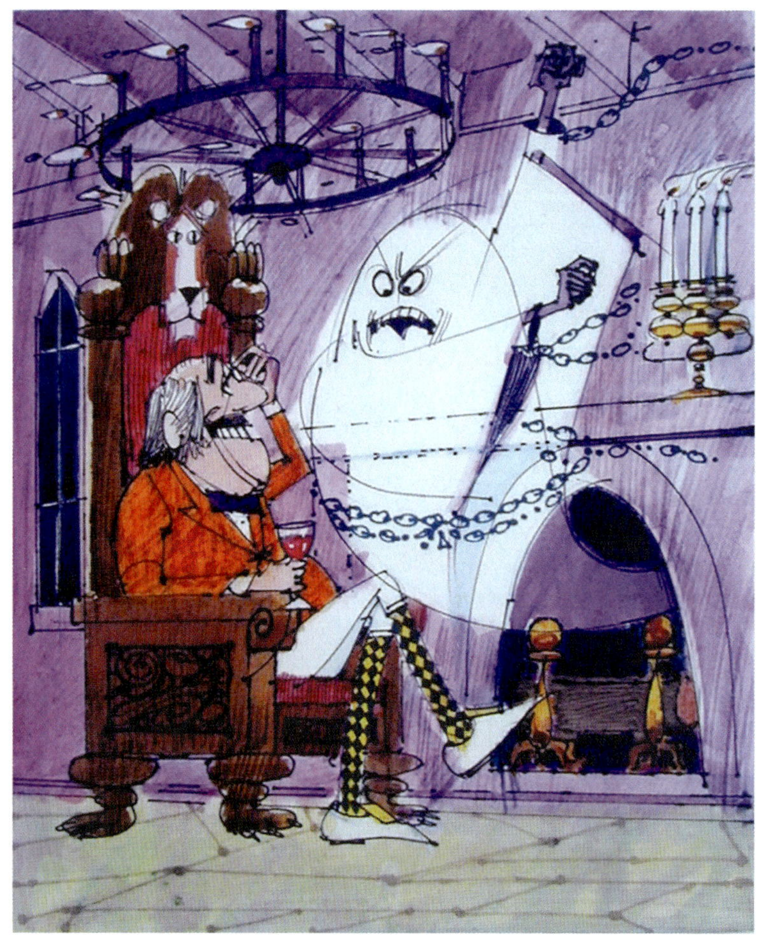

Why does the ghost need an umbrella?

IV

Royal Silverstein

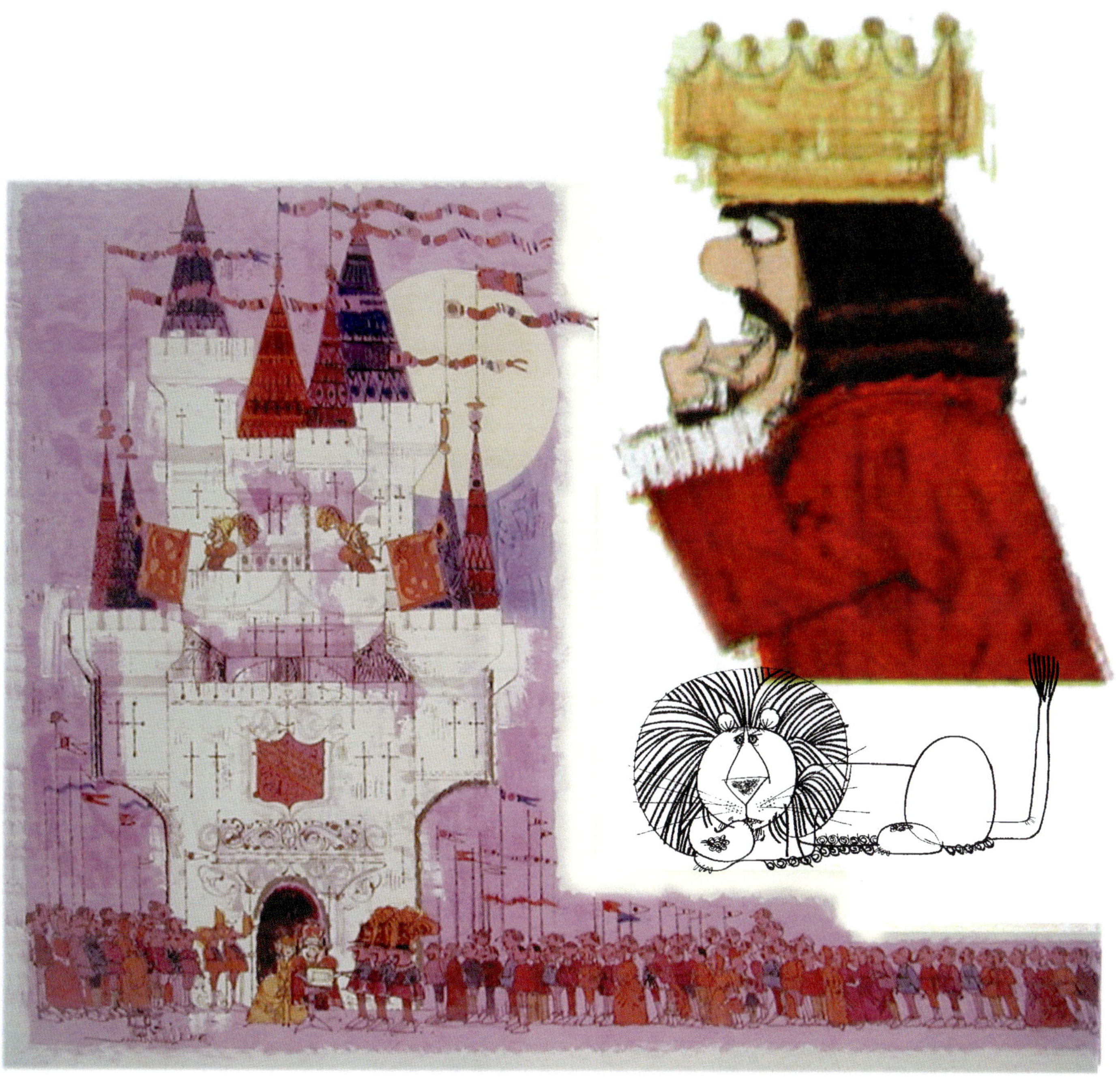

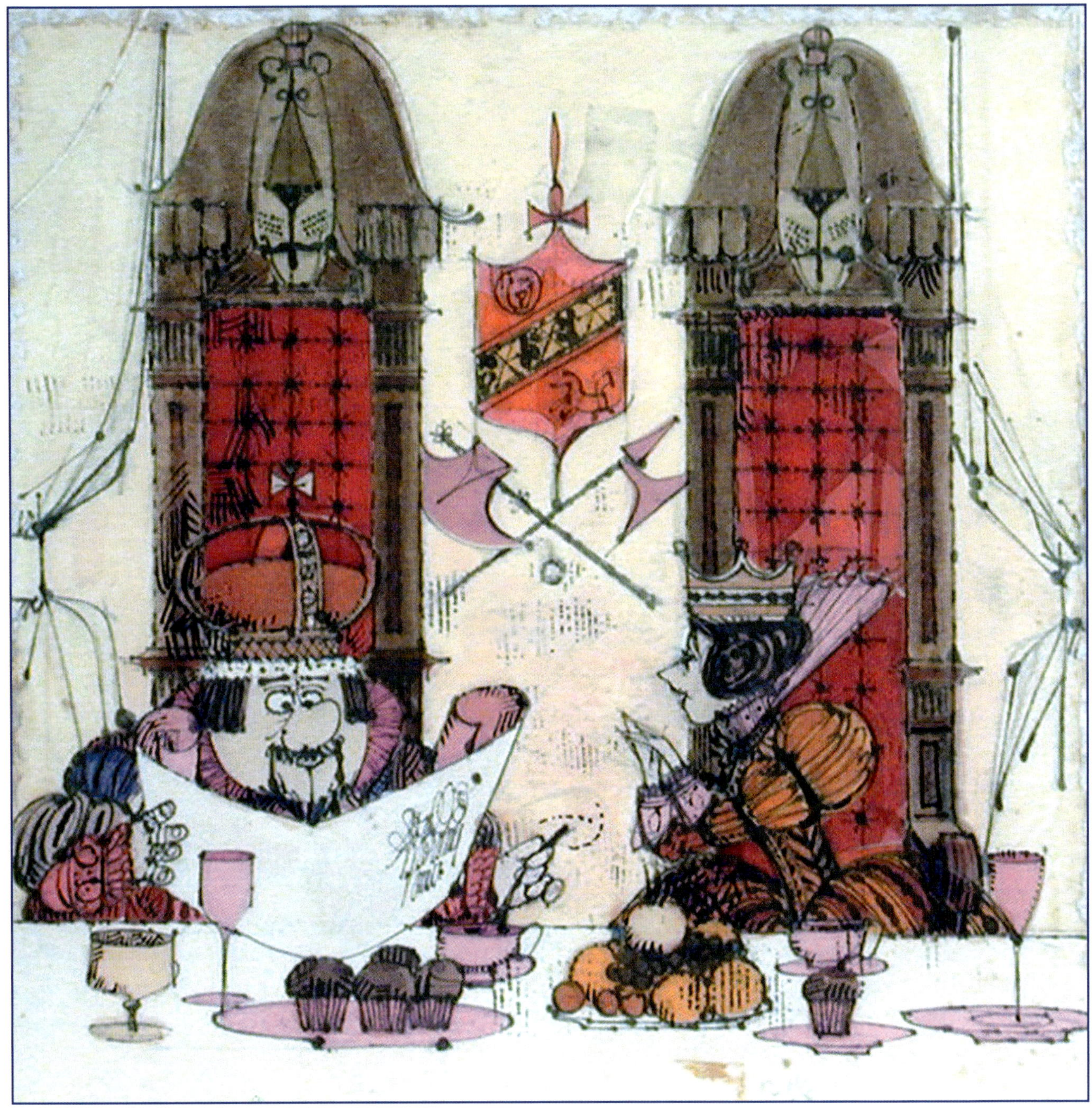

Once upon a time...

Once upon a time, there was a King and a Queen on their thrones.
At the breakfast table, the king liked to read the news, while
the queen wanted to tell him how much she spent on her last shopping spree.

The king dildn't pay much attention to her.

That's how they lived happily ever after.

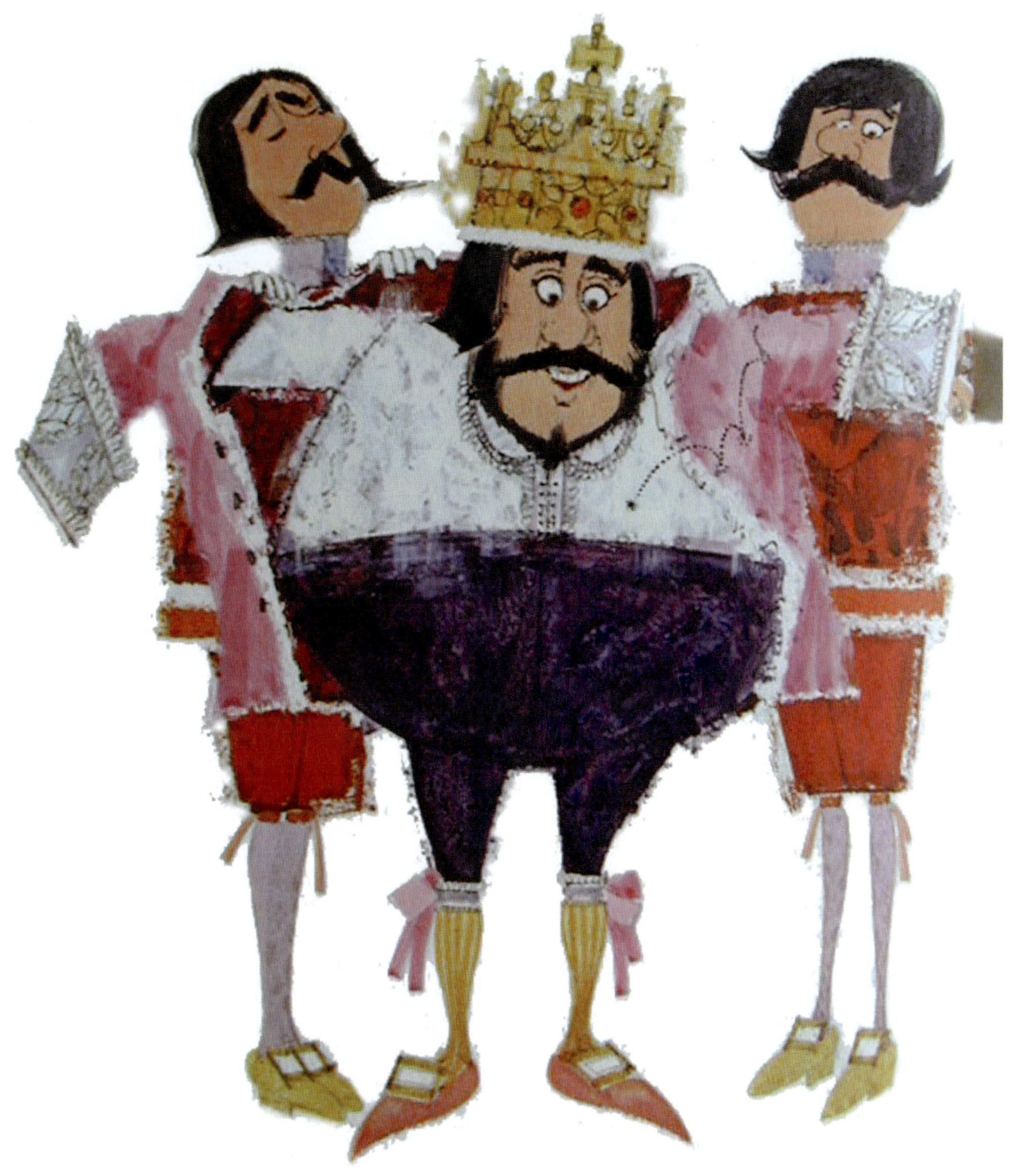

The King has a problem with his girth.

— From "Folktales of Spain and Latin America" *(see also page 60)* —

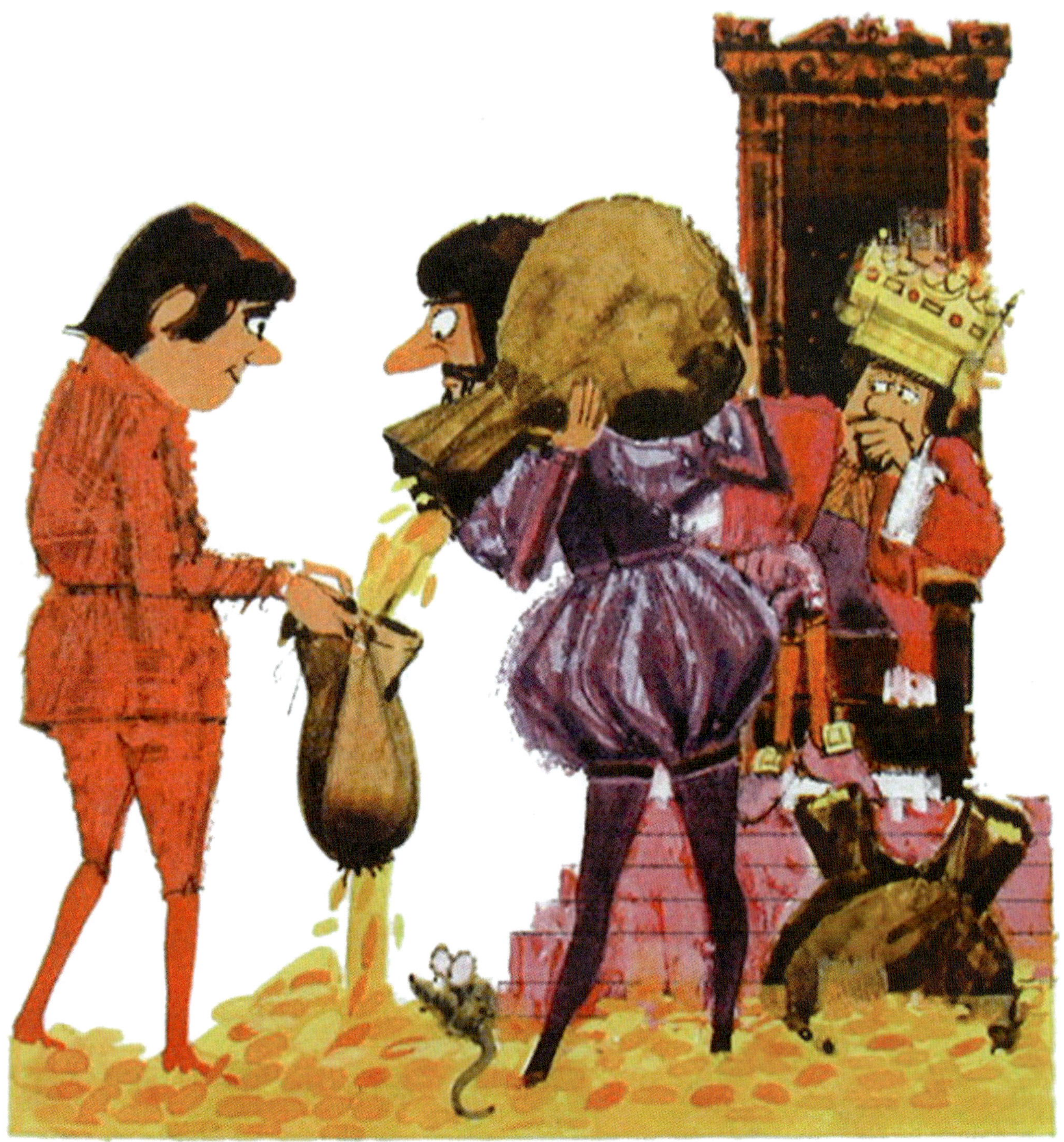

eing King is the easiest task in the world. That's what you think.
He doesn't have to work. People pay him taxes. Farmers bring their
harvest to the King in appreciation for his protection of their field.
The King has power over the people. The King can do anything he wants to.

But, all that's not true.

The King must be clever.

He must be careful not to be double-crossed by a tricky rabbit.
Or wise enough not to be cheated by dishonest merchants.
The hardest part of being a great king is to make the right judgement.

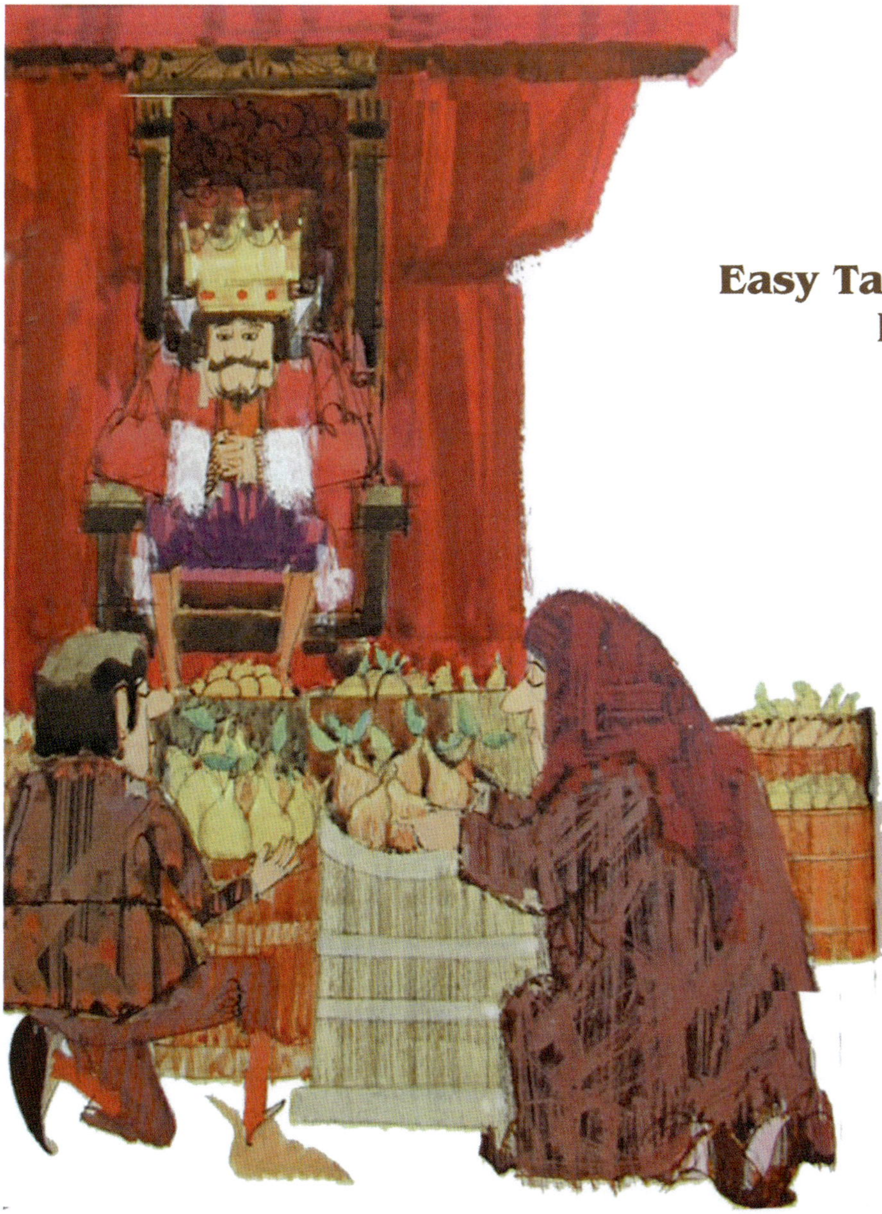

Easy Task, or Hard Decision?

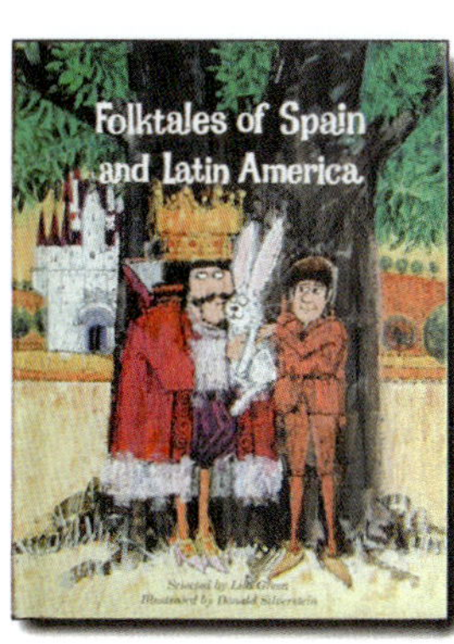

— All three illustrations here are from
"Folktales of Spain and Latin America" —
(see page 60)

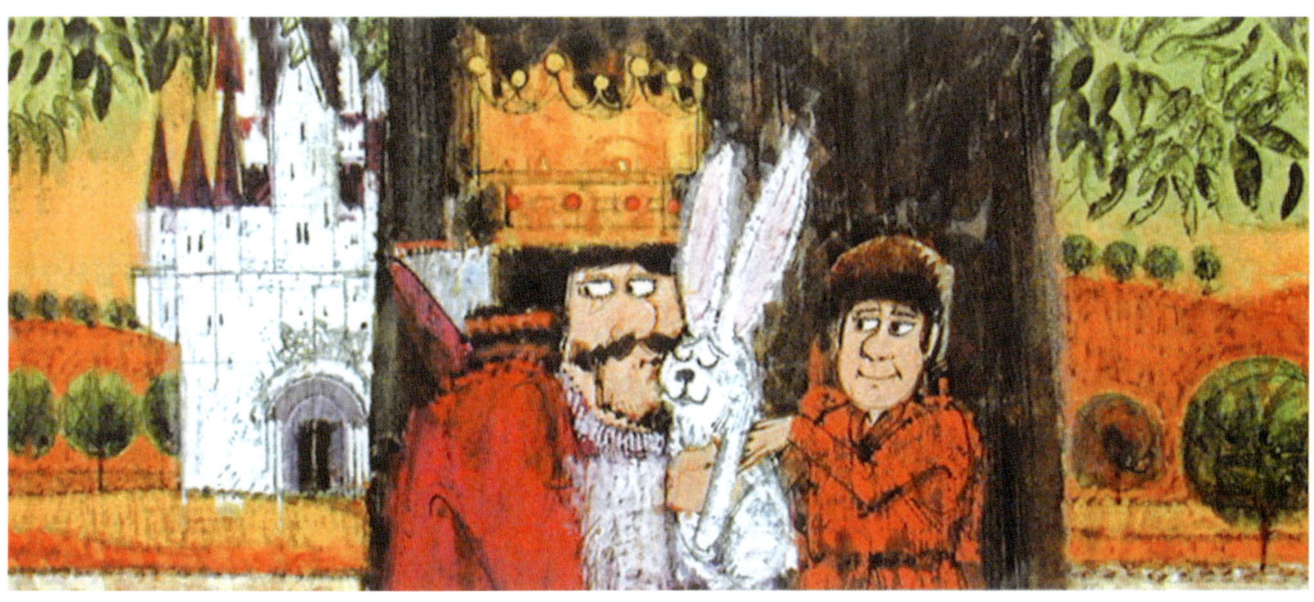

P.S. IV

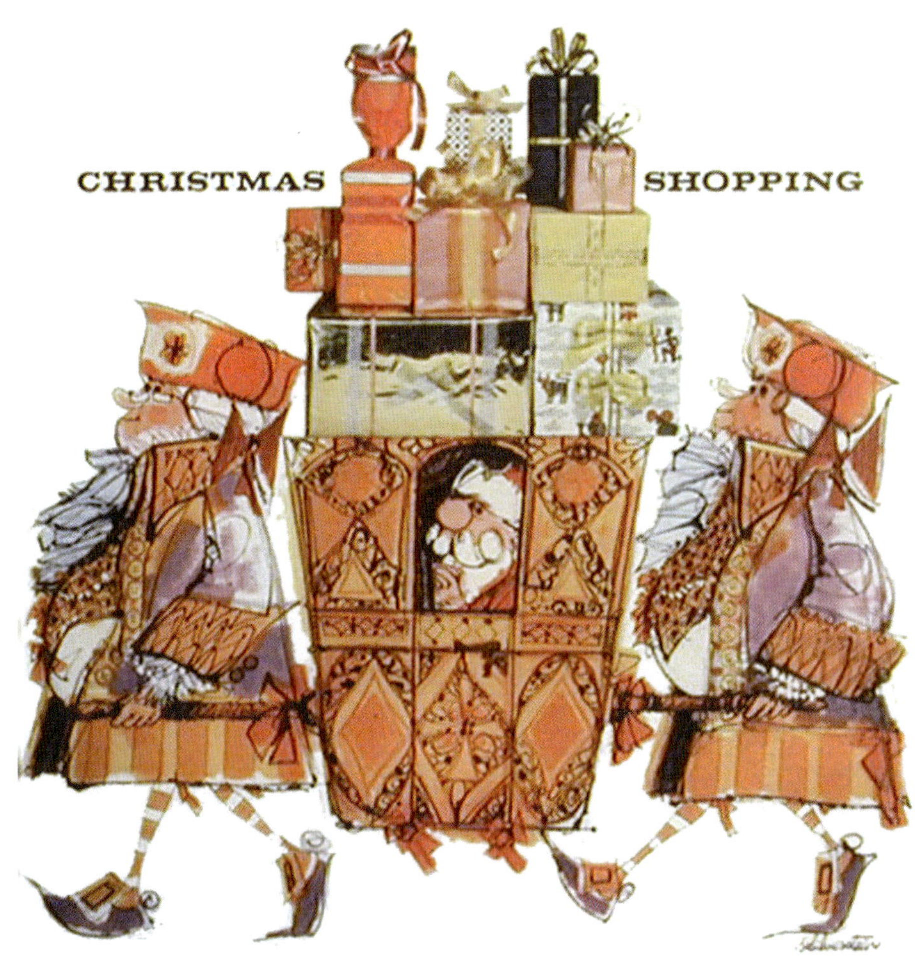

V

Donald in
the Entertainment Community

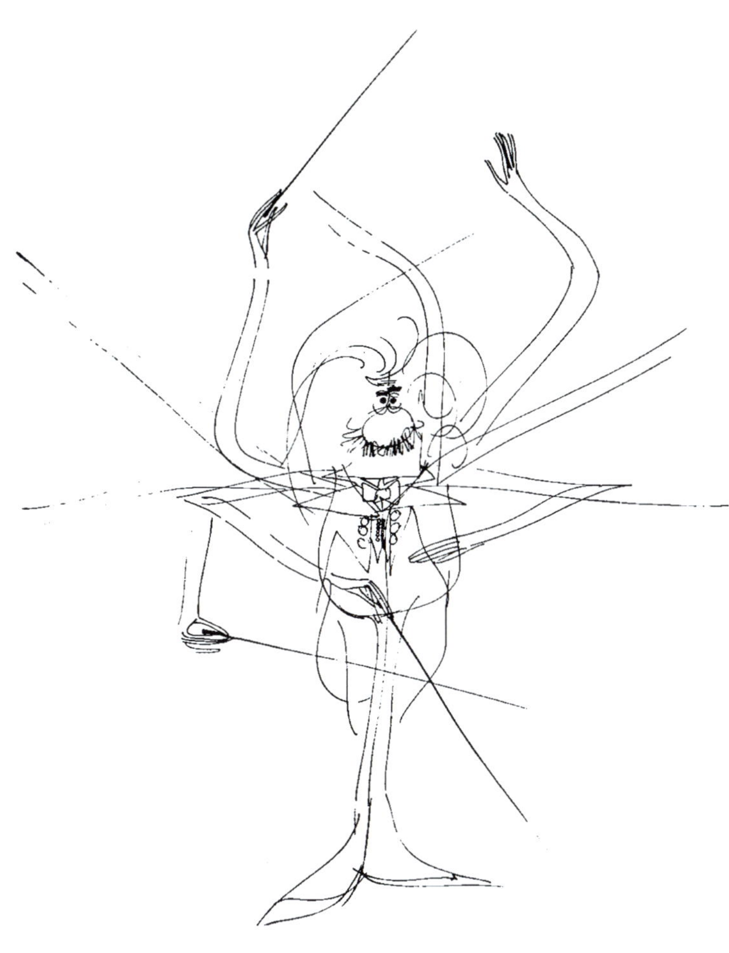

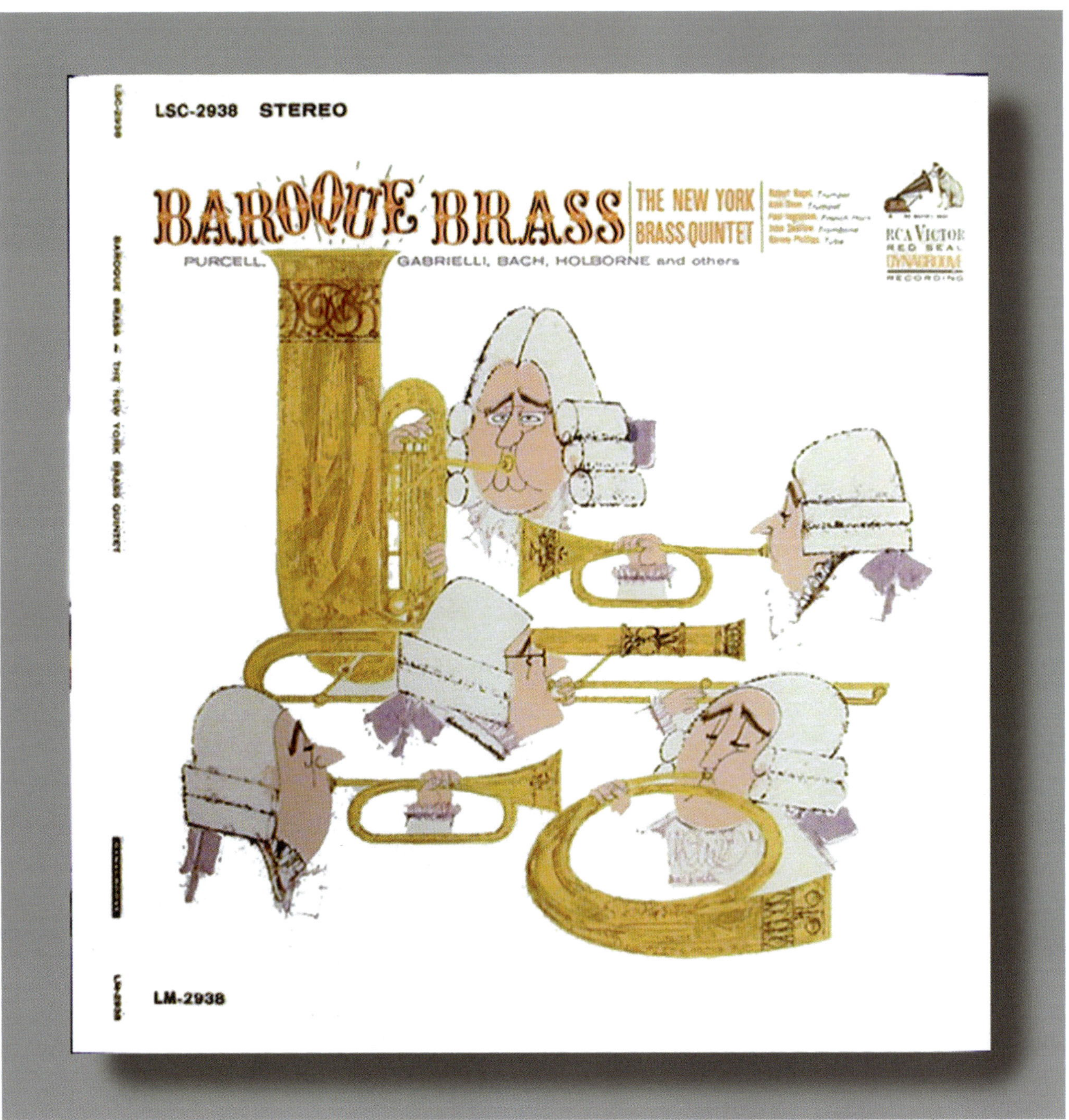

—"Baroque Brass" The New York Brass Quintet; RCA Record; 1966 —

Donald Silverstein collected numerous LP records of both classical and jazz music.
His friends wonder why some are still wrapped.

The Sound of Music

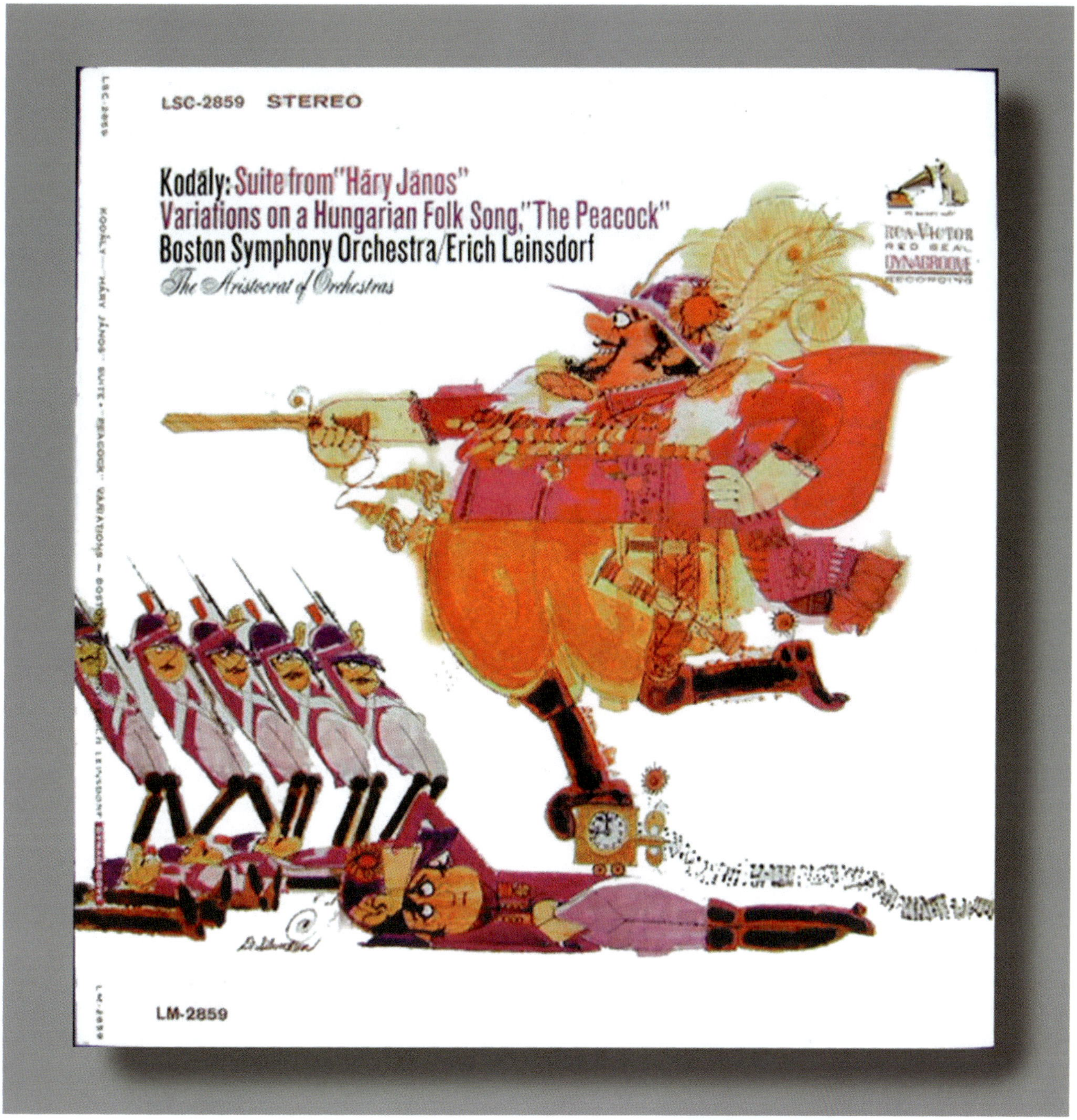

LSC-2859   STEREO

Kodály: Suite from "Háry János"
Variations on a Hungarian Folk Song, "The Peacock"
Boston Symphony Orchestra/Erich Leinsdorf
The Aristocrat of Orchestras

LM-2859

— Kodaly: Salute from "Háry János" and others: RCA Record; 1966 —

Not only was Donald an LP record collector,
he also installed professional stereo systems
which were a luxury in the 1960s.

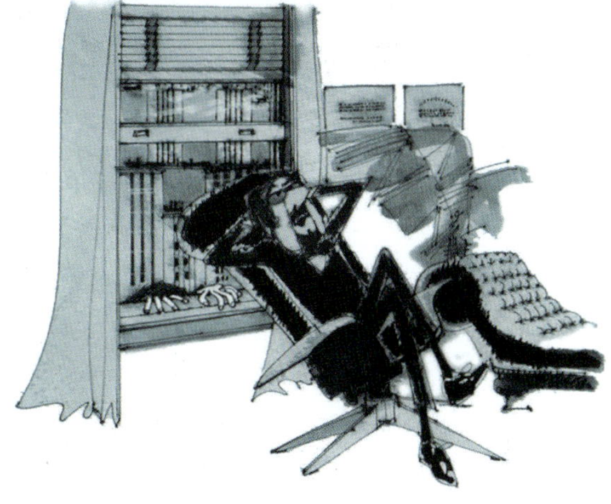

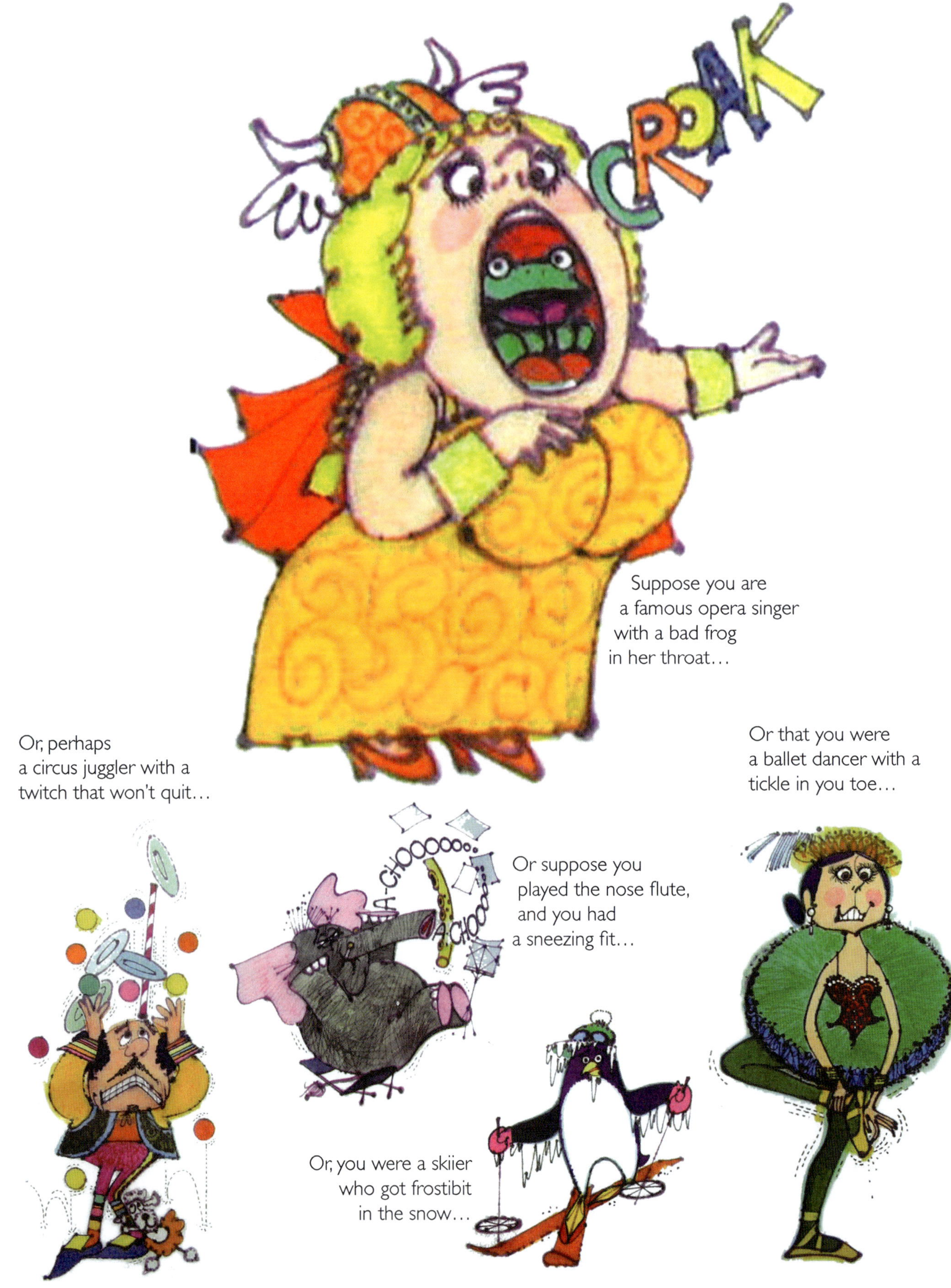

Suppose you are
a famous opera singer
with a bad frog
in her throat…

Or, perhaps
a circus juggler with a
twitch that won't quit…

Or suppose you
played the nose flute,
and you had
a sneezing fit…

Or that you were
a ballet dancer with a
tickle in you toe…

Or, you were a skiier
who got frostibit
in the snow…

Problems, problems, problems, and you don't know what to do.

There's a solution!

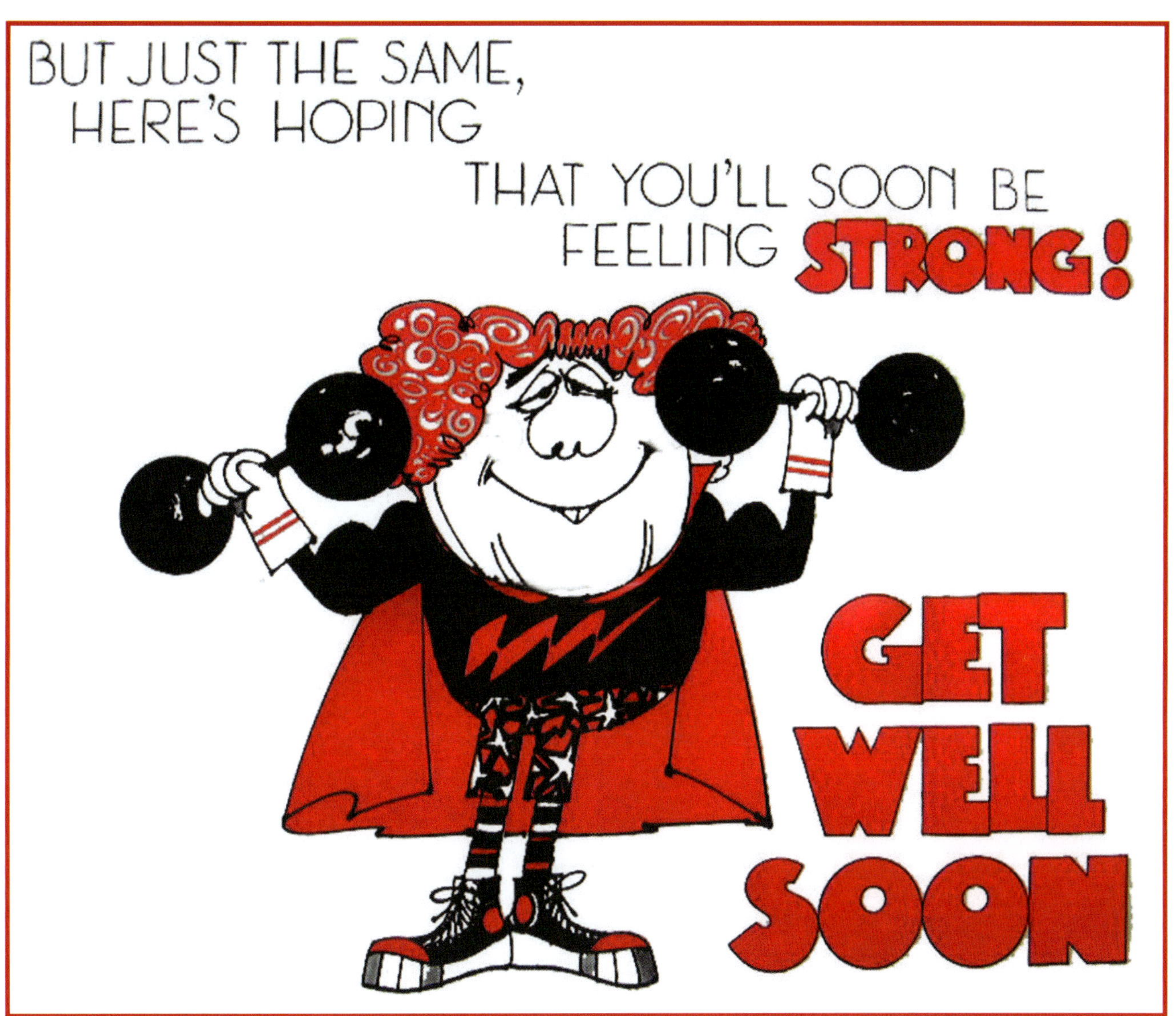

"Get Well Soon" by the American Greetings Corp., Cleveland, Ohio.

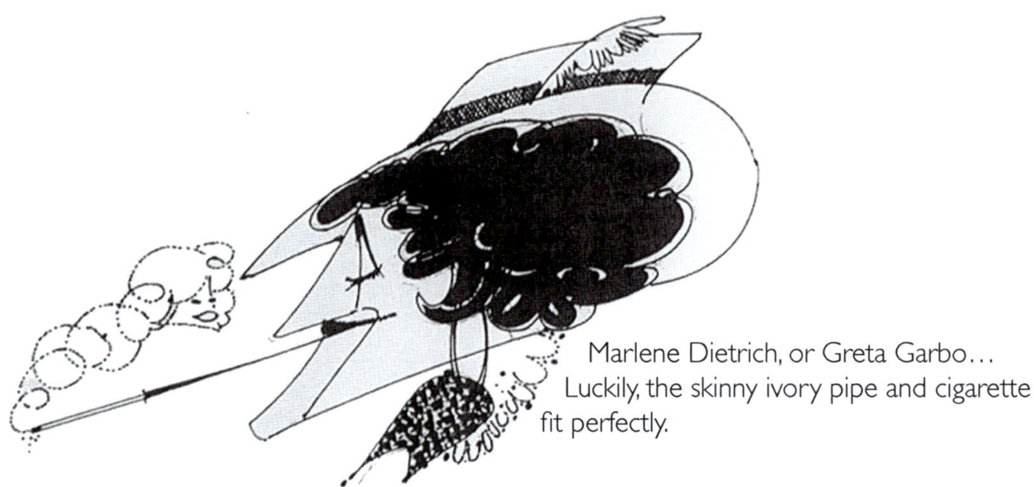

Marlene Dietrich, or Greta Garbo…
Luckily, the skinny ivory pipe and cigarette
fit perfectly.

That's Entertainment, II

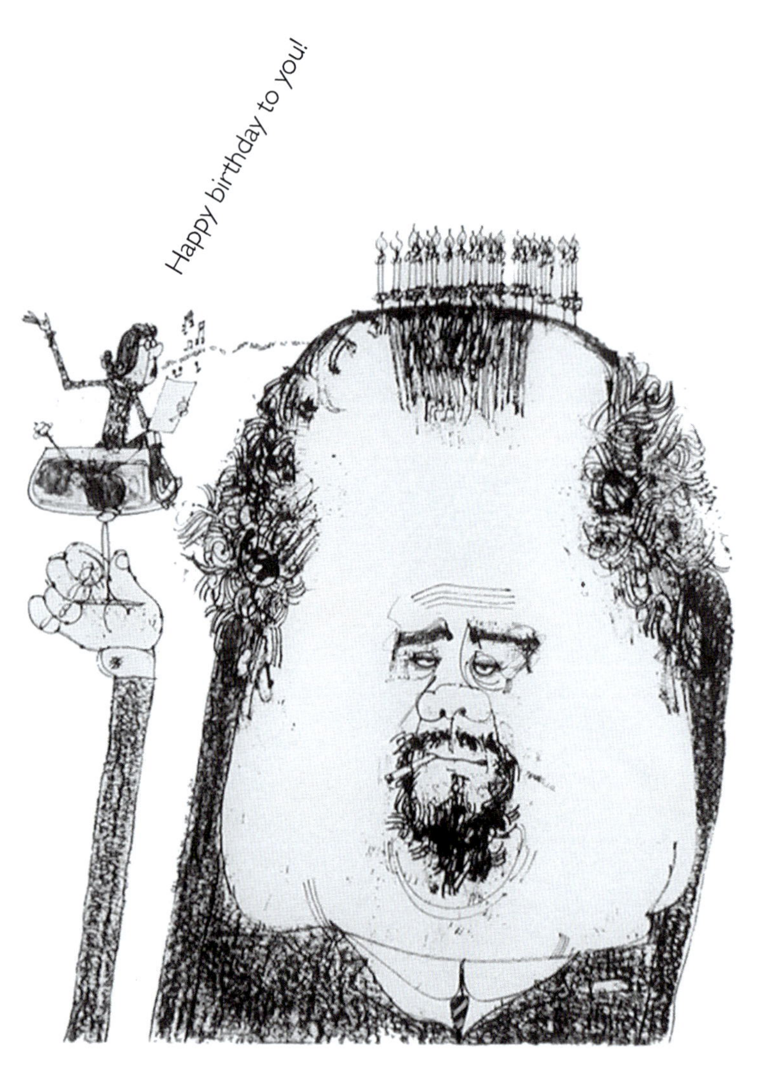

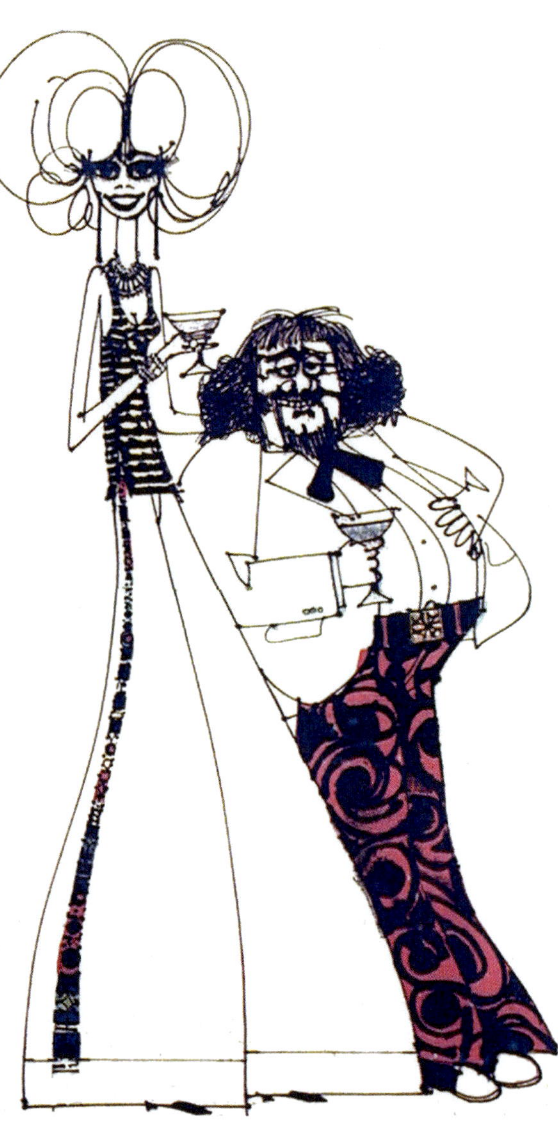

1960's Mods.

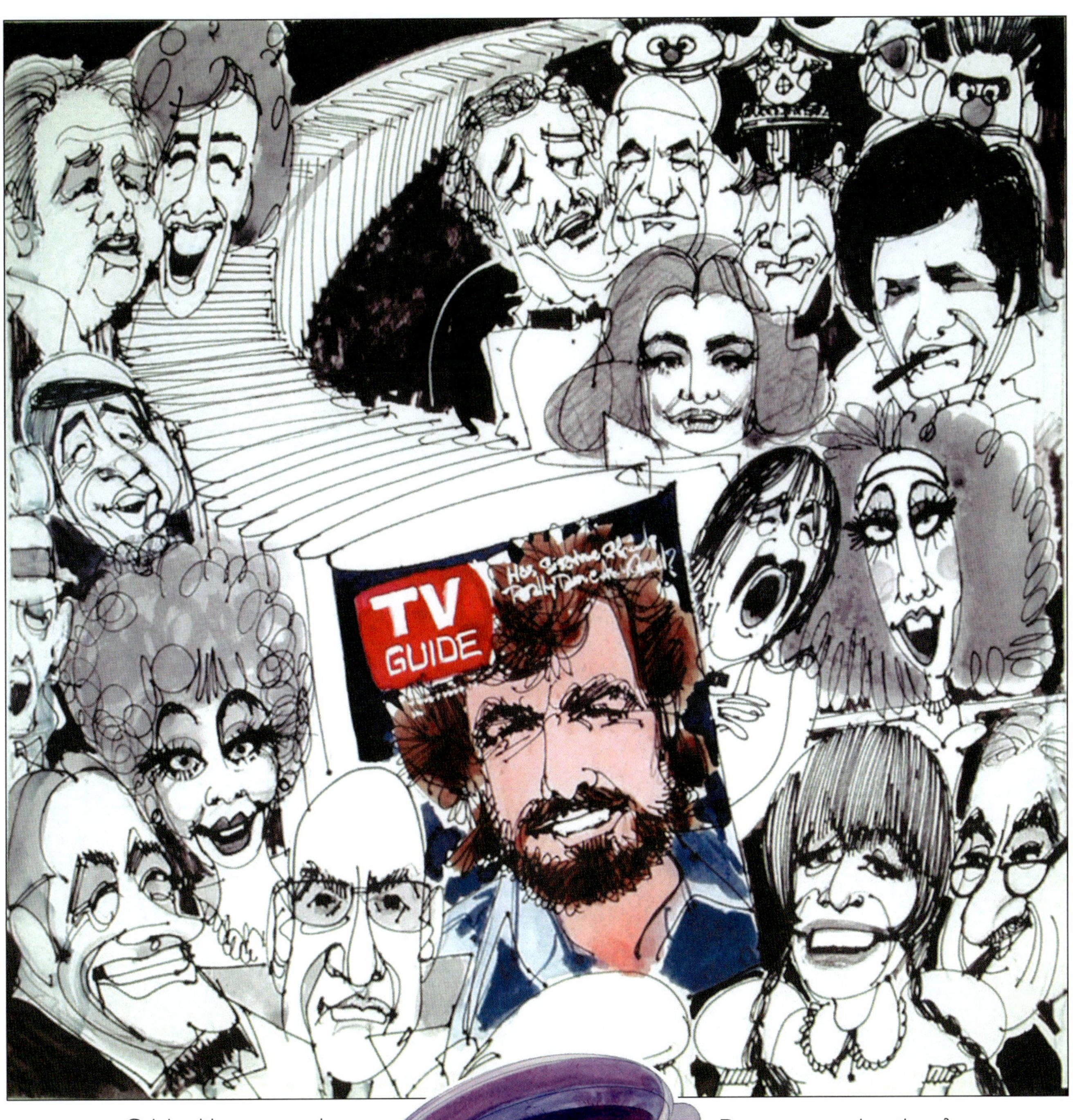

Celeberities on parade.   Do you remember them?

— From the editorial pages of *TV Guide* —

"Caddy, hand me my 9-iron and a blonde wig,"
shouted Dinah Shore at her golf tournament.

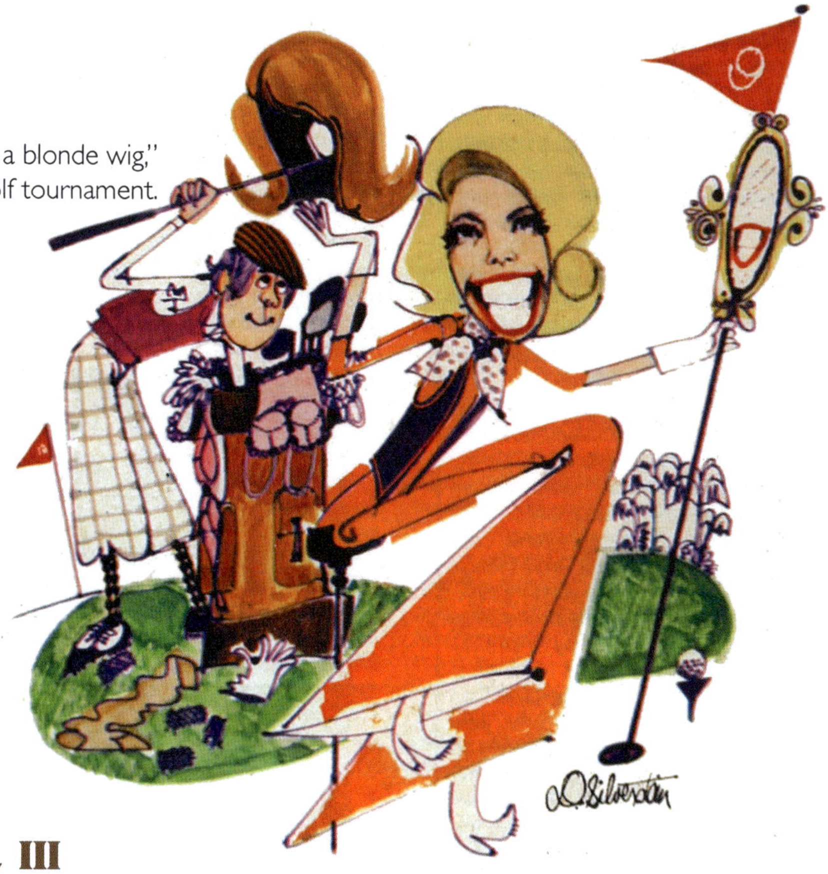

That's Entertainment, III

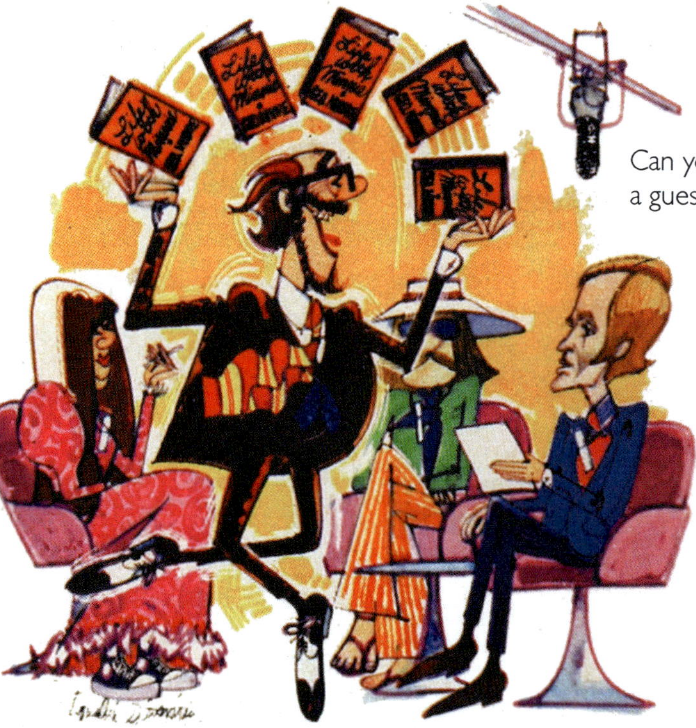

Can you find Zsa Zsa Gabor as
a guest on the Jack Paar Show?

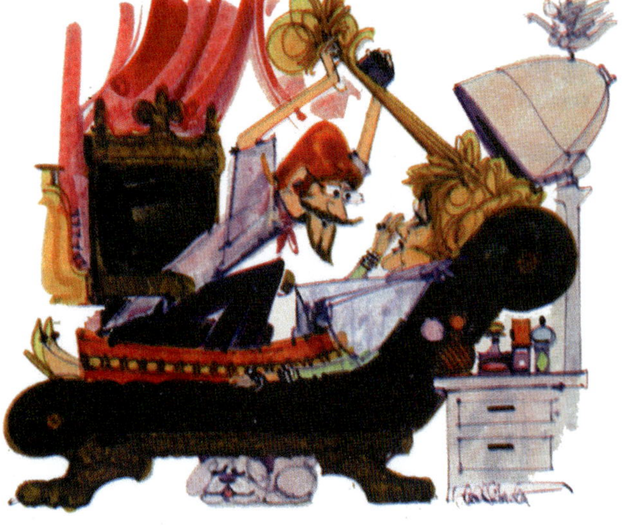

Hollywood hairdresser

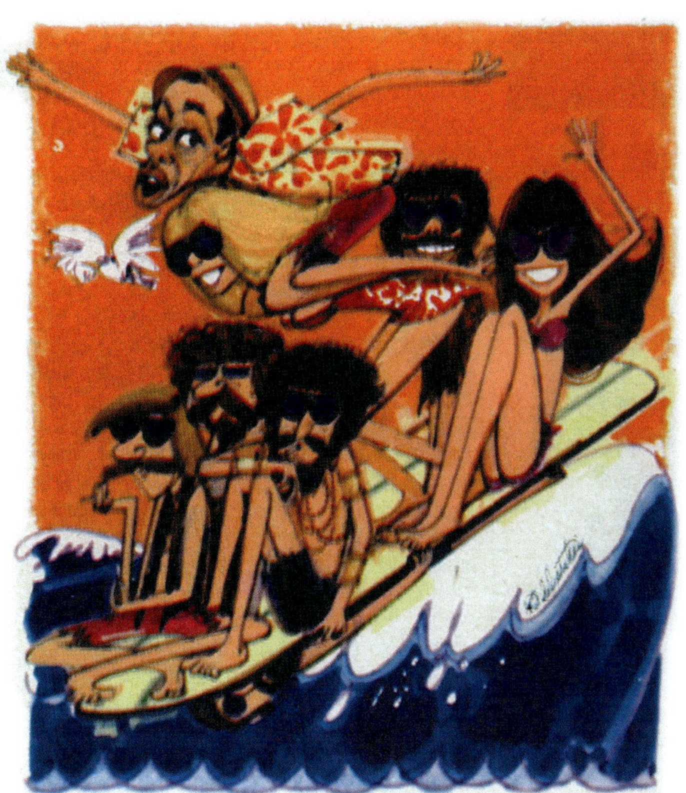

Don Knotts with the Beach Boys-plus.

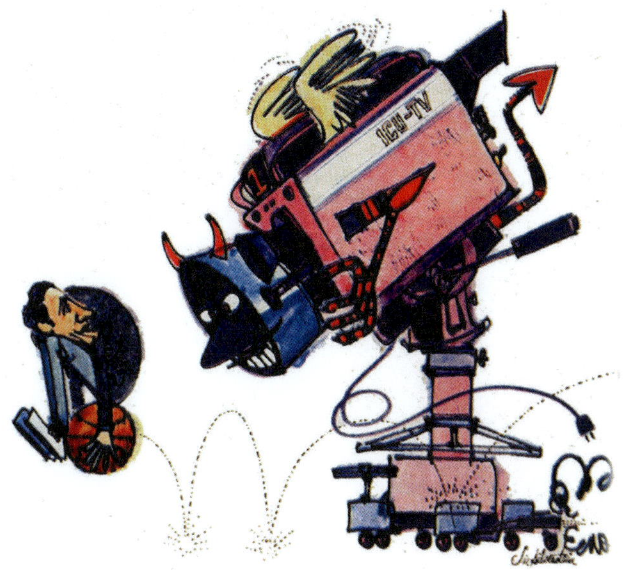

Bill Sherman, basketball player.

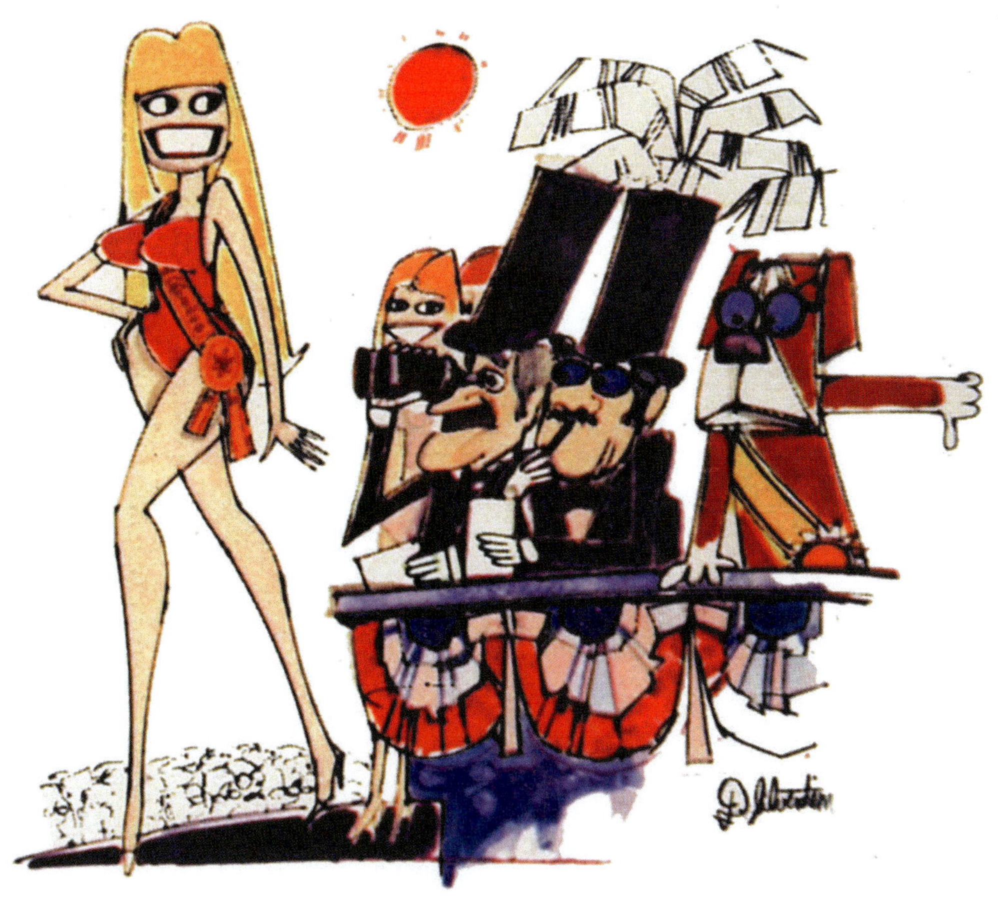

Miss U.S.A. Pageant

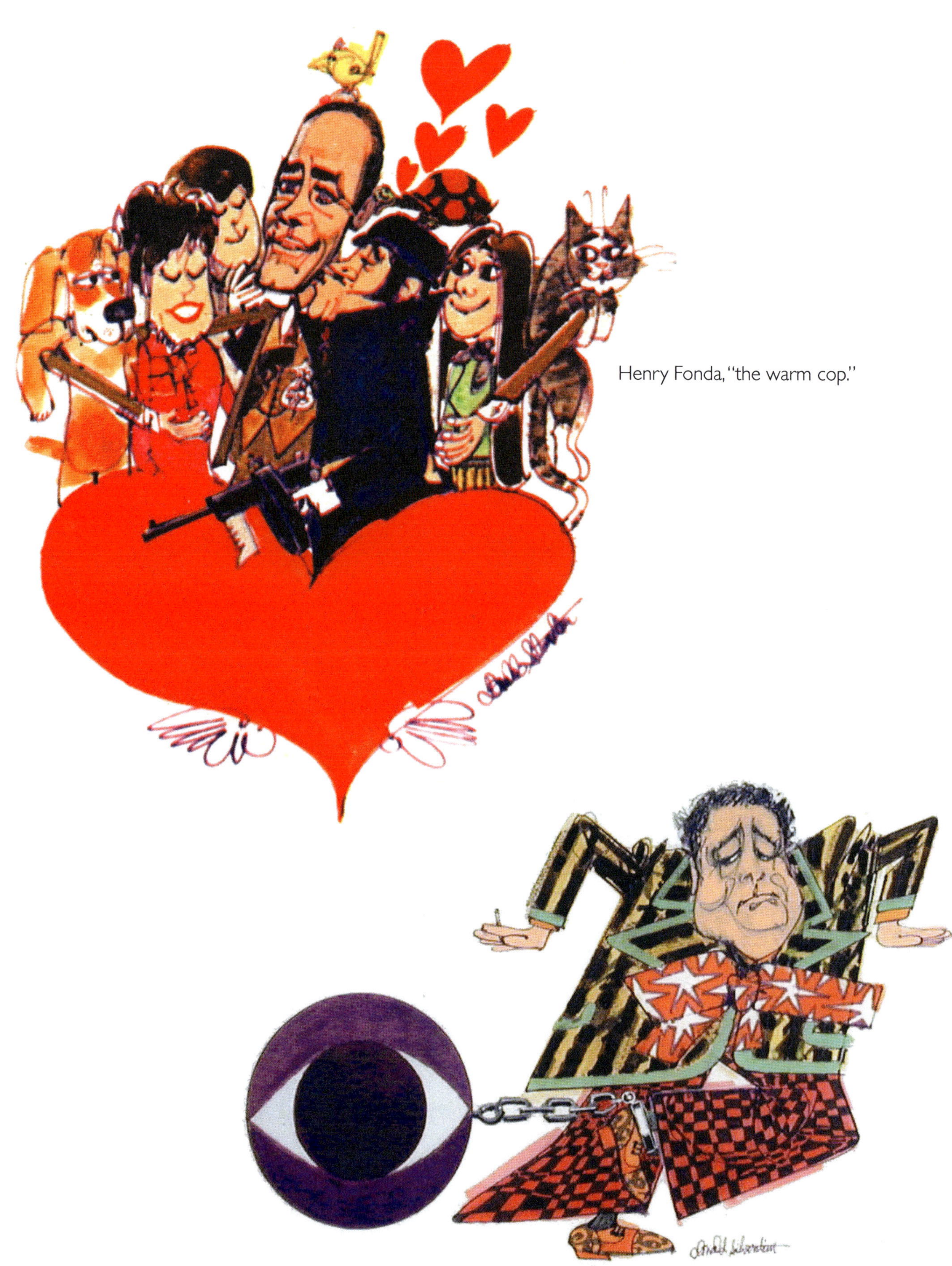

Henry Fonda, "the warm cop."

Jackie Gleason, the prisonor of CBS.

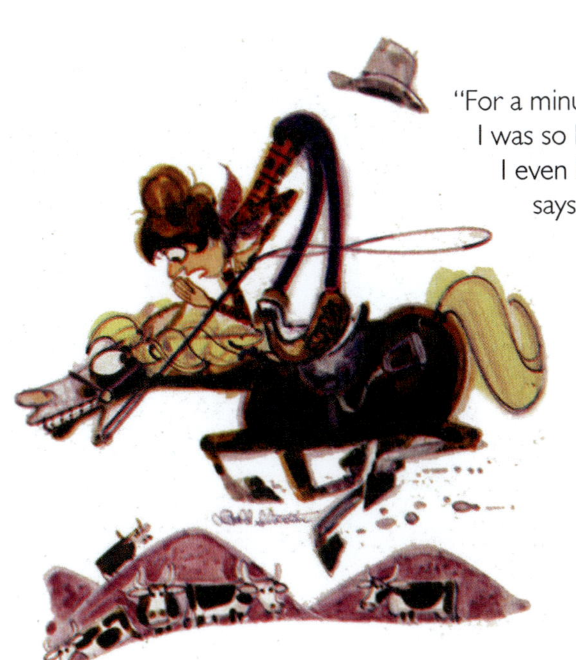

That's Entertainment, IV

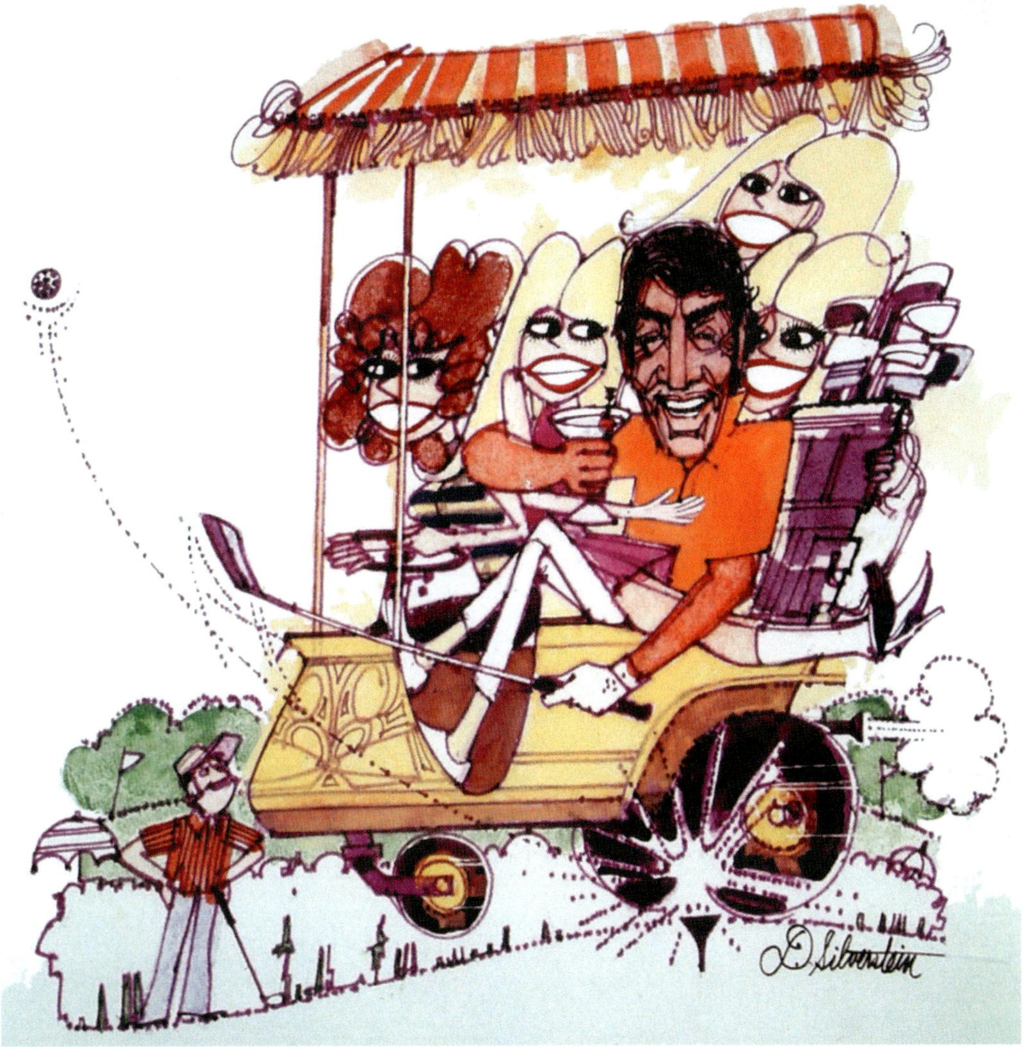

Golf and girls… Dean Martin.

P.S. V

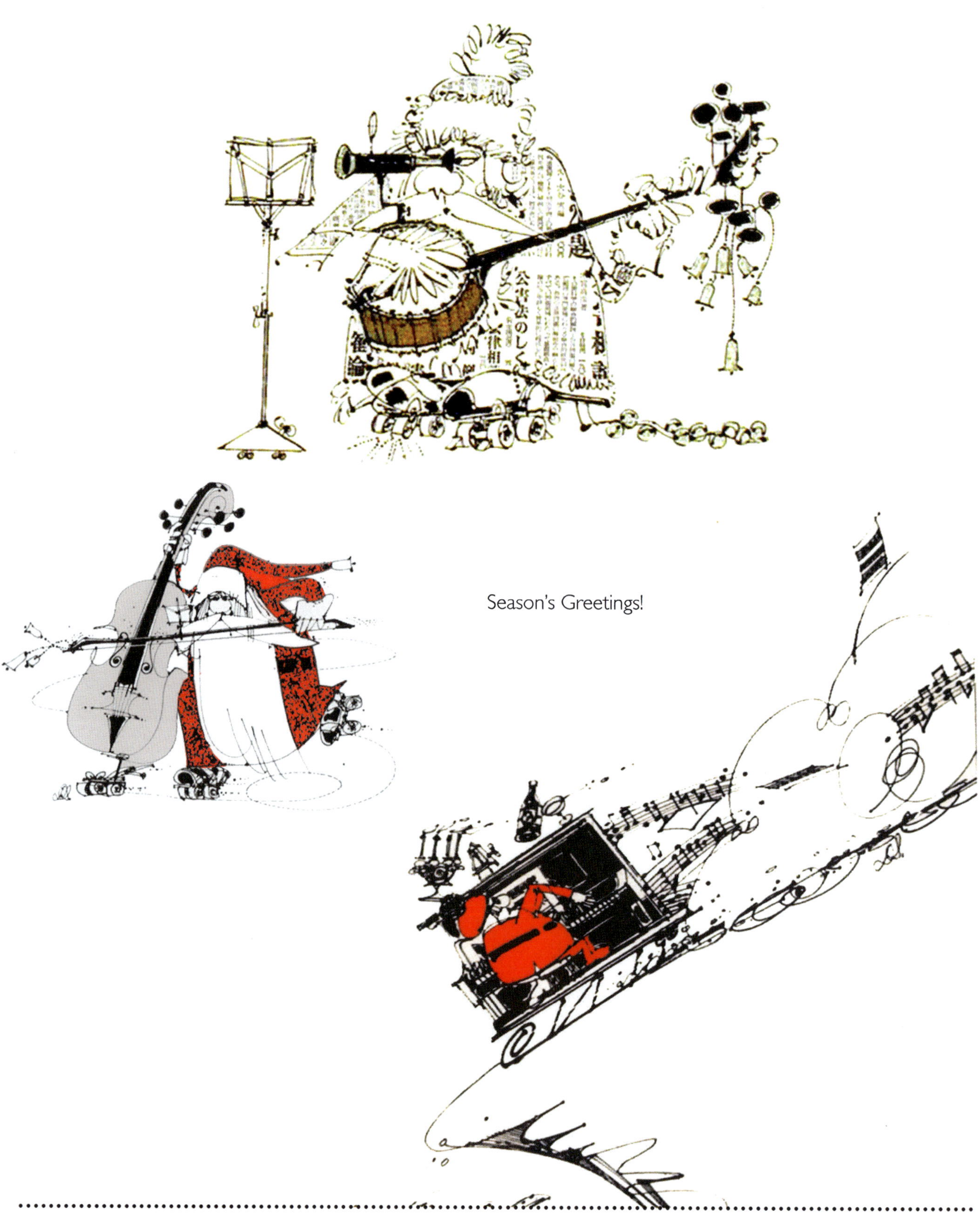

Season's Greetings!

VI

Donald's Zoology

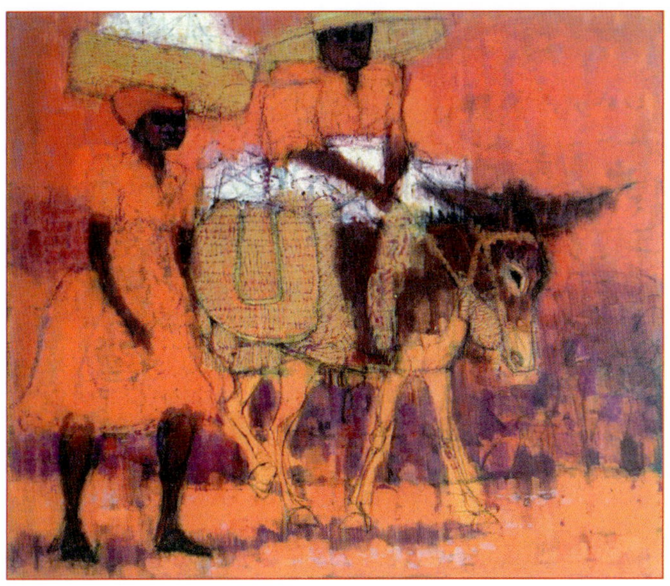

This particular African scene, a donkey transporting a man and his load, along with a woman carrying a basket on her head, was drawn by Donald Silverstein sometime in the early 1960's. Such an impressionistic quality and touch didn't last long.

As you go on in this book, you will see Donald's unique personality and sense of humor emerging in his drawings.

The evolution of Donald's cats

At the beginning, Donald was observing cats…, durable and innocent.

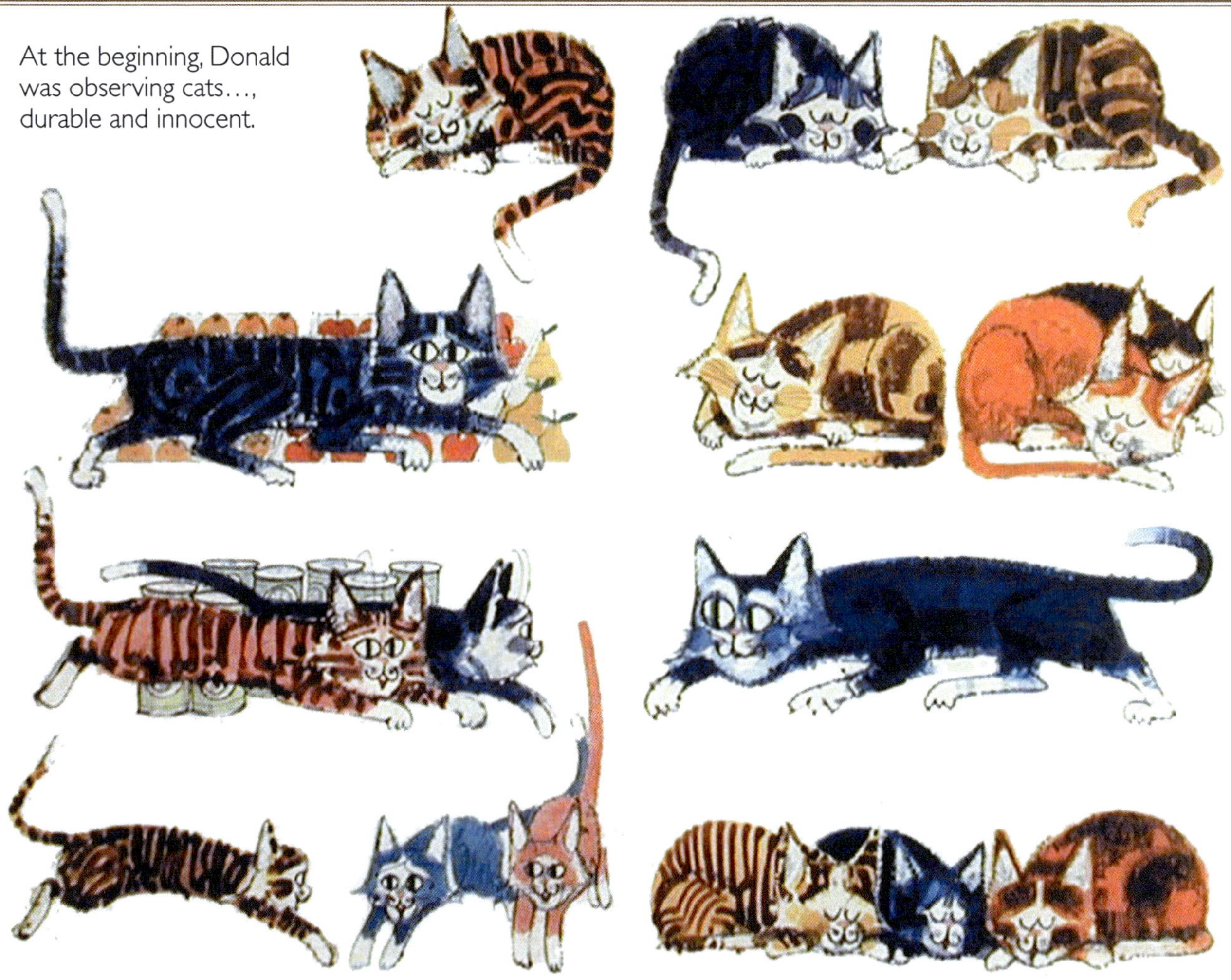

Donald began pursuing "his" cat.

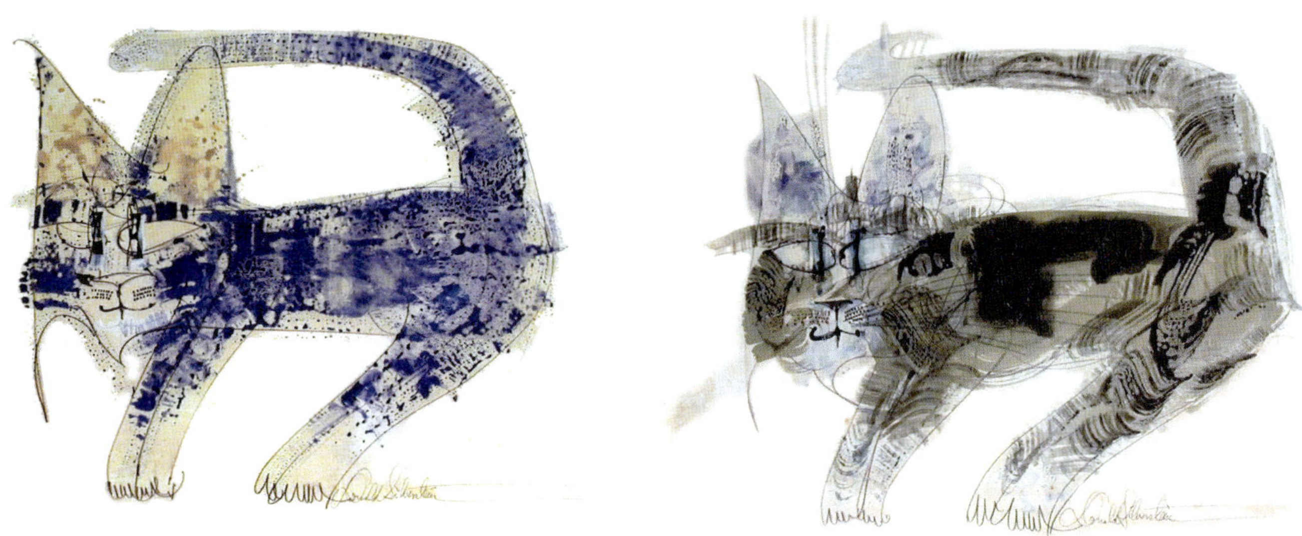

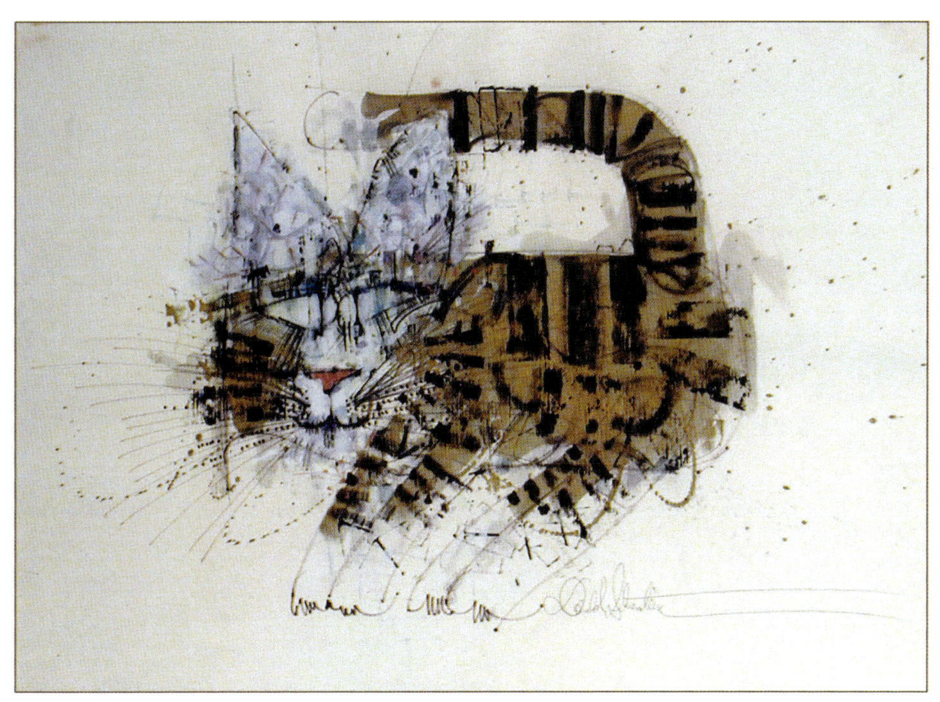

Transition from cat to tiger:
Nobody knows if Donald was satisfied with "his" ultimate cat.
You be the judge..

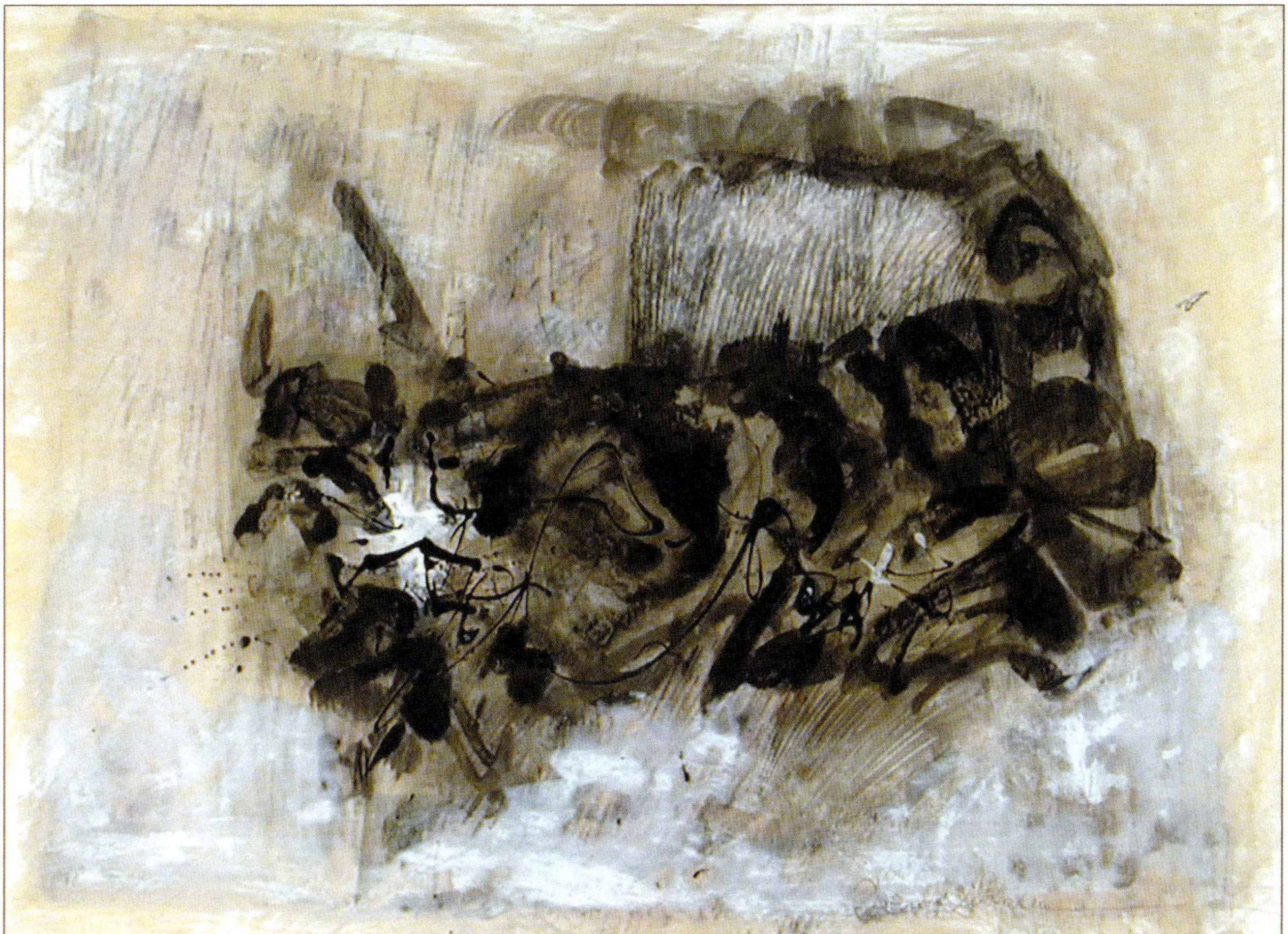

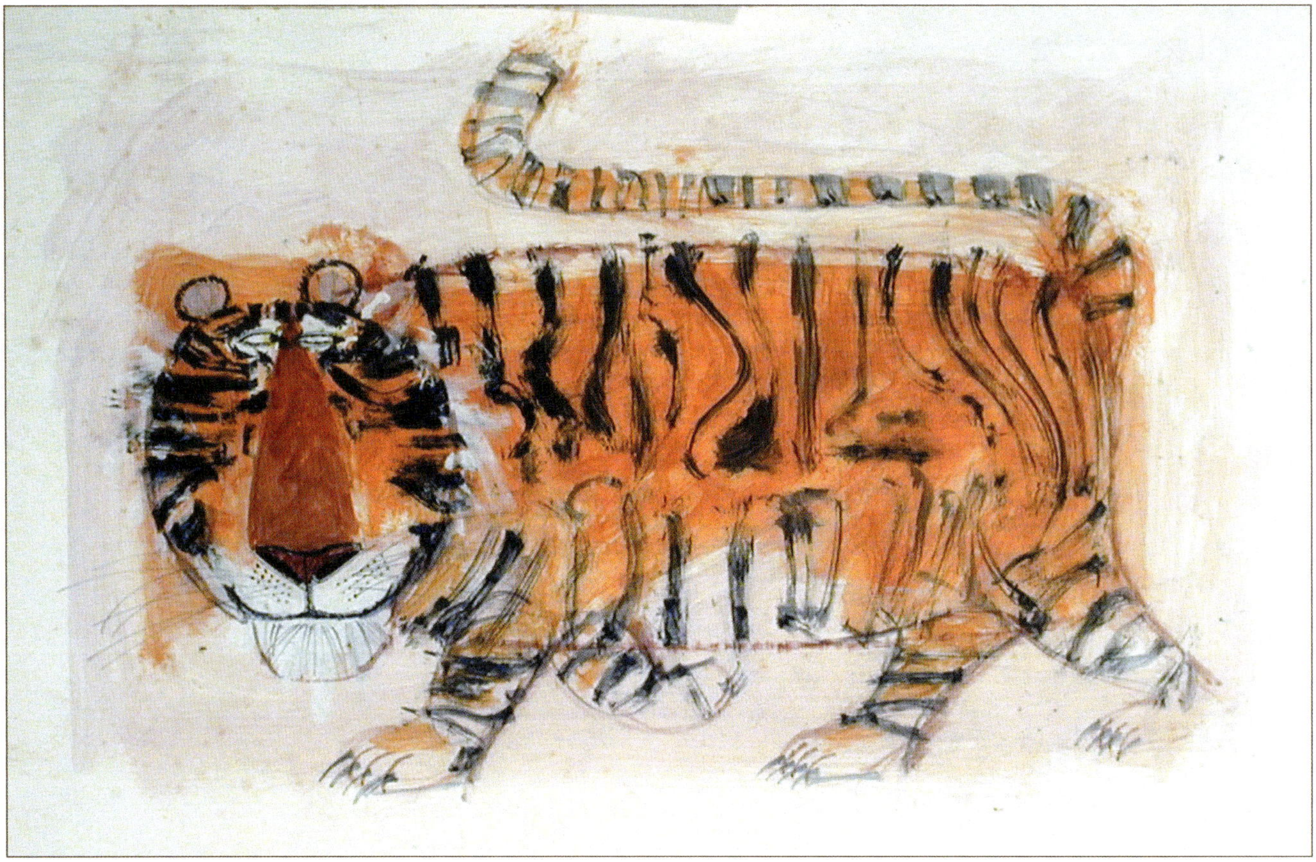

Big Cats

Donald's fascination with cats, shifts to tigers and back, from time to time.
However he saw more personality in tigers, their boldness, and
rudeness, and how tigers interrelated with other animals and even with
human beings.

Donald's tigers do not really scare kids, or rabbits, or majestic kings.
In most cases, tigers act silly, and ridiculously friendly. Sometimes, they're
taken advantage of which results in dumb disasters.

Some stories were folktales from Spain or Mexico. It is certain that
Donald sympathized with those unfairly treated tigers.

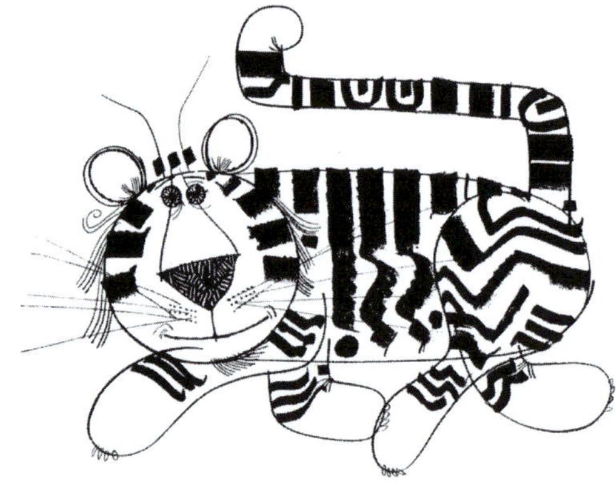

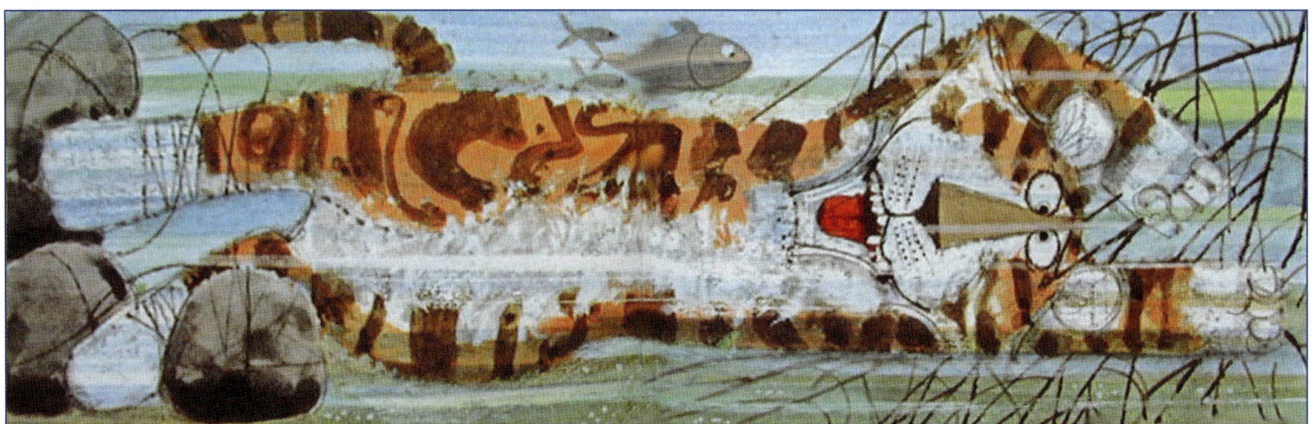

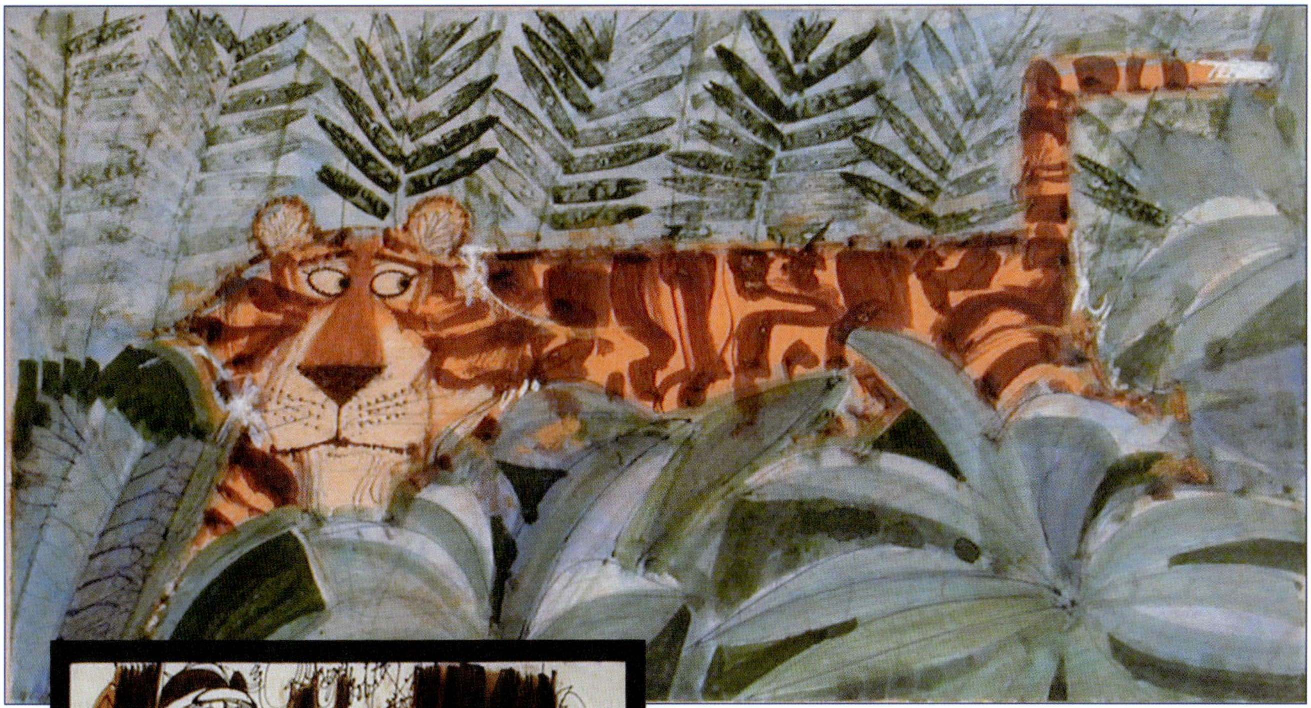

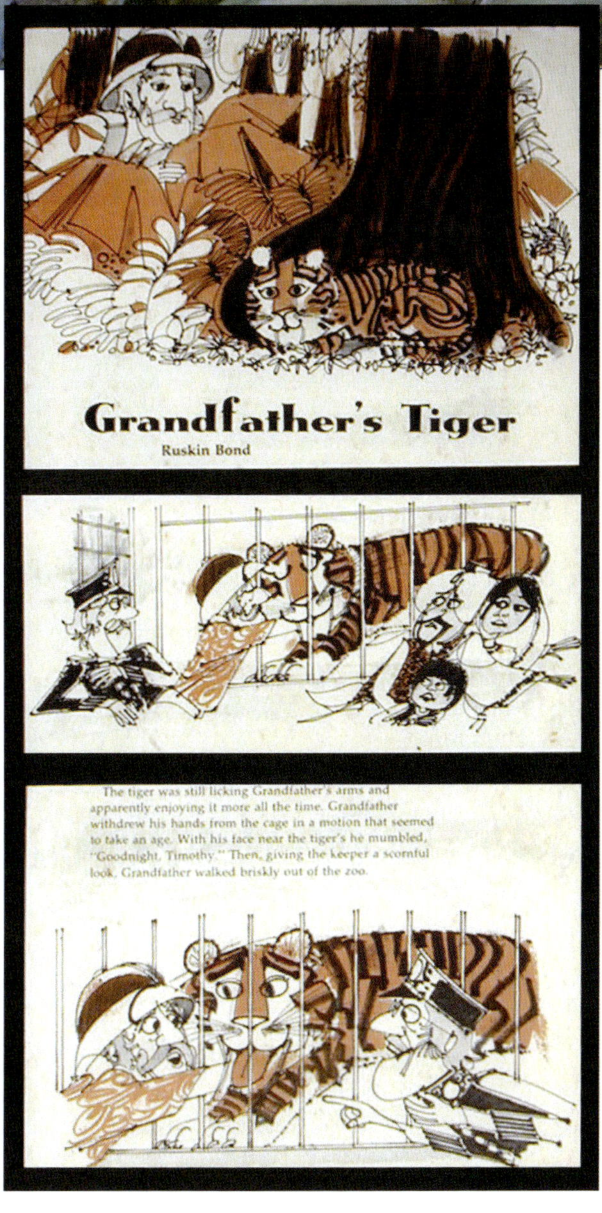

Sometimes Donald's tiger encounters some curious wacky people.

The adventures of tiger and rabbit.

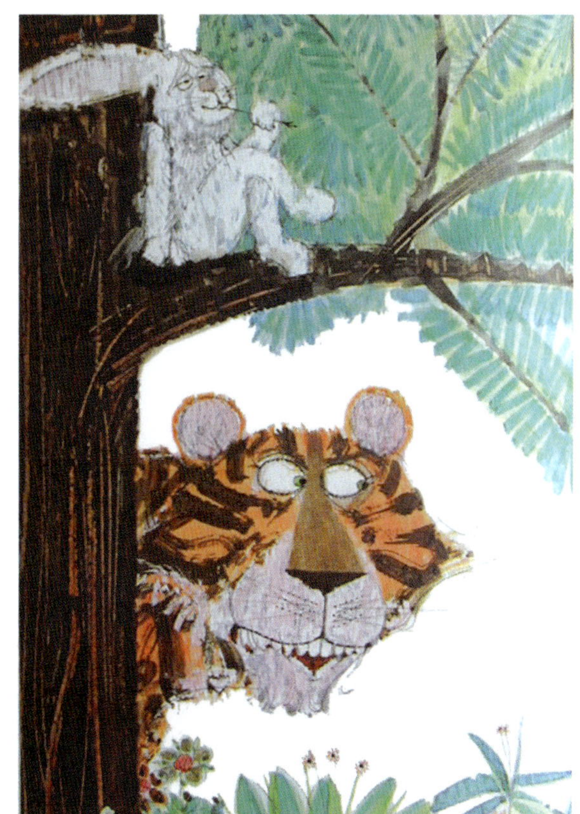

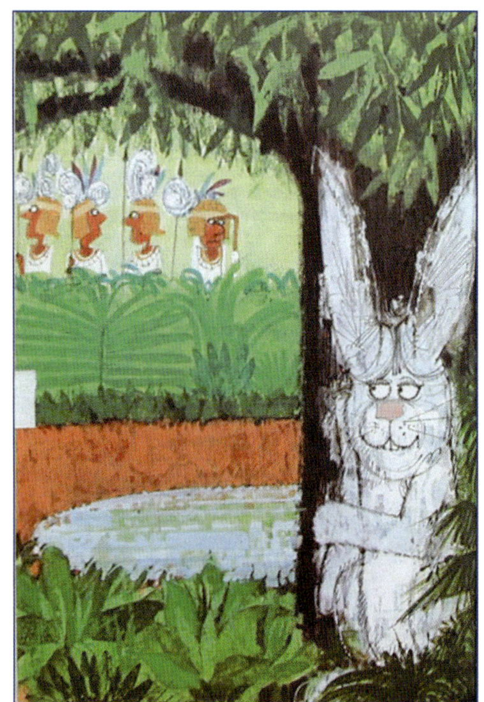

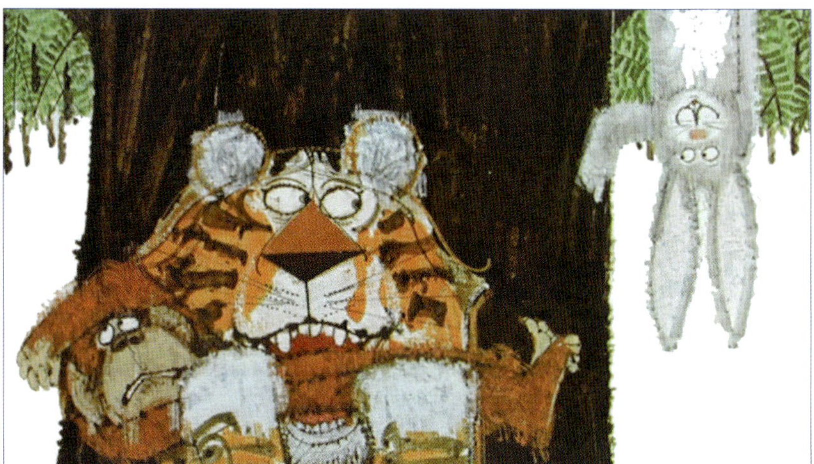

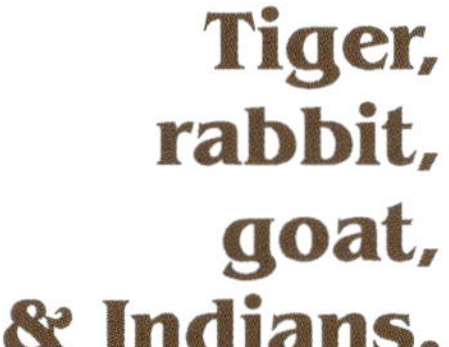

**Tiger,
rabbit,
goat,
& Indians.**

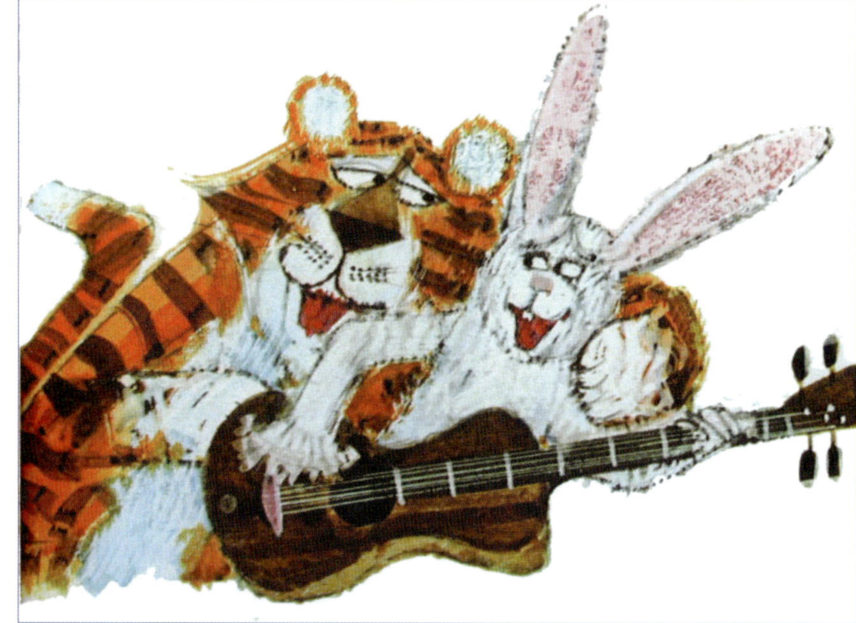

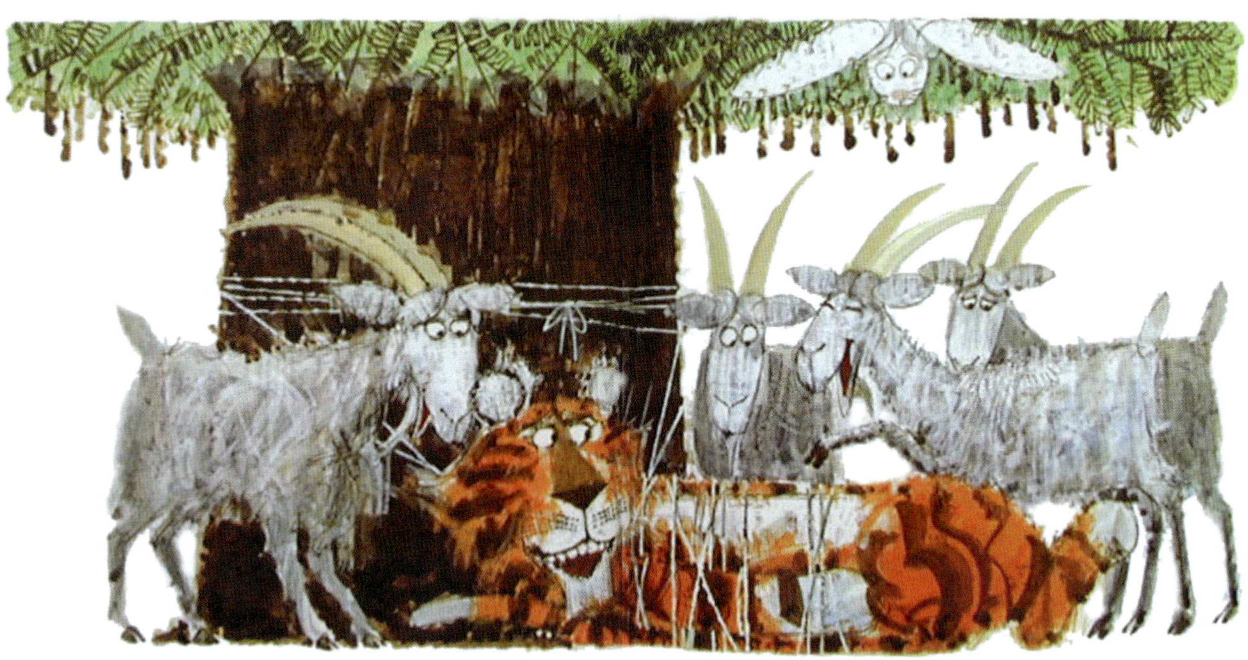

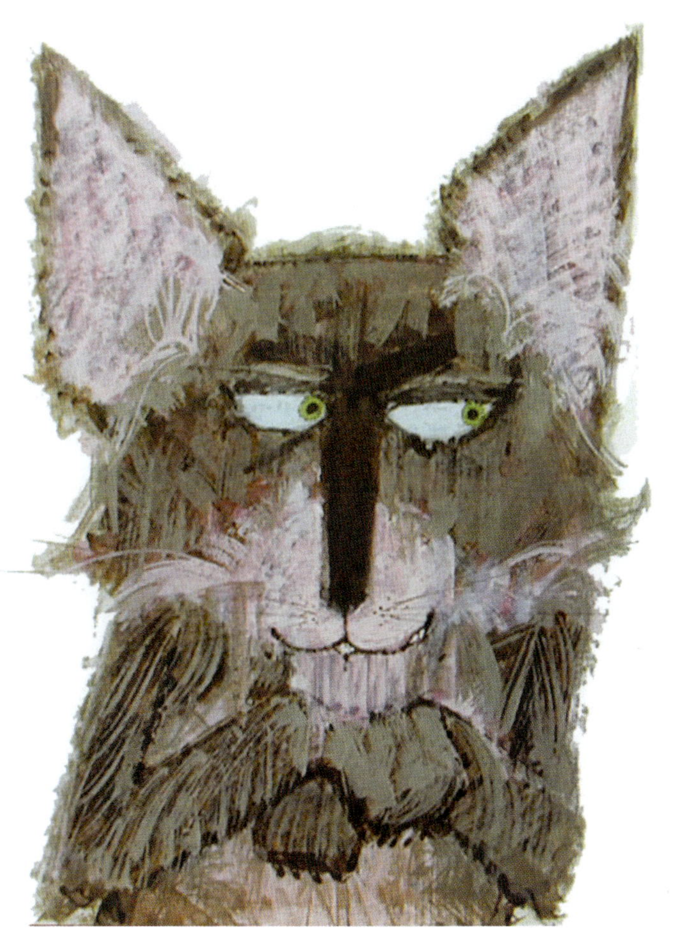

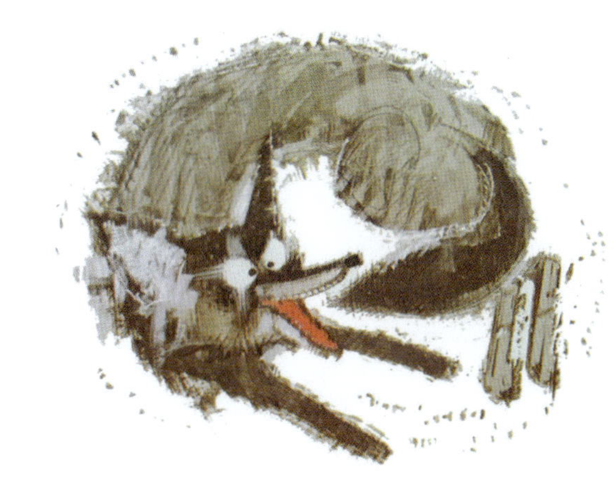

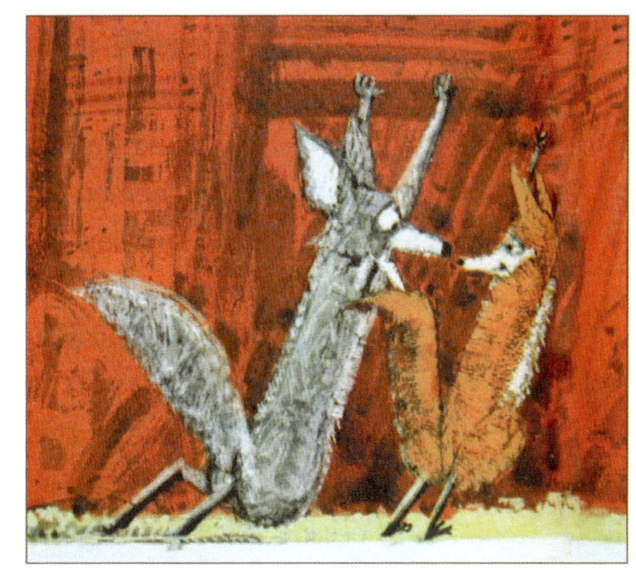

Coyote, Fox, Cock, & Dogs

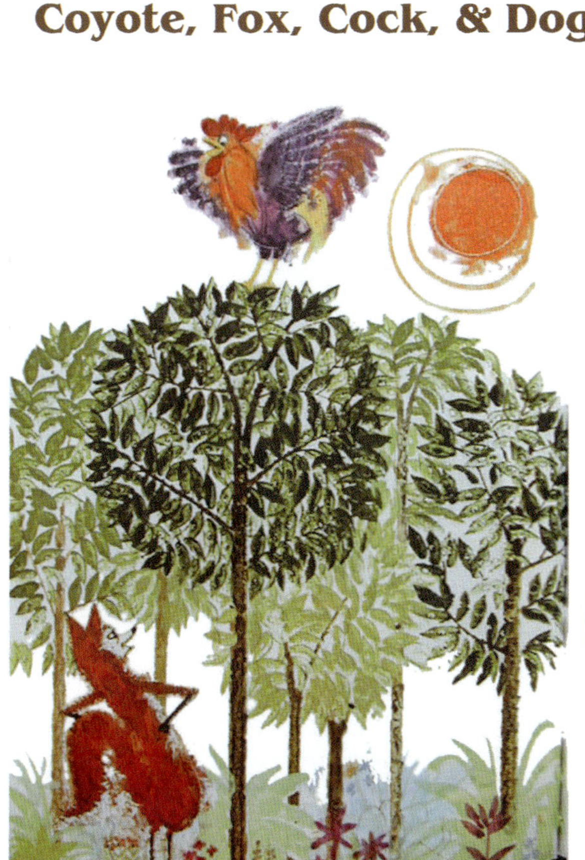

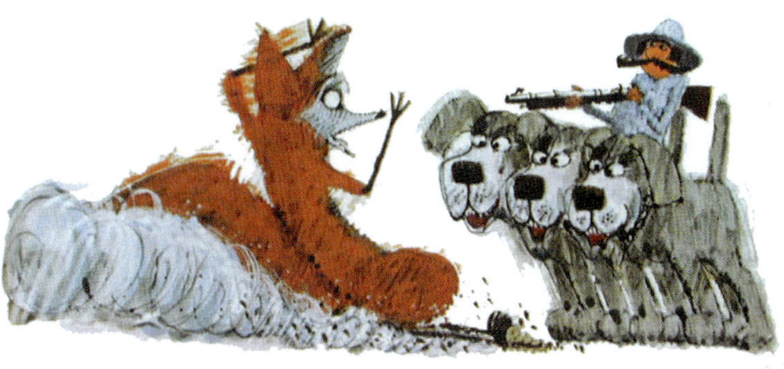

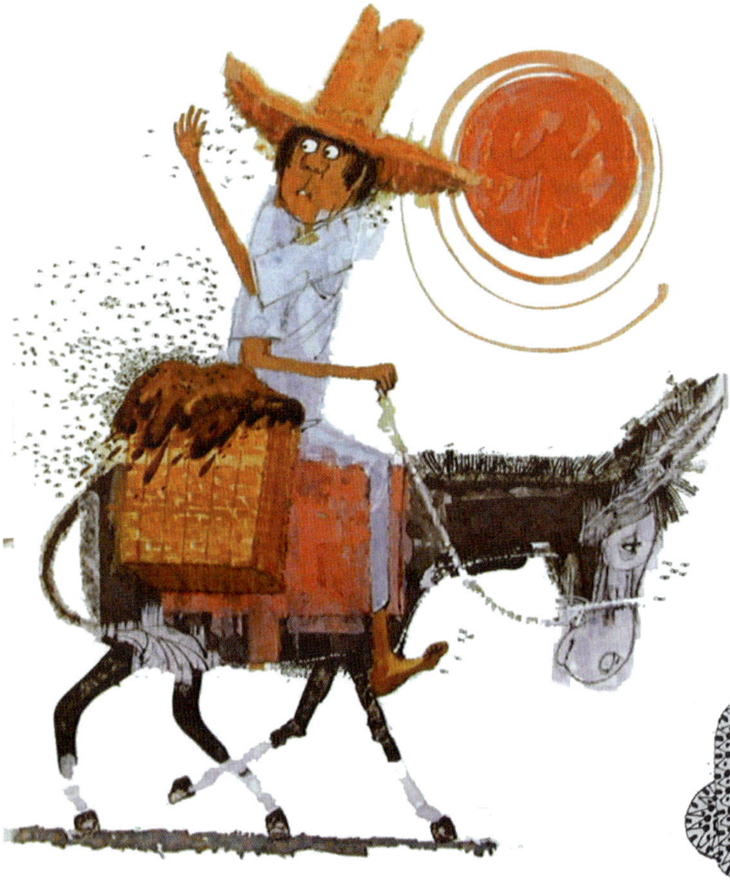

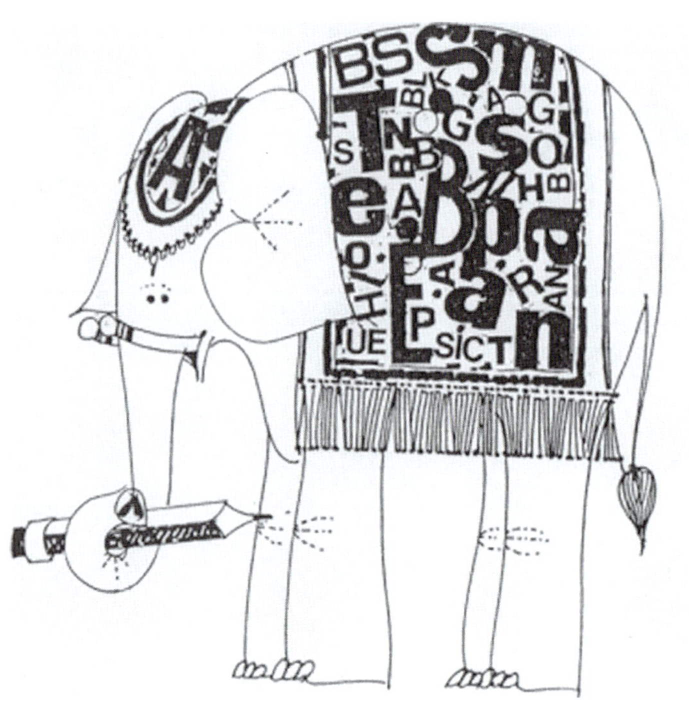

Sun scream

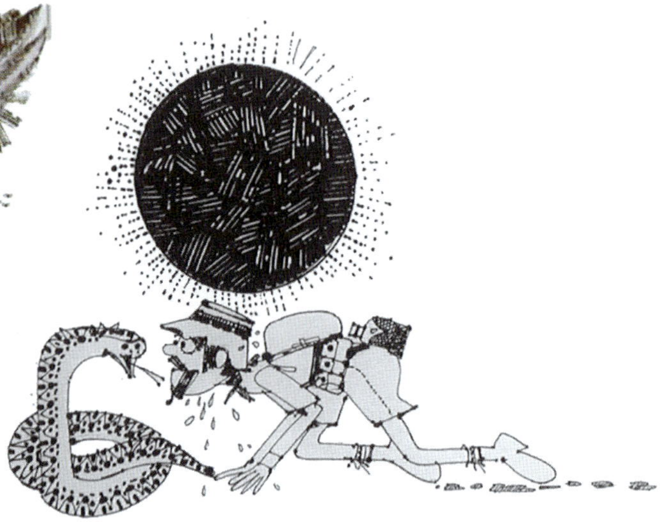

Progressive self-portraits

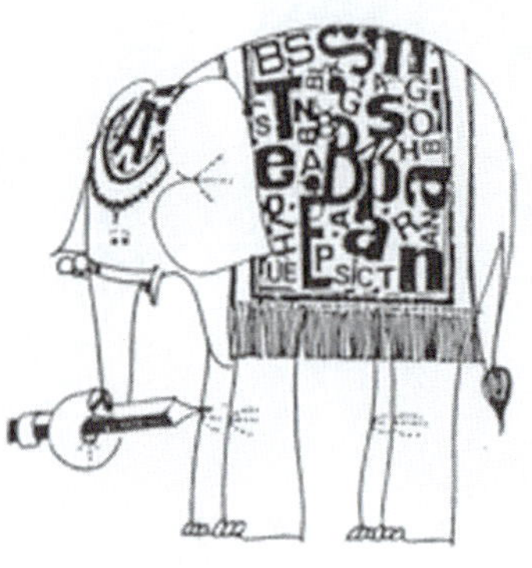

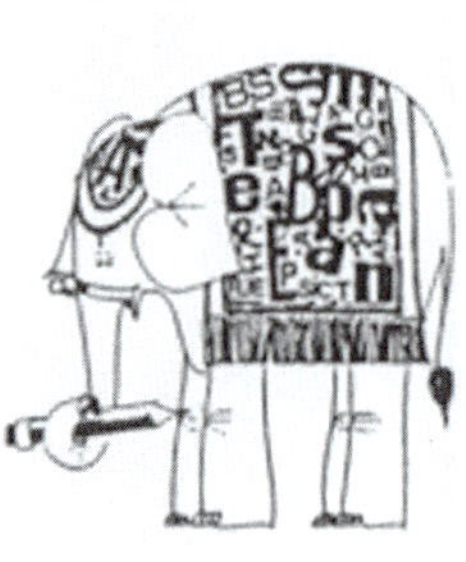

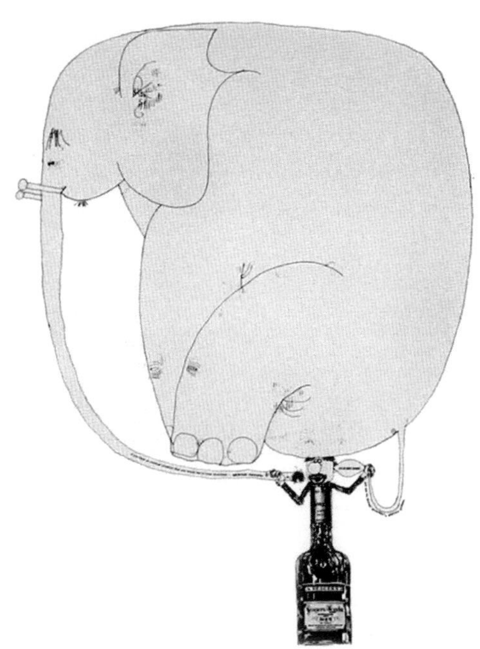

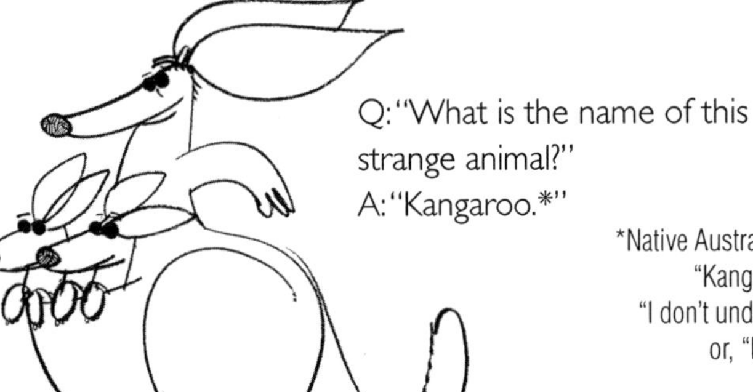

Q: "What is the name of this
strange animal?"
A: "Kangaroo.*"

*Native Australian's answer
"Kangaroo" means,
"I don't understand you,"
or, "I don't know."

abba-dabba-dabba-dabba-dabba-dabba zebra...

Passion Show

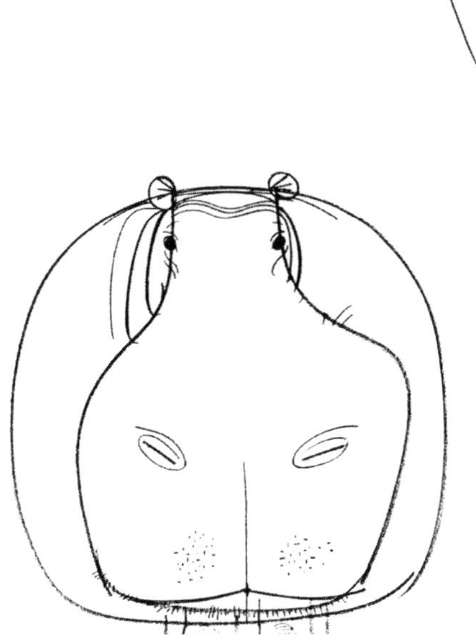

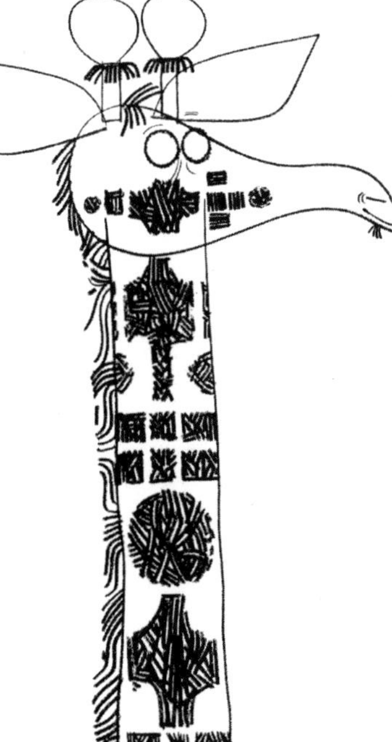

A fashion-minded giraffe
designed its neck, and
called it "neck-dye."

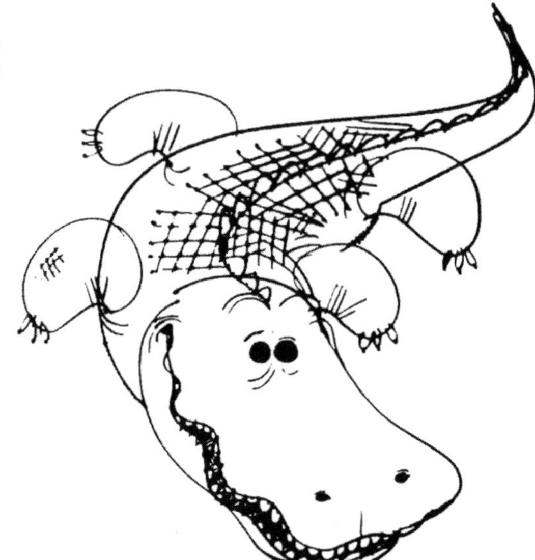

"See you later alligator!"

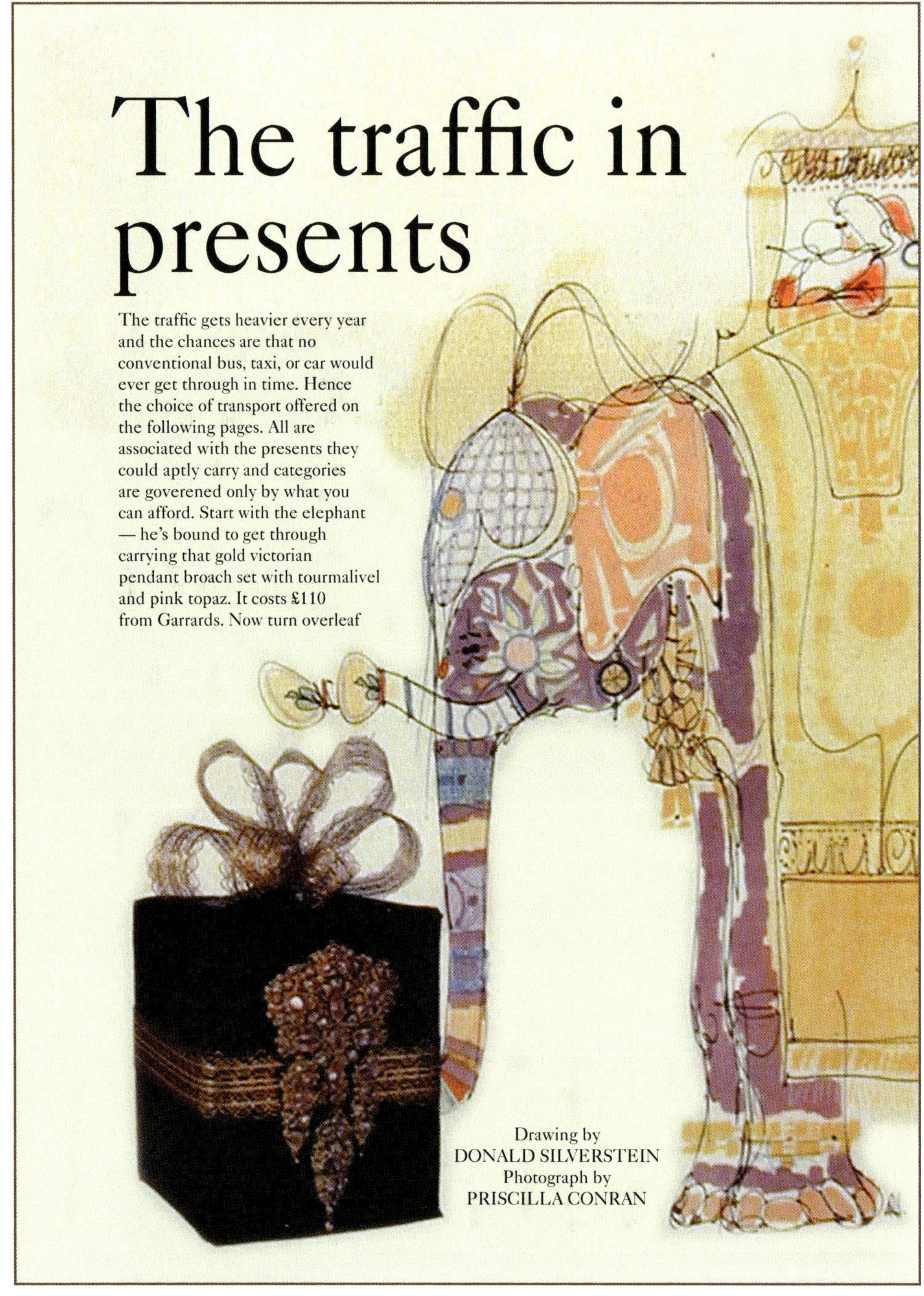

The traffic in presents

The traffic gets heavier every year and the chances are that no conventional bus, taxi, or car would ever get through in time. Hence the choice of transport offered on the following pages. All are associated with the presents they could aptly carry and categories are goverened only by what you can afford. Start with the elephant — he's bound to get through carrying that gold victorian pendant broach set with tourmalivel and pink topaz. It costs £110 from Garrards. Now turn overleaf

Drawing by
DONALD SILVERSTEIN
Photograph by
PRISCILLA CONRAN

VII
Fairytales and Books

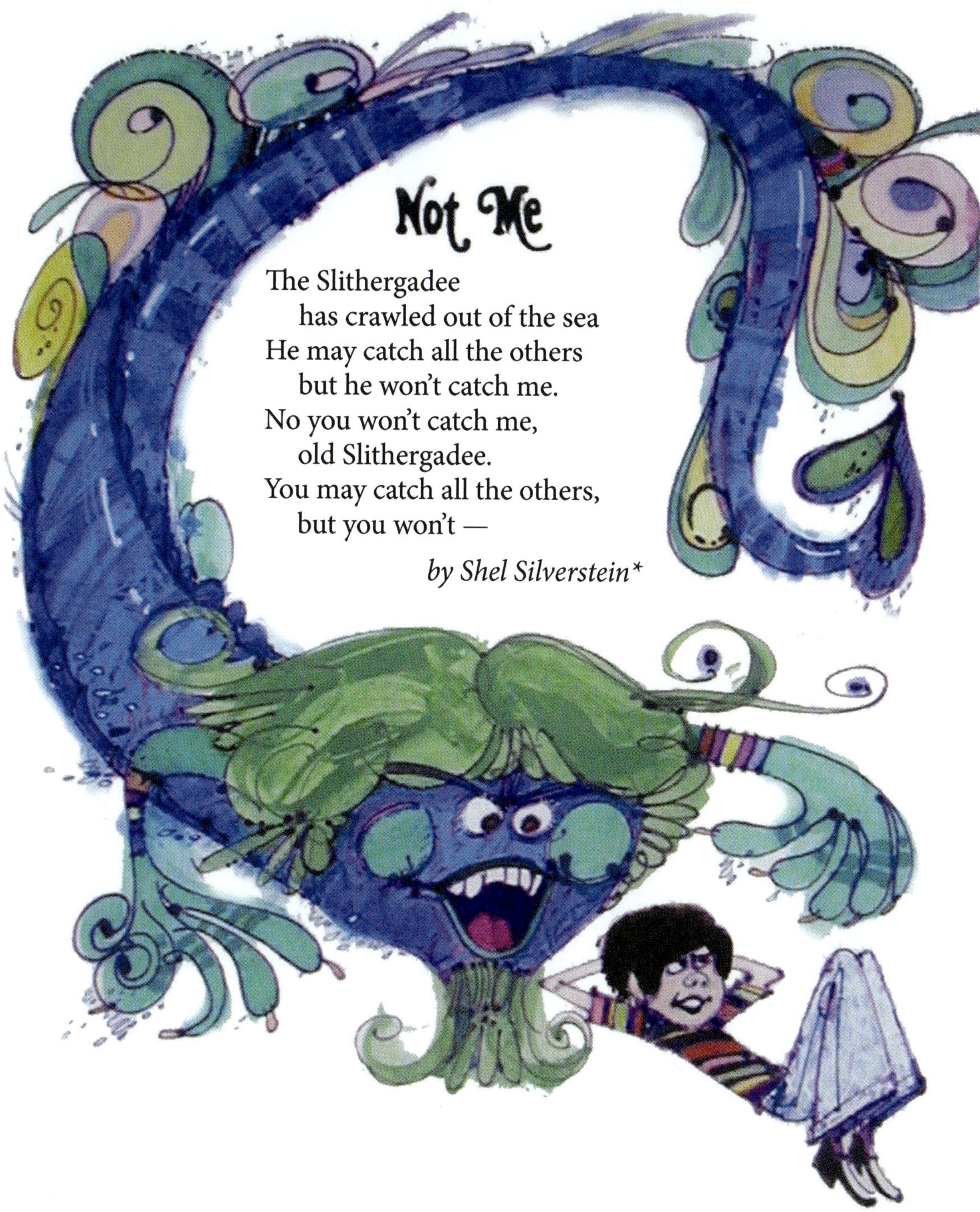

* Shel Silverstein, a well-known story writer, is not related to the illustrator, Donald Silverstein.

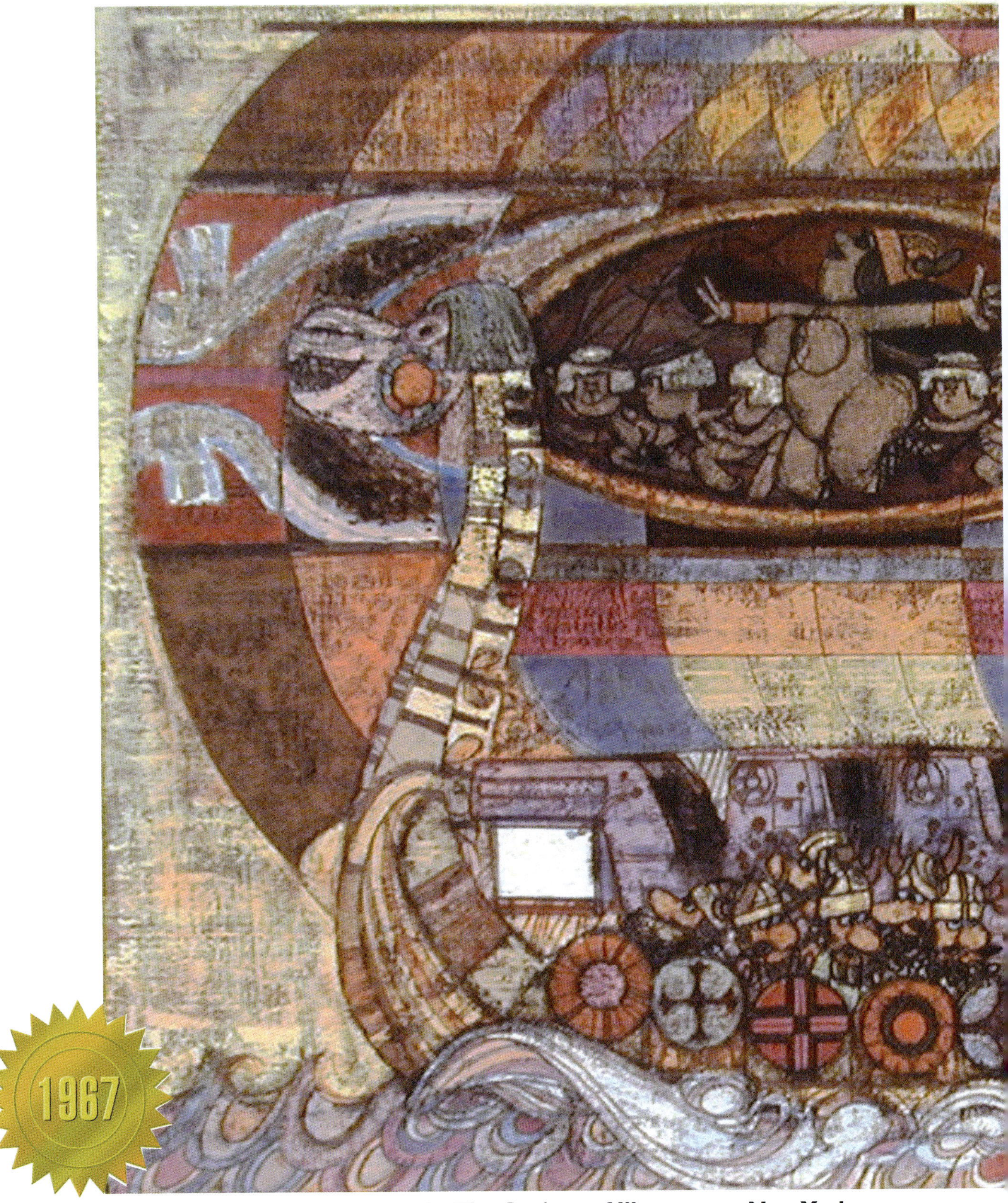

1967 Award of Excellence by The Society of Illustrators, New York

This fully orchestrated, graphic display of Nordic Majesty depicts the highly ceremonious Trans-Atlantic crossing from Switzerland to the U.S. by the highly unusual, but unique, unbelievably odd Viking expediting service, — named strangely enough, the highly unusual but unique unbelievably odd Viking expediting service of Stockholm, carrying the cargo of a 4 color press to Harrison Color Process in Philadelphia. To insure maximum speed, prompt delivery and dry beards among the lovely crew, the Viking ship was loaded aboard the fast Greek freighter, Yokishama Ugashu Jr. and was carried across the Atlantic to New York where upon entering the harbor the Viking ship complete with crew, beards and cargo was lowered into the water to make its own triumphant finale to pier 444 under its own sail. The sail was raised and a strong breeze immediately filled it out making the delicious figure painted on it more voluptuous than ever.

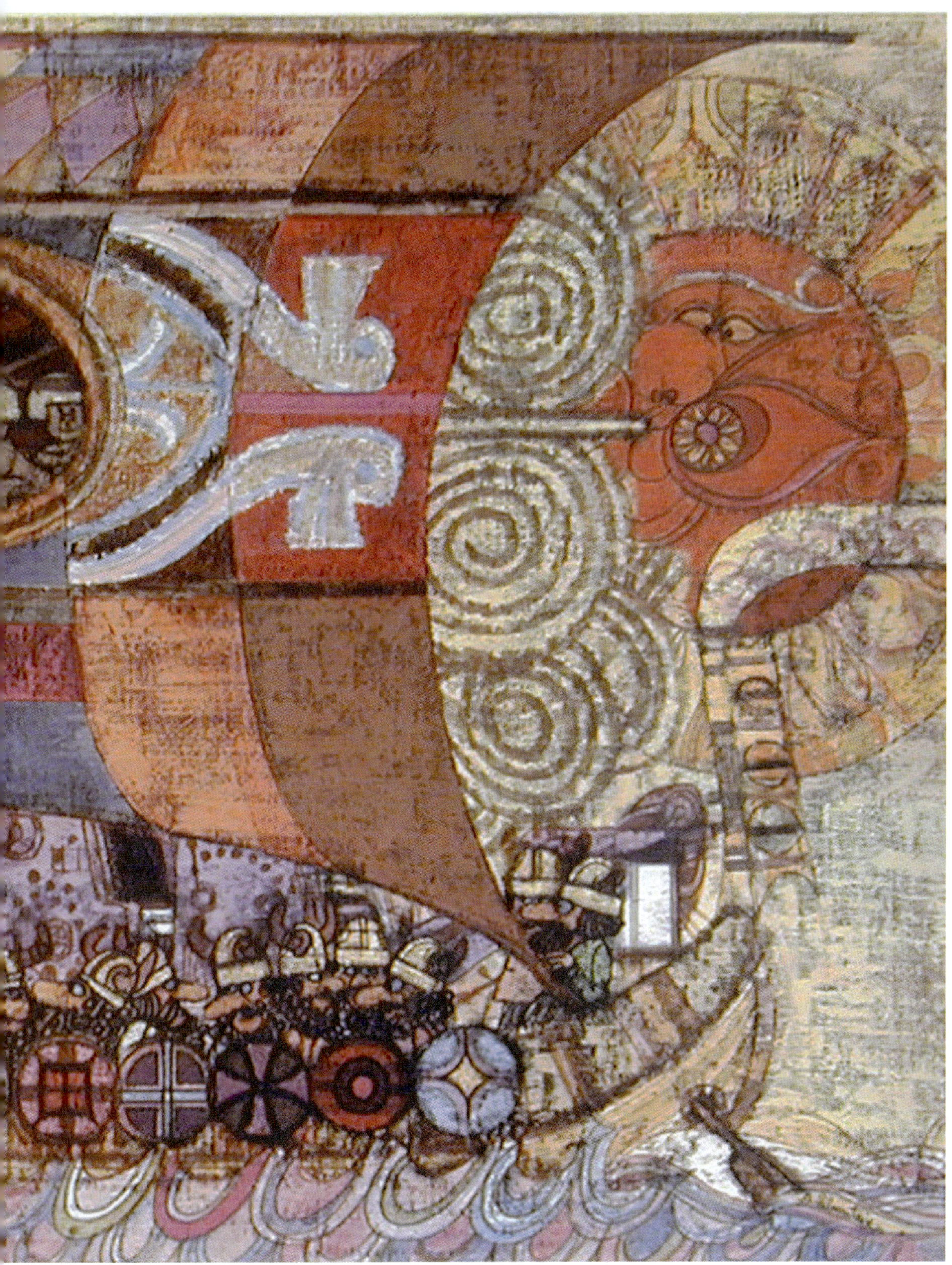

After a few moments of quivering ecstasy, the hairy crew caught sight of land and immediately mutinied; The navigator became slightly unbalanced and ate 6 yards of delicious sail cloth and a side order of stewed oars as the ship sailed majestically towards and eventually through pier 444. Straight on to 10th Avenue, where the press was unloaded and shipped to Philadelphia, and is now fully operative, printing full color Chinese Editions of the Philadelphia telephone directory for America's leading universities.
Credits: Artist: Donald Silverstein/Represented in New York and the free world by Darwin M. Bahm, 29 Fifth Avenue, New York, NY 10003/Art director: Larry Alten/Printed by Harrison Color Process; 2032 North 16th St., Philadelphia, PA 19121/ Copywriter: Rodney G. Twitchwell/ Type consultant: Jeeves L. Nowicki/Color consultant: Paul Gauguin/ Printing supervisor: Benjamin Franklin.

Folktales

Donald's award-winning fairytale books were well received by parents and children worldwide.

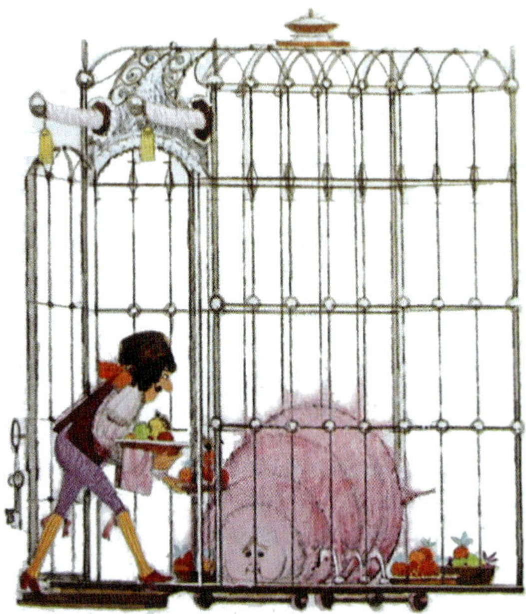

Feeding the giant flea

"Folktales of Spain and Latin America" selected by Lila Green ©1974; General Learning Corporation" 7.5" x 9.5" hard cover; 96 pages.

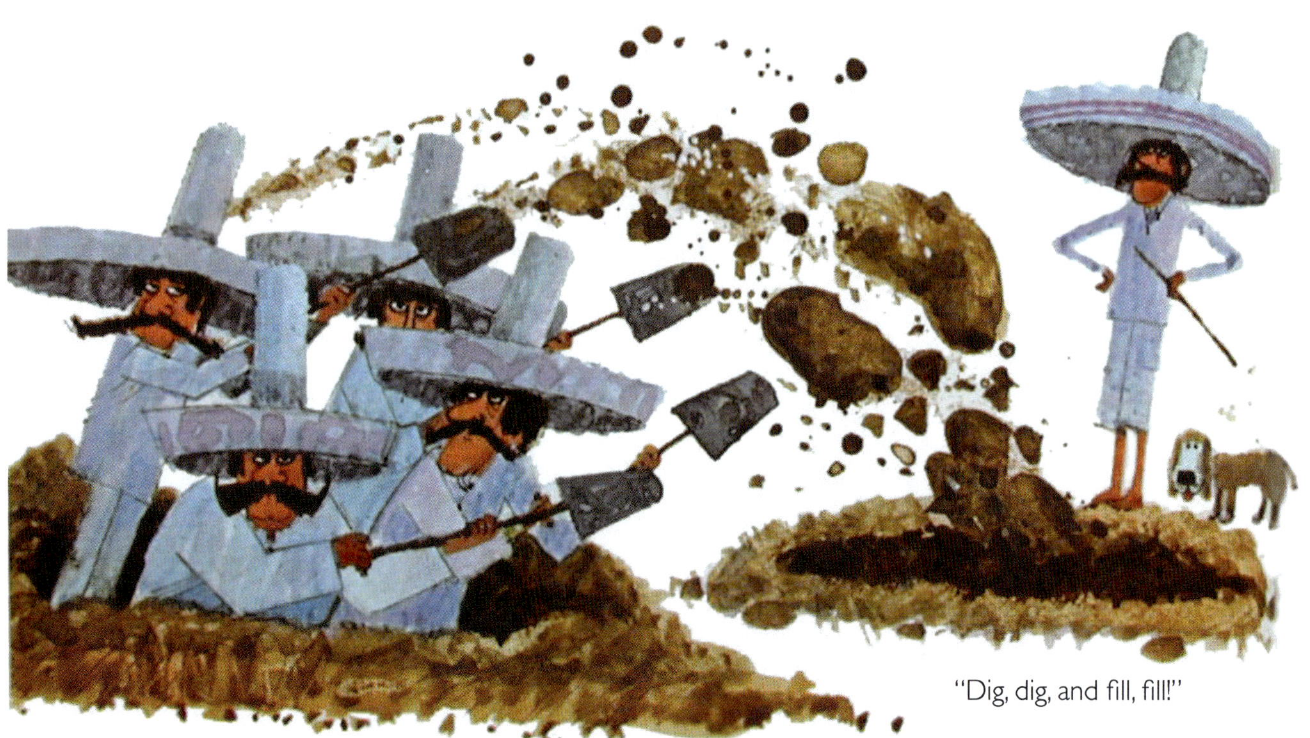

"Dig, dig, and fill, fill!"

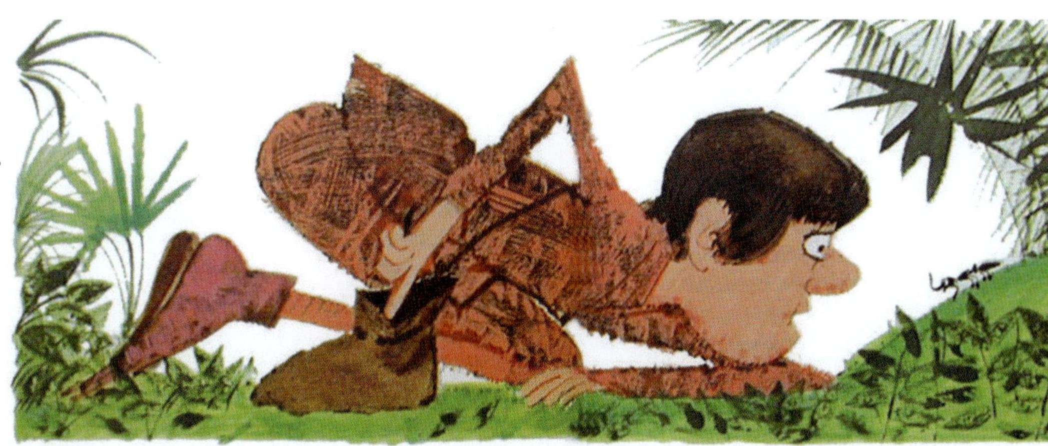

A man and an ant.

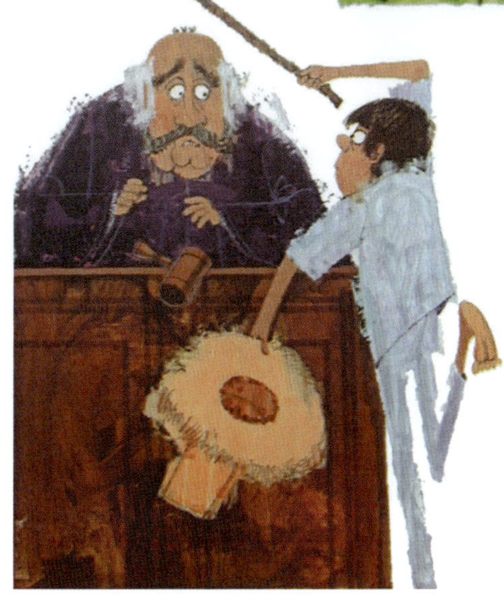

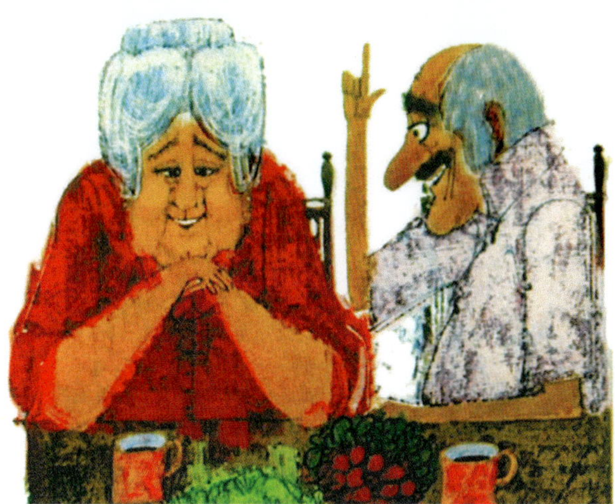

Grandpa and grandma are still enjoying their lives.

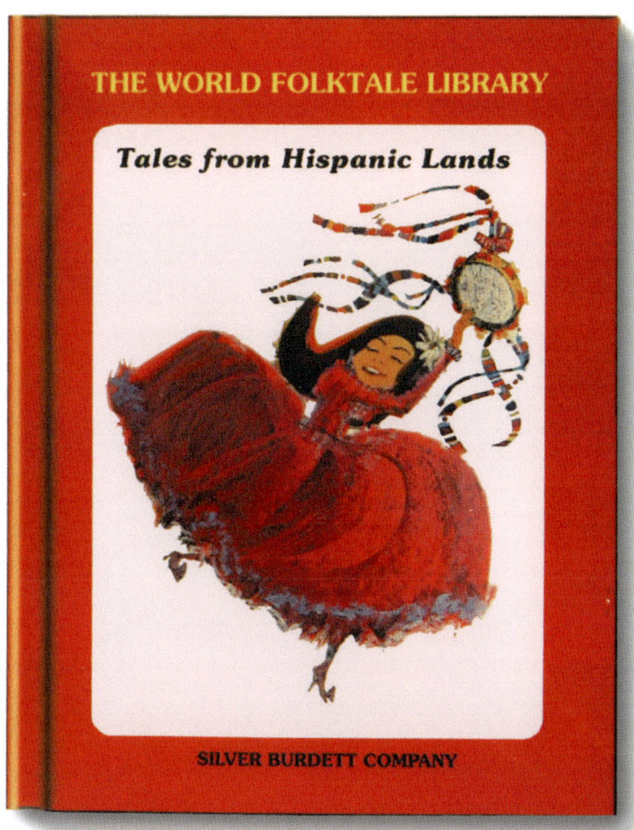

Folktales are old. They are easy to remember, and fun to listen to and to tell. Most folktales are stories that were told and retold long before the invention of books and printing. That is how they got their names. they were passed along by word of mouth — one folk told another folk. Fathers told children. Neighbor shared with neighbor Merchants told innkeepers. Innkeepeers told visiting sailors and sea captains, who carried the stories to the far corners of the world.

Folktales may come from unfamiliar people and different parts of the world, but there is something in each one that makes people see that we are very much alike the world over. Well, if you are about to be eaten by a tiger, maybe you had better read about Donald's rabbit right away!

—From "*Tales from Hispanic Lands*"

"Tales from Hispanic Lands" ©1979 Silver Burdett Company

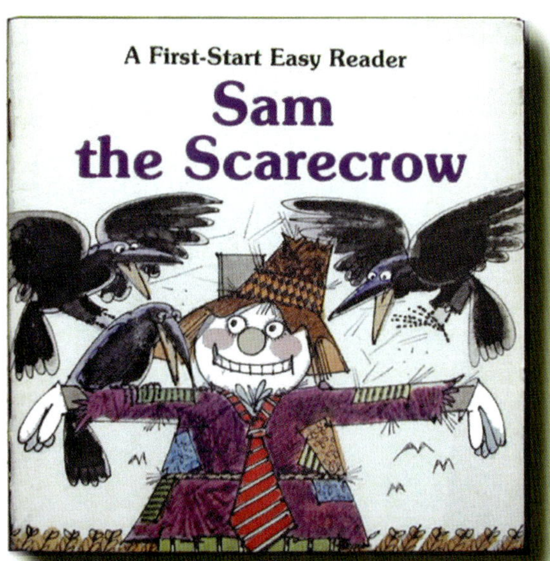

"Sam the Scarecrow" Written by Sharon Gordon ©1980
Troll Associates, Nahwah, New Jersey.6"x6"; 28 pages

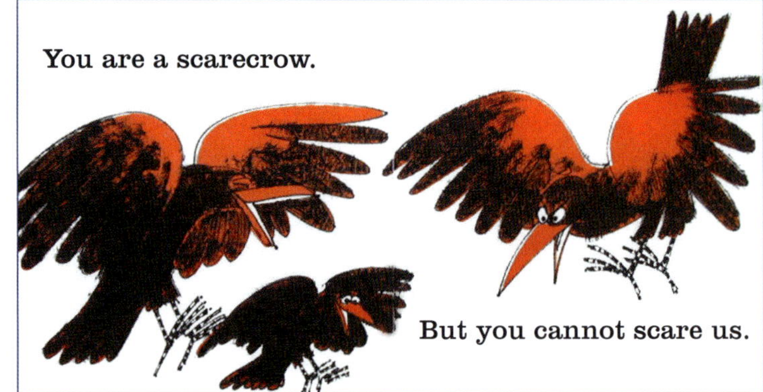

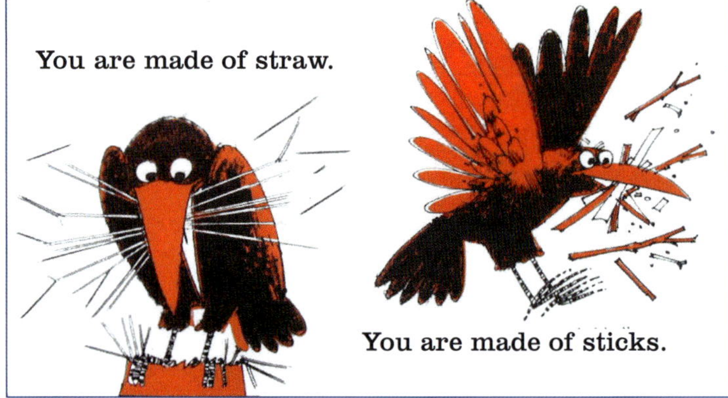

So, how did Sam scare the crows?
Find the book and read, and you will see how.

Straggling animals and even a scarecrow

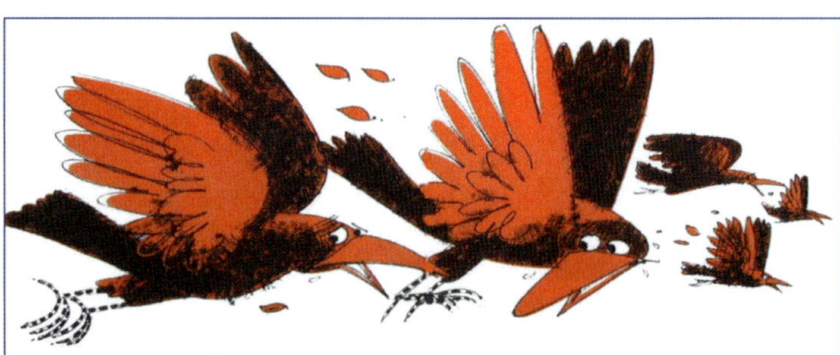

King Kong

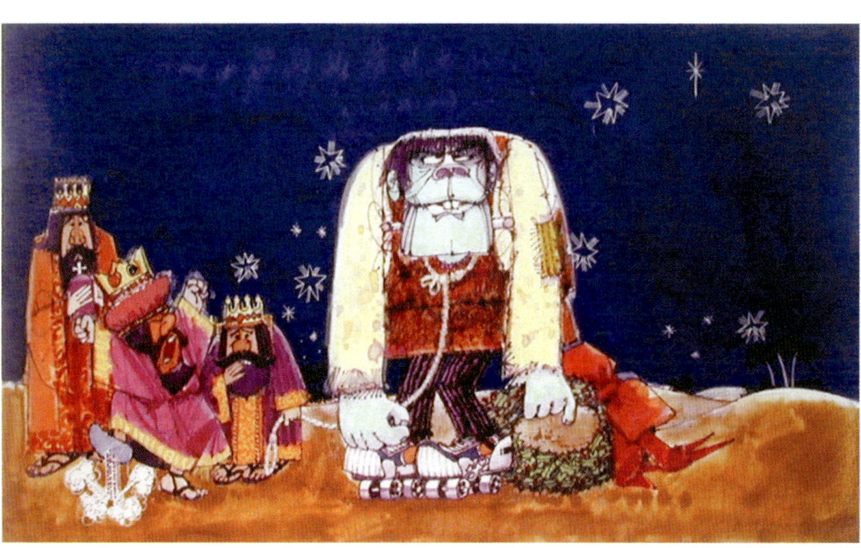

Three Kings and a gorilla.
A gorilla?

Monster?!

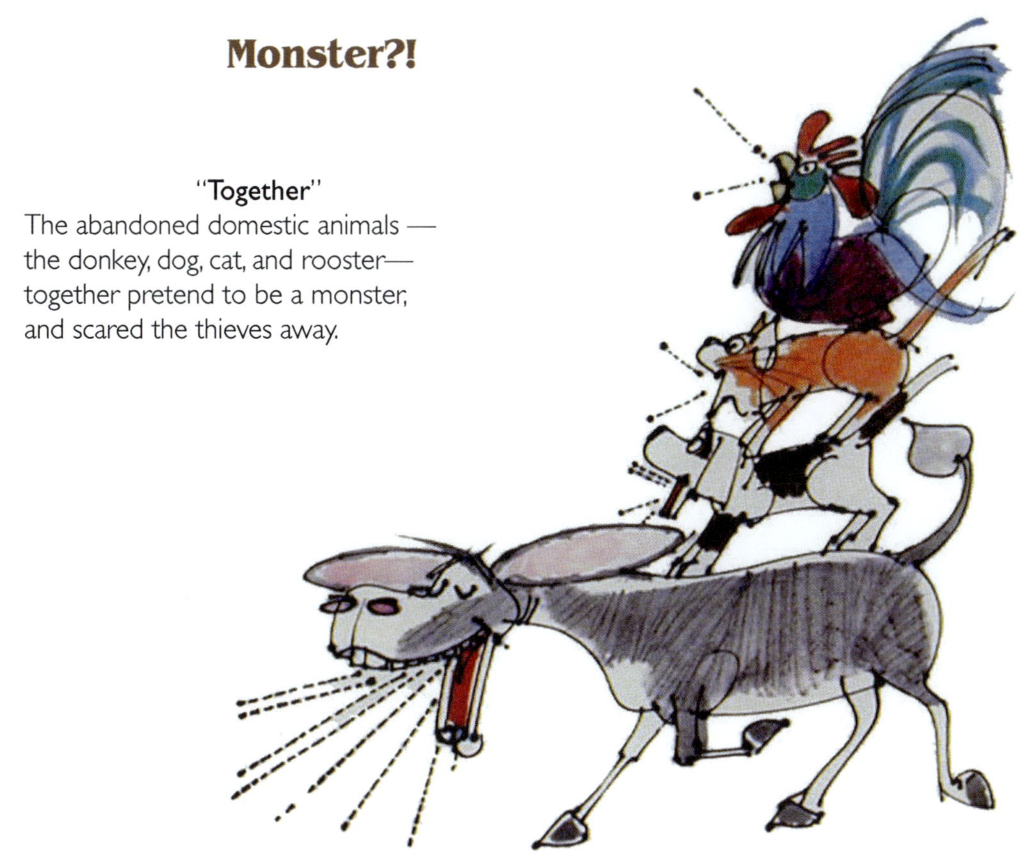

Dog's Best Friend

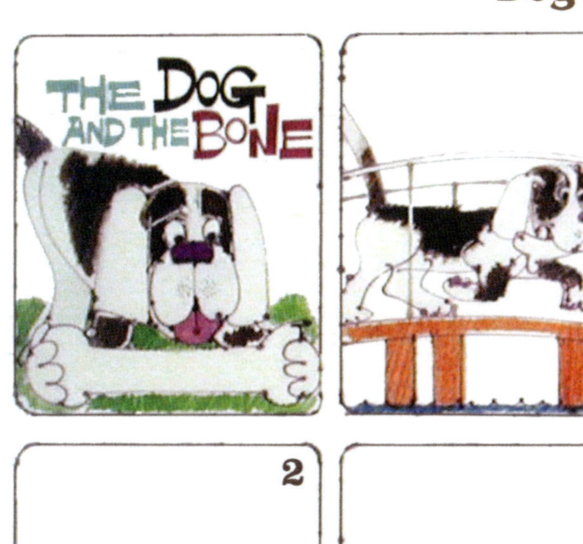

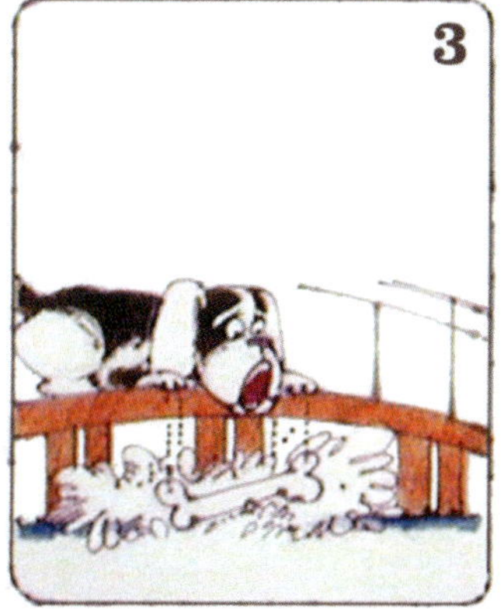

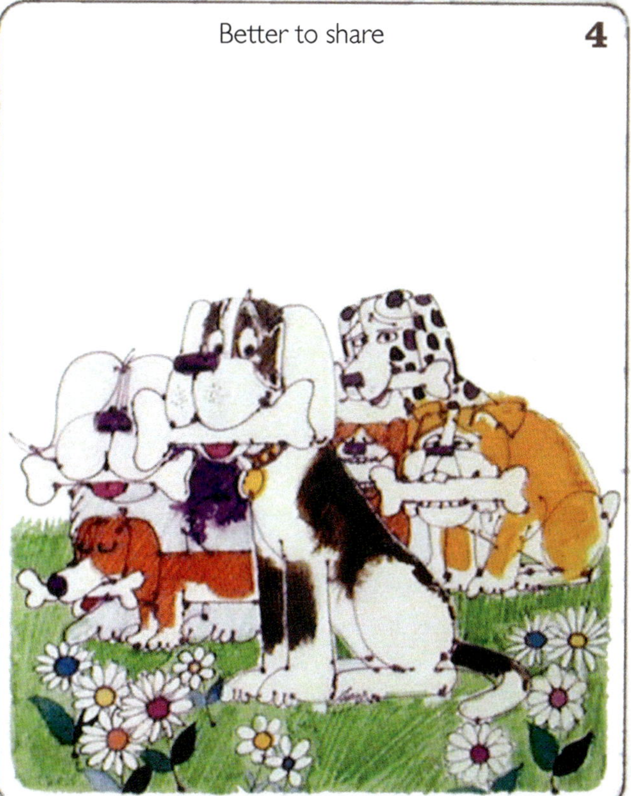

"The dog and the Bone"

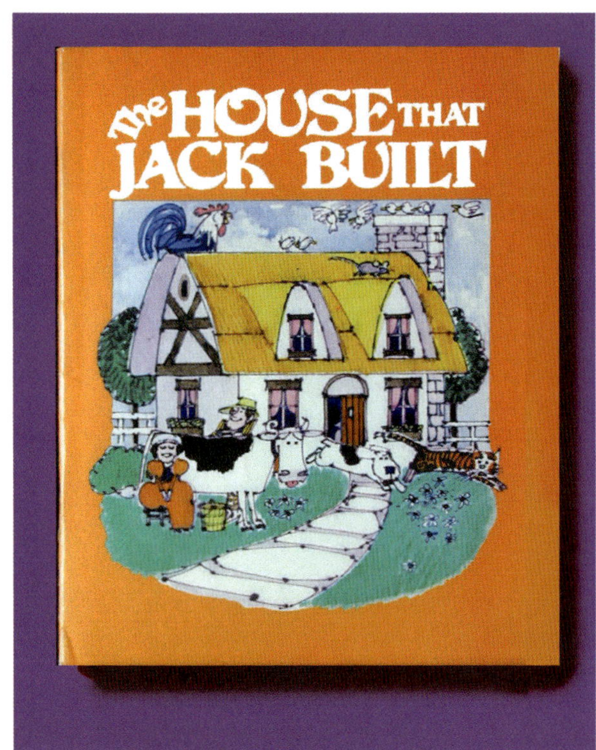

"The House that Jack Built" retold by David Cutts
©1979 Troll Associates; 7.25" x 9.125 hardcover, 32 pages.

Household Chore

To make a long story short in reversal order.

- The End
- This is the farmer sowing his corn,
- That kept the cock that crowed in the morn,
- That waked the parson all shaven and shorn,
- That married the man all tattered and torm,
- That kissed the maiden all forlorn,
- That milked the cow with the crumpled horn,
- That tossed the dog,
- That worried the cat,
- That killed the rat,
- That ate the malt,
- That lay in **the house,**
- **That Jack built.**

The Farmer

The Cock

The Parson

The Man

The Cow

The Maiden

The Dog

The Cat

The Rat and the malt

The House that Jack built

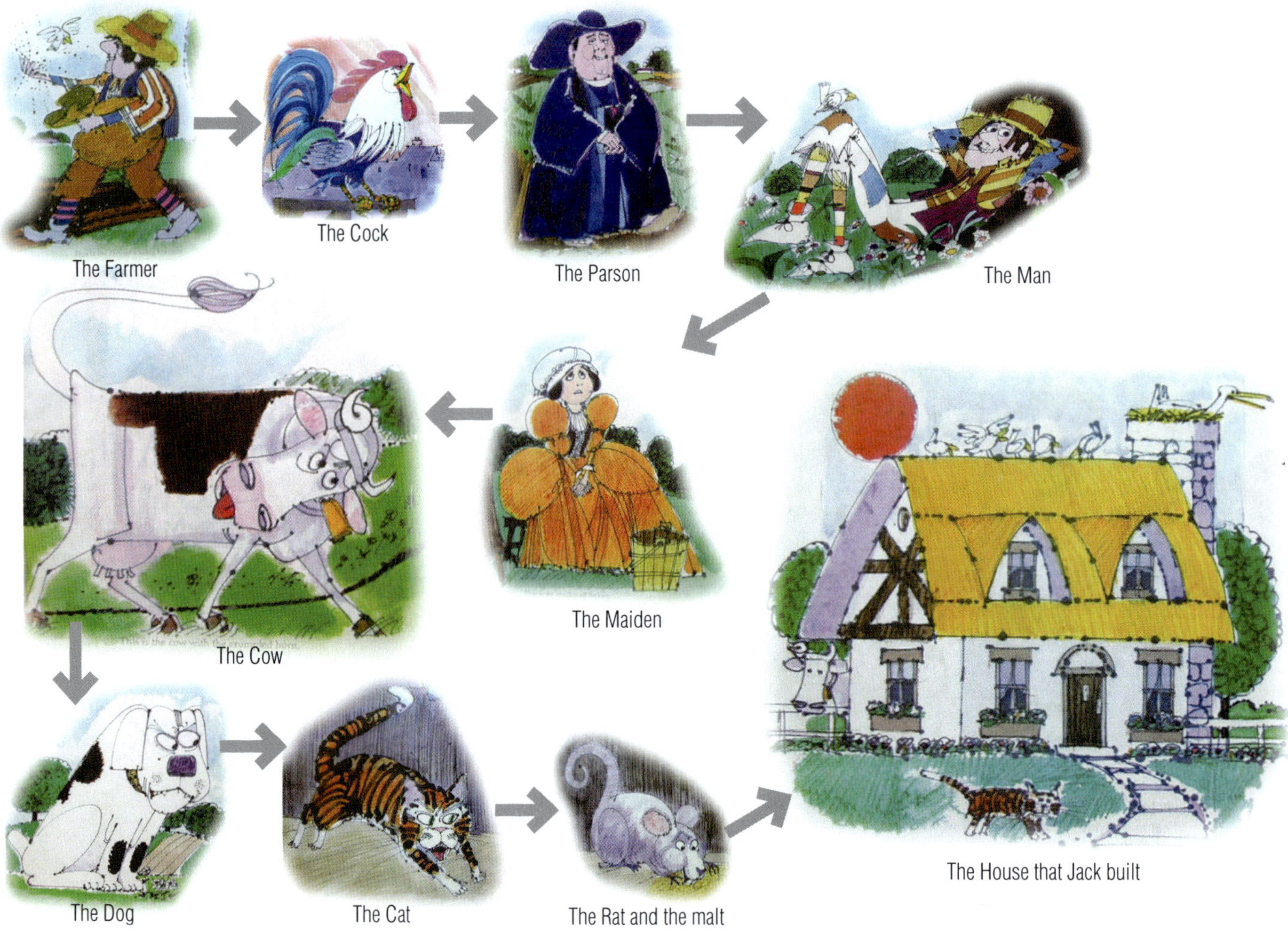

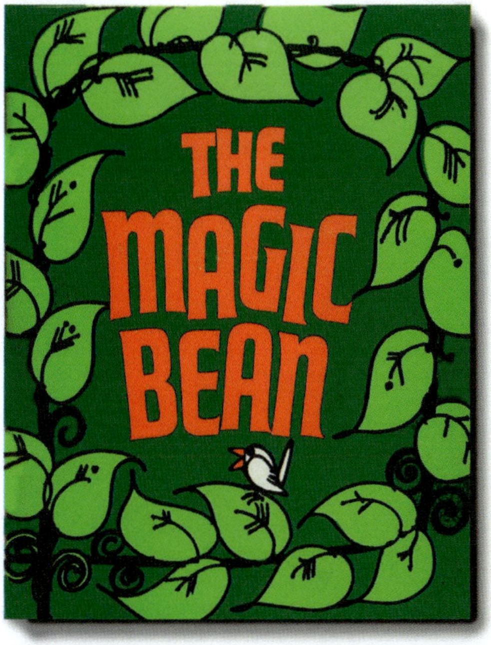

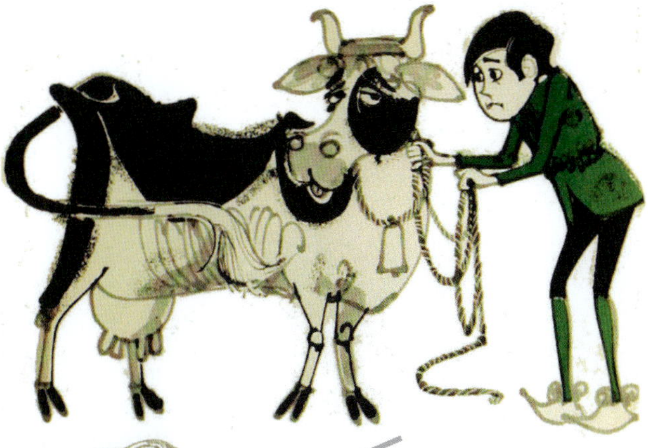

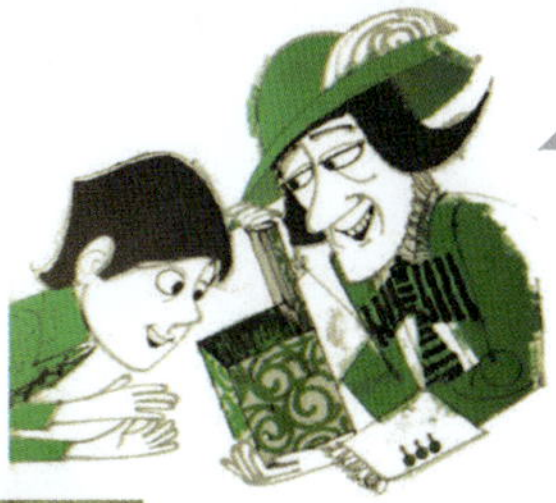

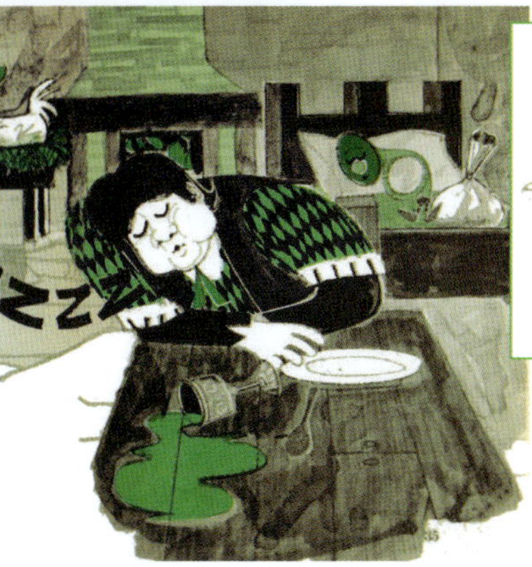

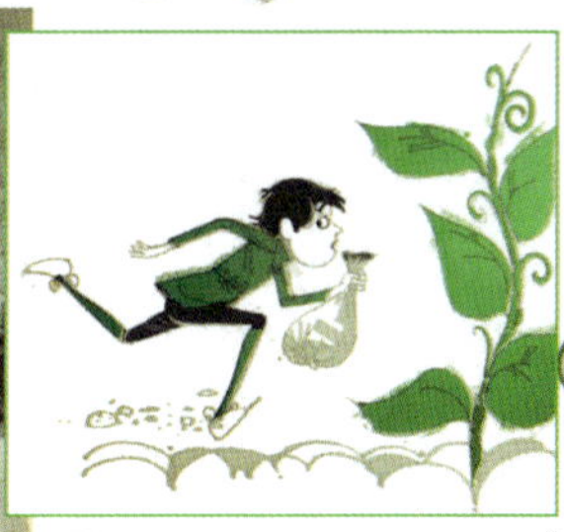

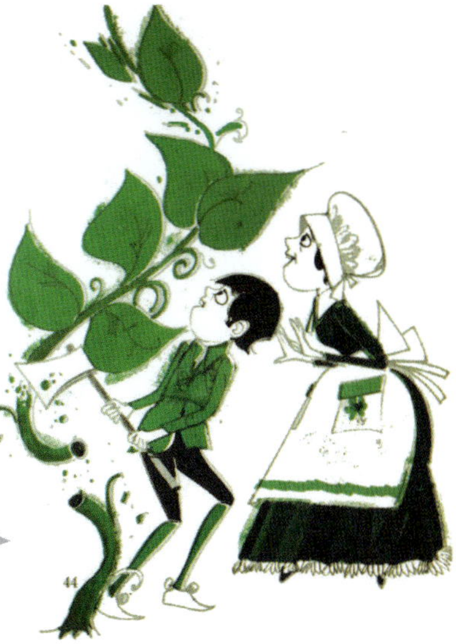

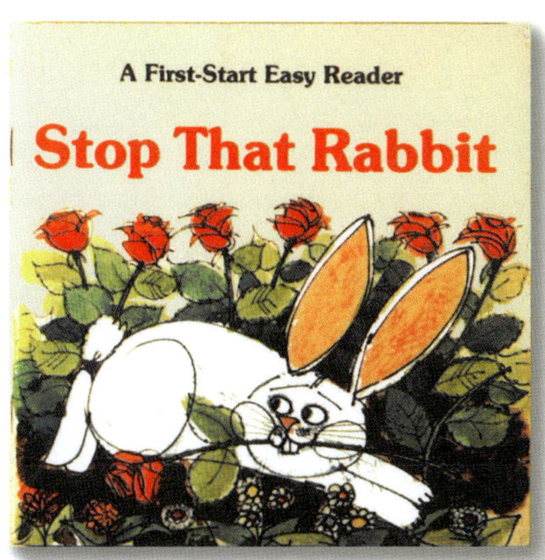

"The Magic Bean"
Known as "*Jack and Beanstalk*"
©1970 Raytheon Education Co.
7" x 9" paperback, 48 pages.

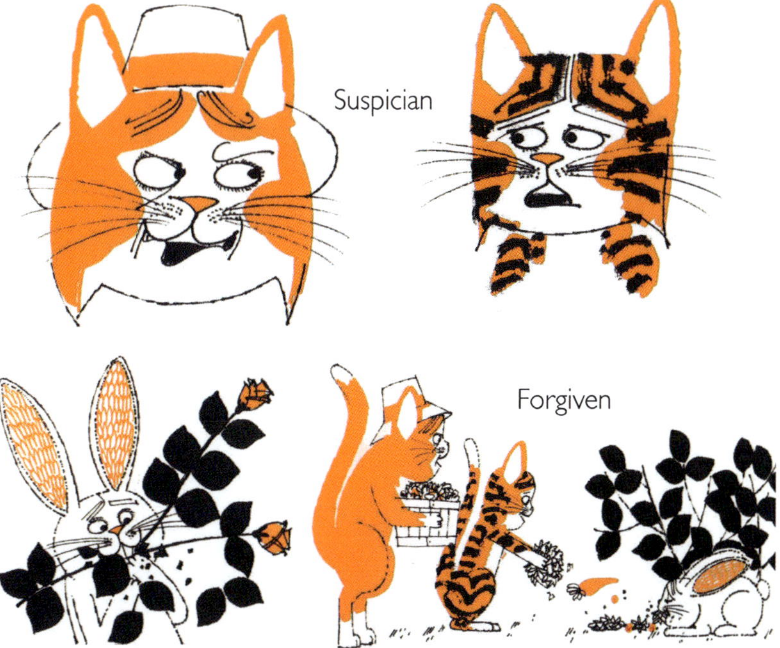

"Stop That Rabbit" written by Sharon Peters
©1980 Troll Associates, Mahwah, New Jersey
6" x 6" paperback; 30 pages

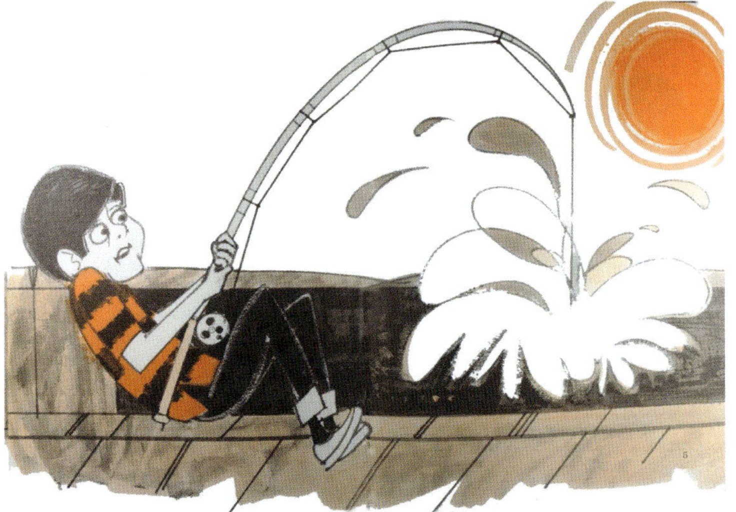

"My Fish Got Away!" written by Donna Lugg Pape
©1969 The L. W. Singer Company, New York
8.5" x 11" hard cover, 32 pages

When I felt my line jerk. I pulled and I pulled….

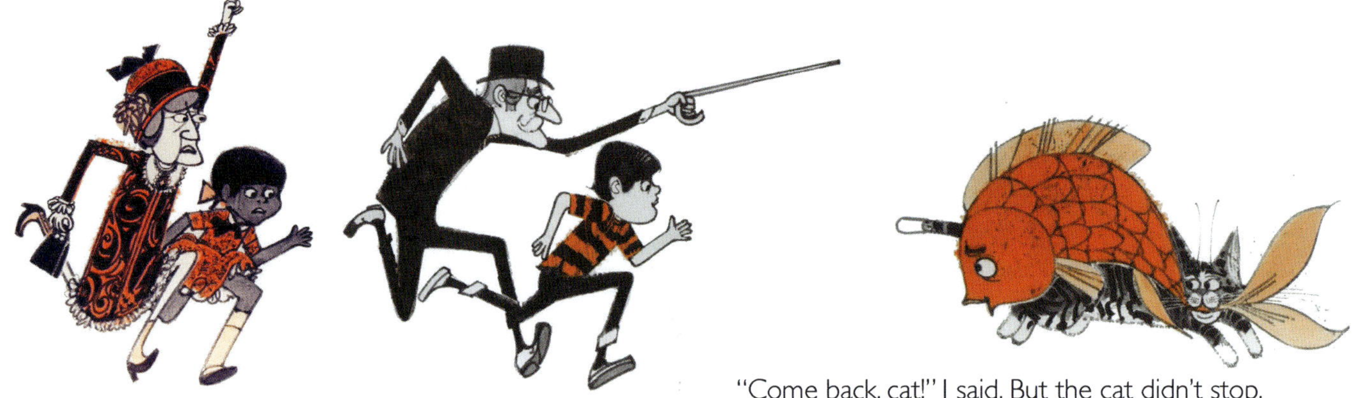

"Come back, cat!" I said. But the cat didn't stop.

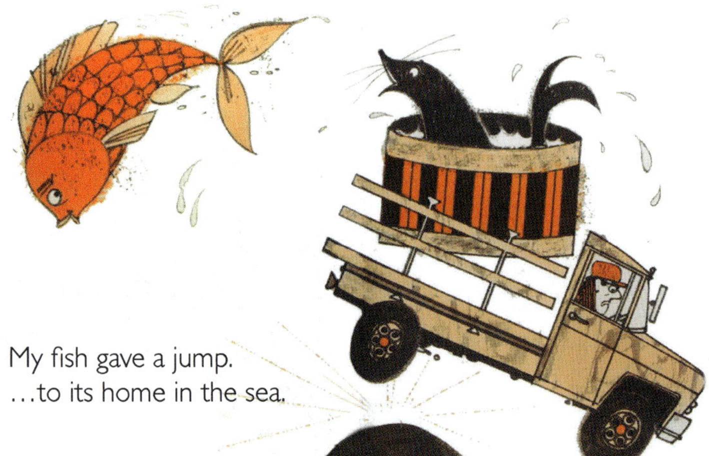

My fish gave a jump.
…to its home in the sea.

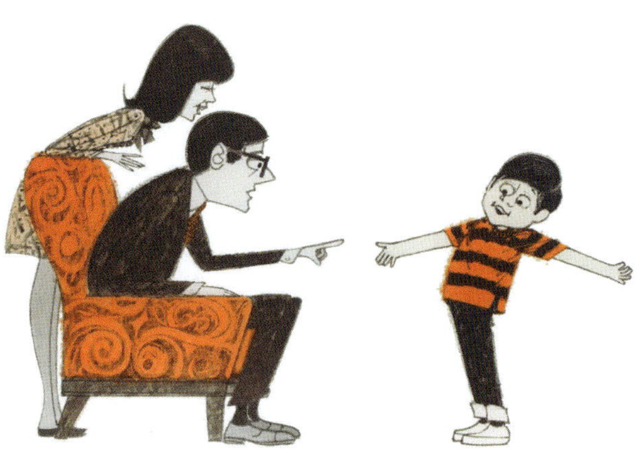

Dad wouldn't believe me.
"That's not true," said he. Mom laughed….

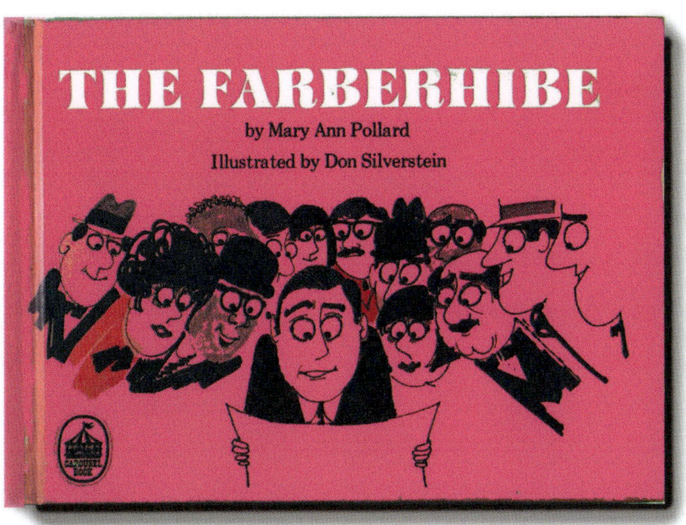

"The Farberhibe" written by Mary Ann Pollard: ©1968 The L. W. Singer Co., 9.2" x 6.5" hard cpver, 48 pages.

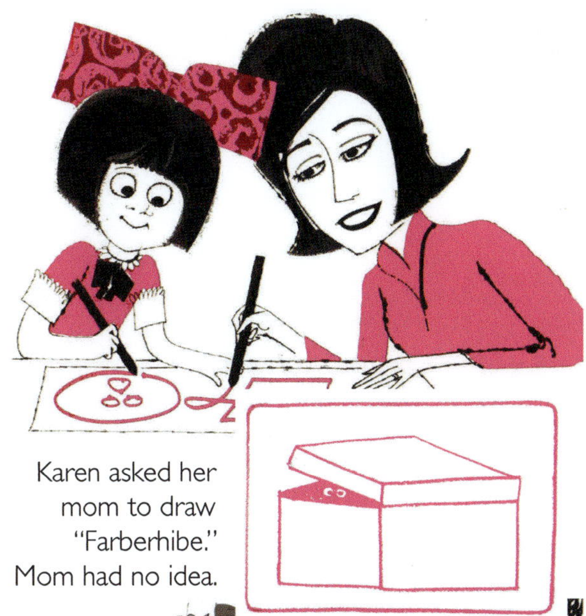

Karen asked her mom to draw "Farberhibe." Mom had no idea.

Nobody knows what the Farberhibe is. Only Karen's cousin Jo knew it and drew it, and made Karen happy.

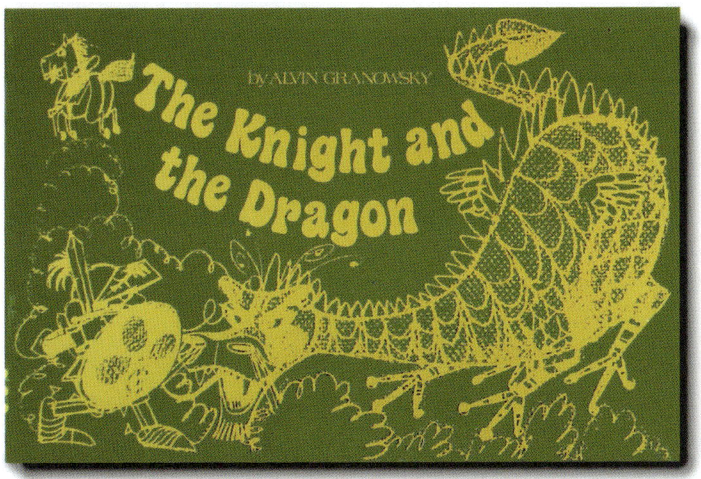

"The Knight and the Dragon" written by Alvin Granowski ©1975 D. C. Heath and Company; 9.2" x 6" paperback, 32 pages.

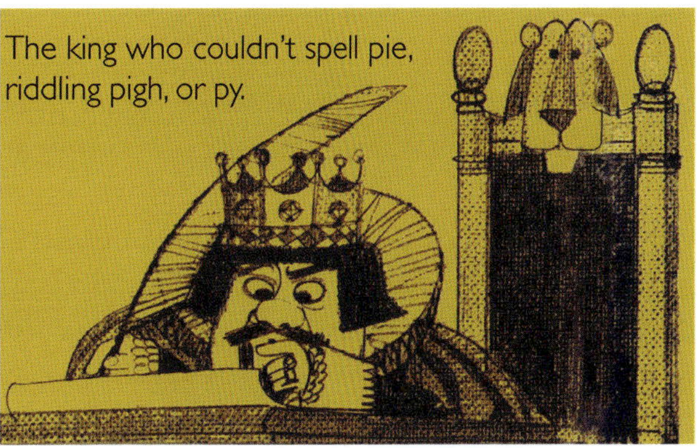

The king who couldn't spell pie, riddling pigh, or py.

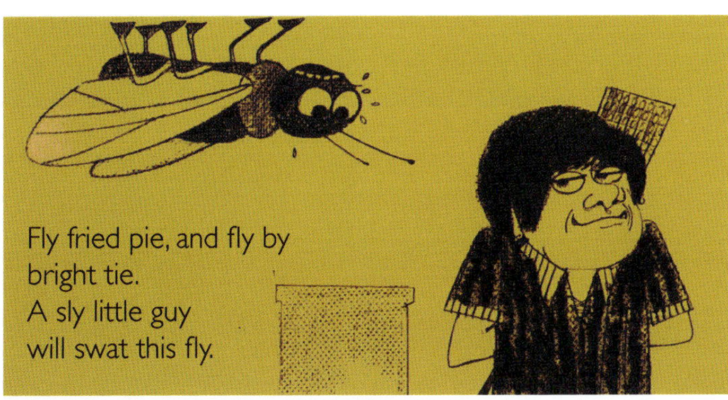

Fly fried pie, and fly by bright tie. A sly little guy will swat this fly.

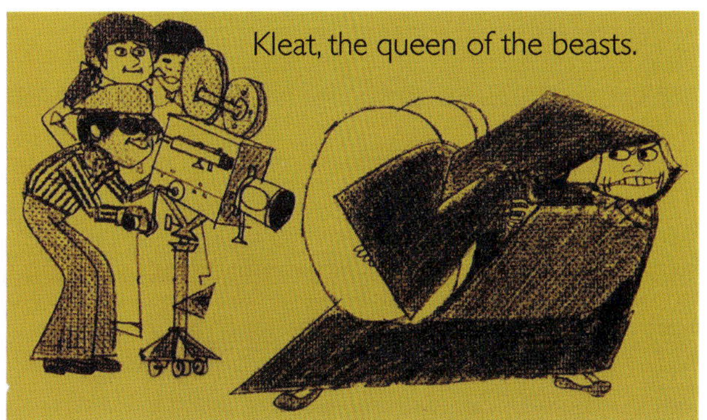

Kleat, the queen of the beasts.

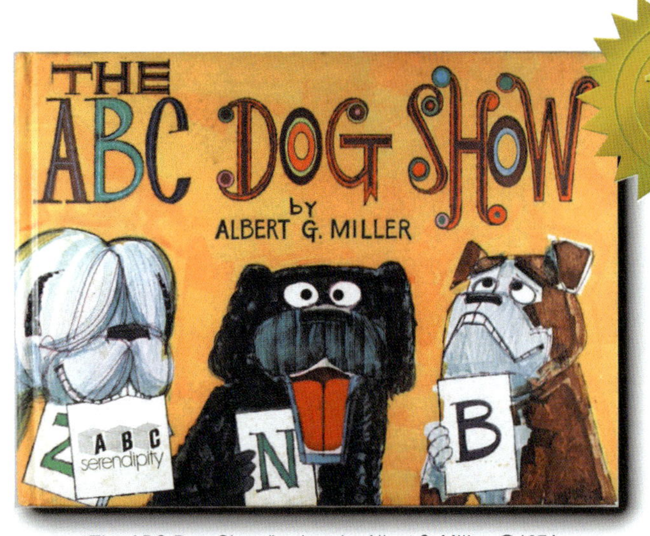

"The ABC Dog Show" written by Albert G. Miller; ©1974
Bowma, Glendale, California: 10.75" x 7.75" hard cover, 52 pages

The Best Children's Book Illustration of the Year

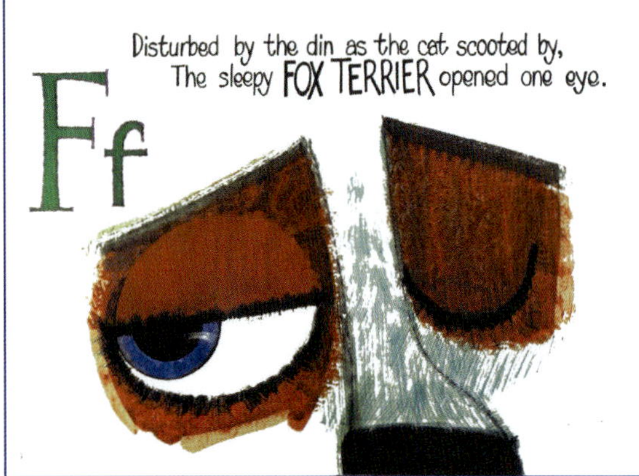

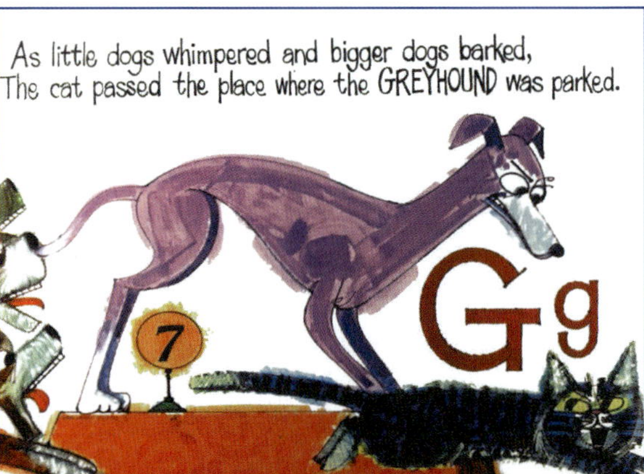

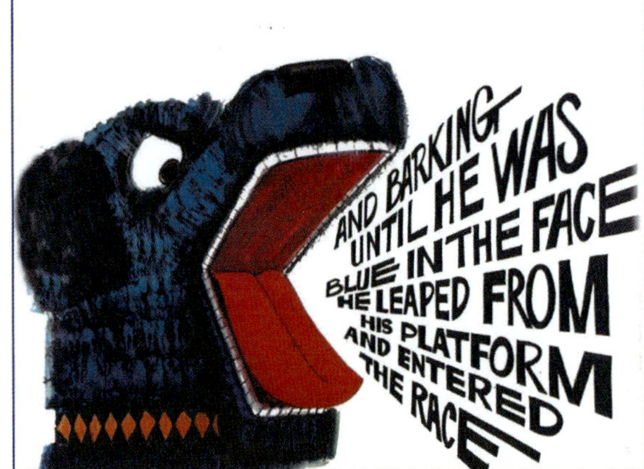

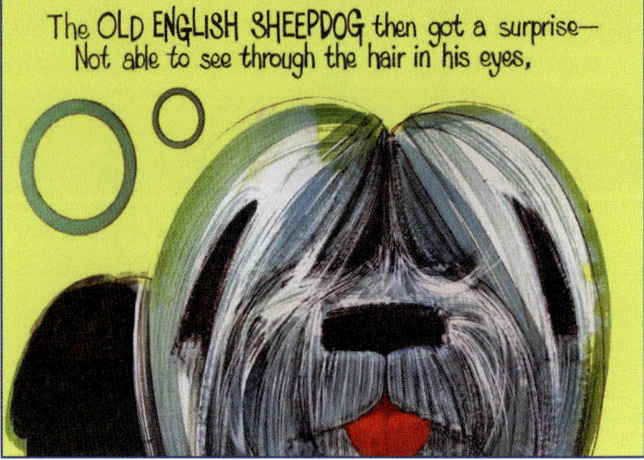

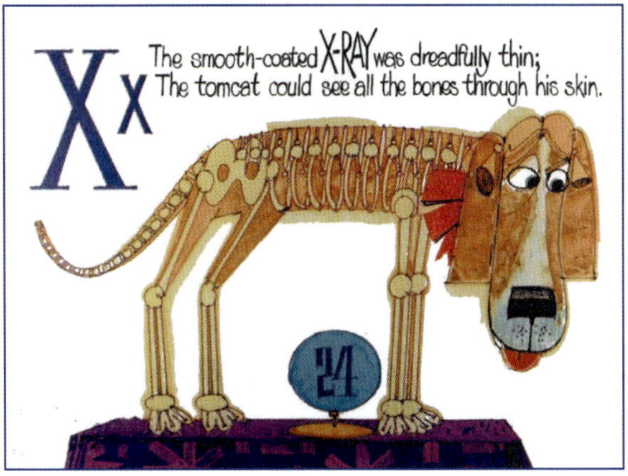

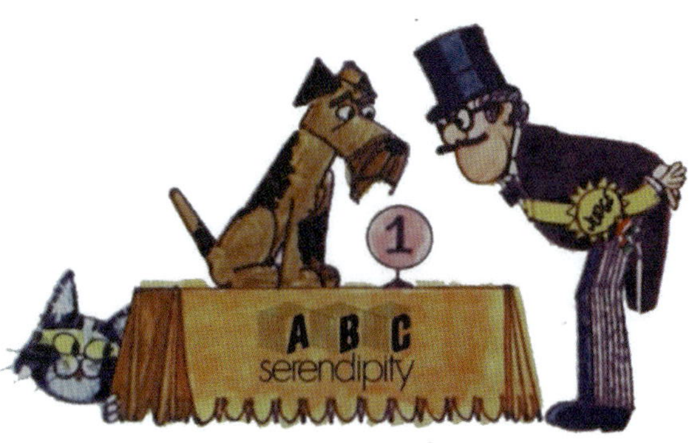

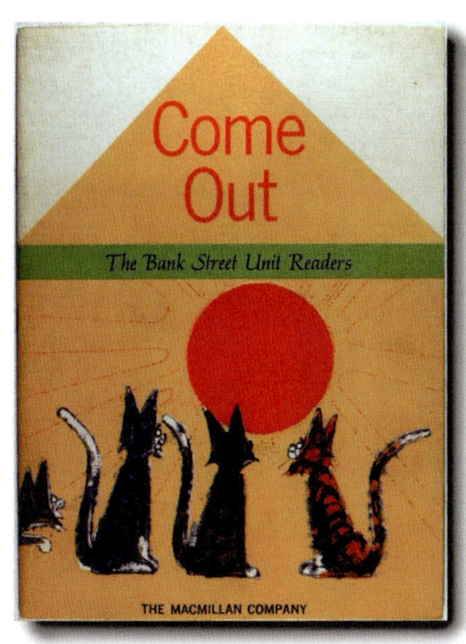

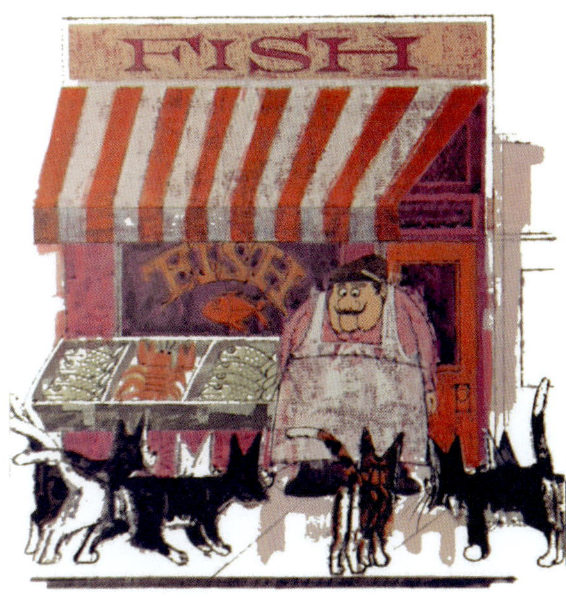

"**Come Out**" prepared by
The Bank Street Unit Readers
©1969 The McMillan Co.
6.5" x 9" paperback, 24 pages.

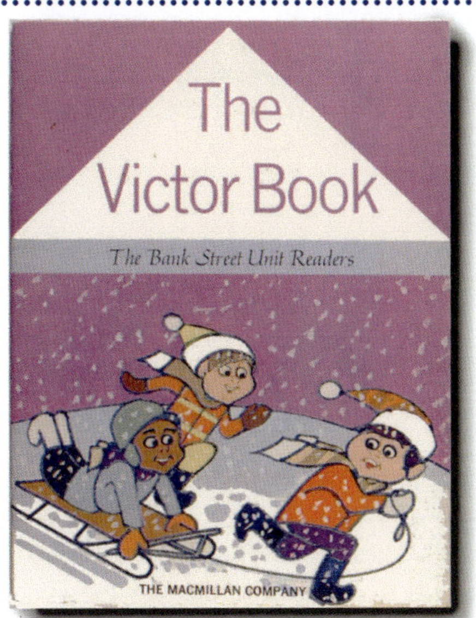

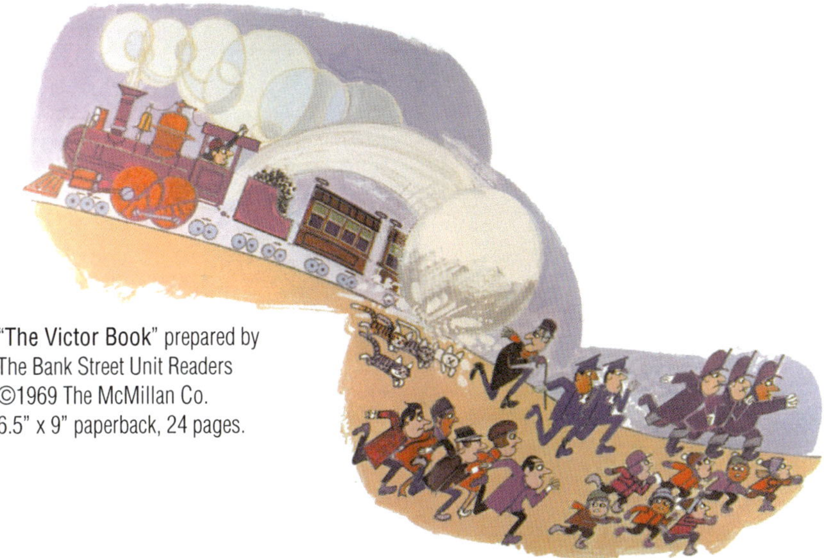

"**The Victor Book**" prepared by
The Bank Street Unit Readers
©1969 The McMillan Co.
6.5" x 9" paperback, 24 pages.

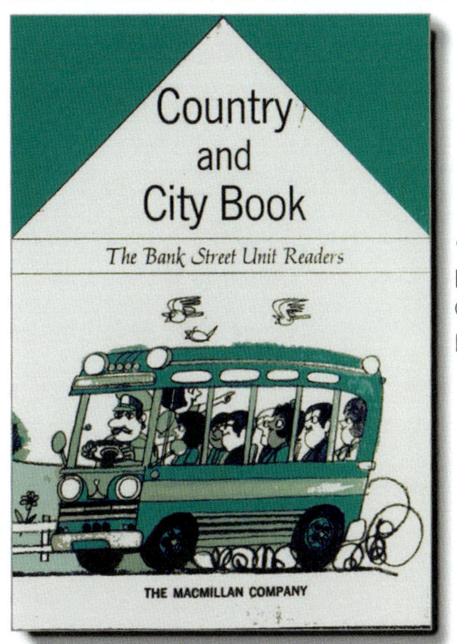

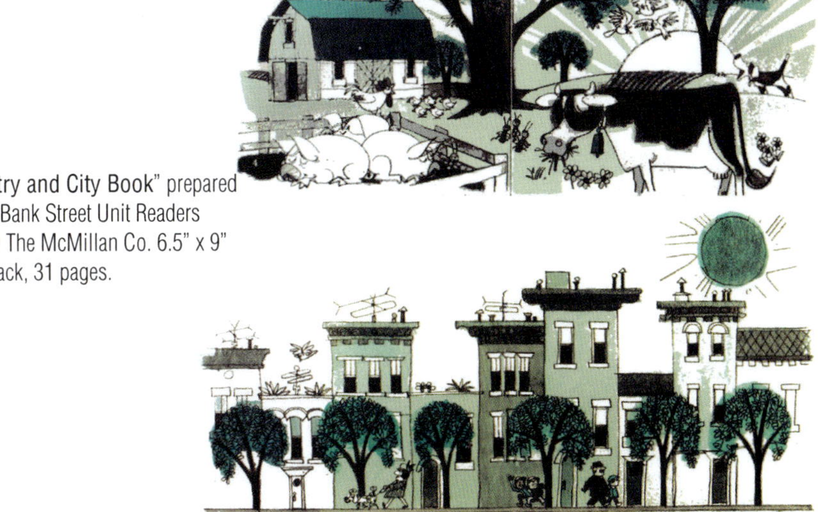

"Country and City Book" prepared
by The Bank Street Unit Readers
©1969 The McMillan Co. 6.5" x 9"
paperback, 31 pages.

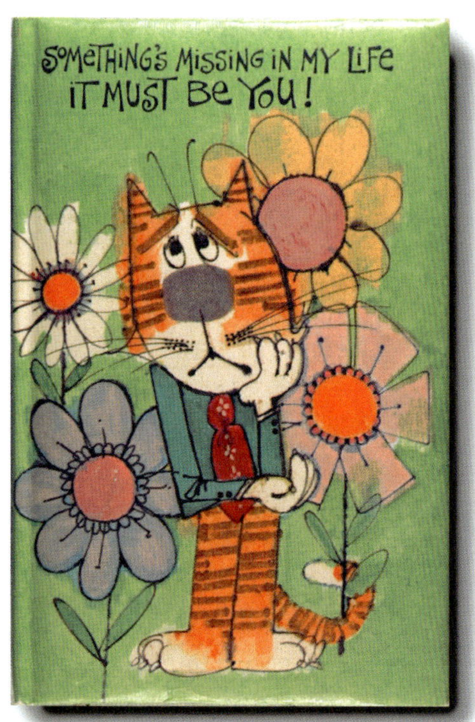

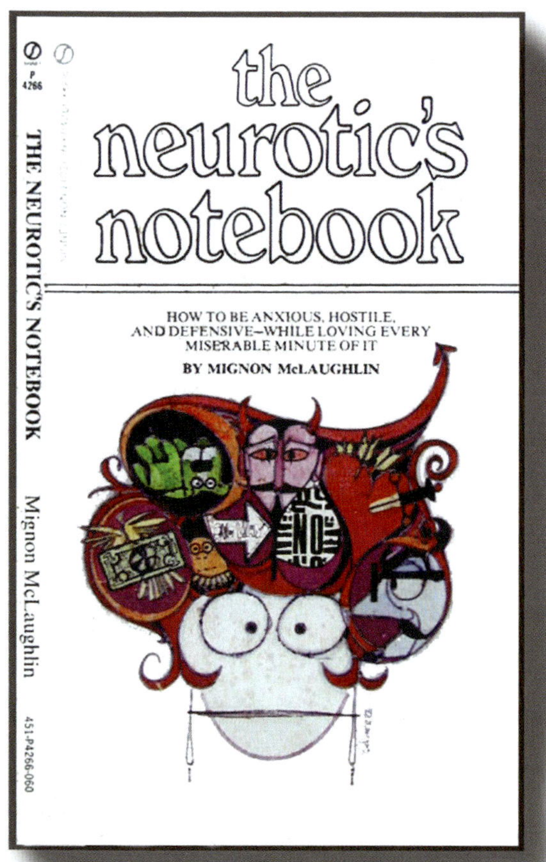

"Something's Missing in My Life" collected by Jean Kyler McManus ©1979 American Greeting Corp., Cleaveland, Ohio 4.5" x 6.75 hard cover, 24 pages

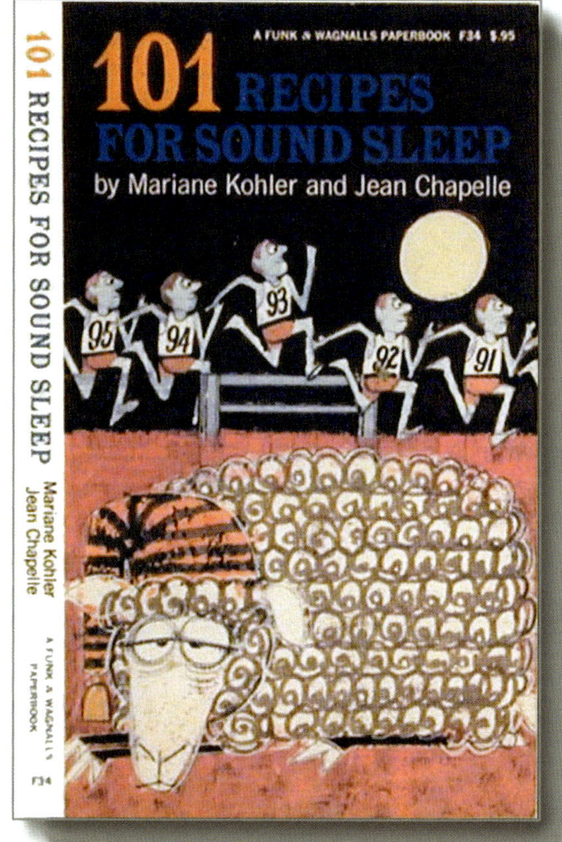

"The Neurotic's Notebook" Written by Mignon McLaughlin
Cover design: Donald Silverstein:
©1970 The New American Library, Inc.

"101 Recipies for Sound Sleep"
Written by Mariane Kohler and Jean Chapelle
Cover design: Donald Silverstein

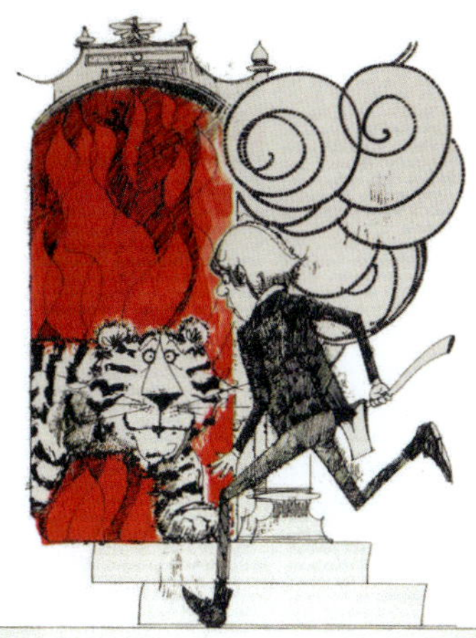

July 13, 1865, fire broke out in Barnum's Museum on Broadway, New York City.

The Museum housed an amazing waxwork collection… lions, tigers, snakes, crocodiles, whales, elephants, fat women, dwarfs, and so on. Most of the animals were saved but not the 425 pound fat woman — because she couldn't walk.

Then, John Denham, one of the runners at the fire department, volunteered to save her. He managed to drag her out to safety.

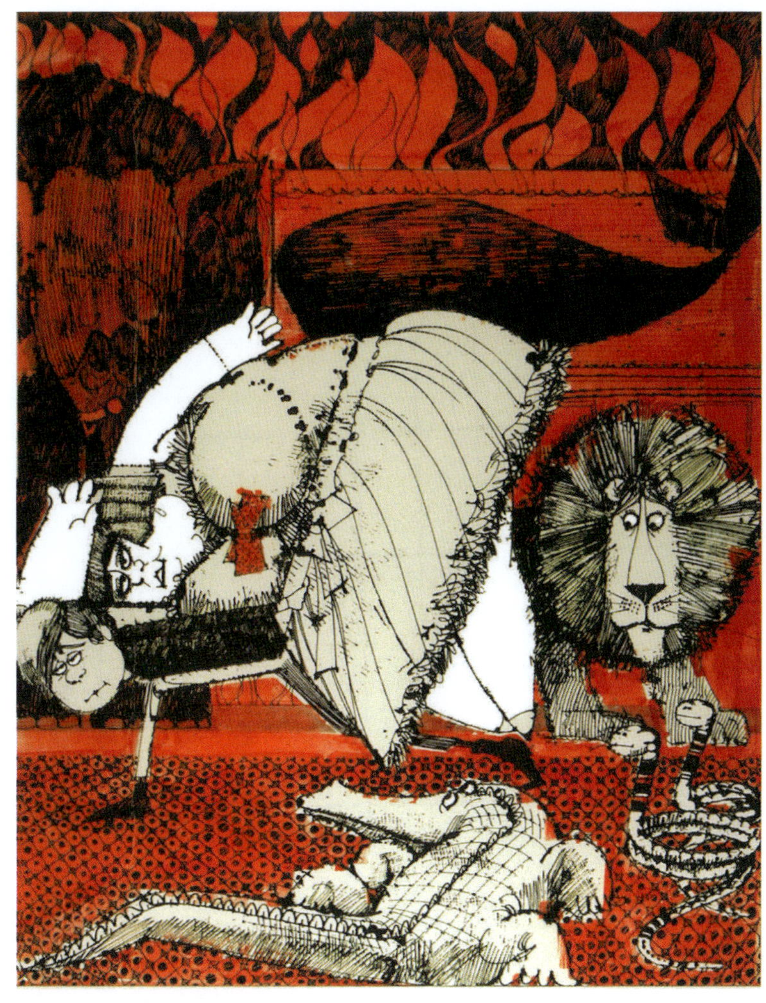

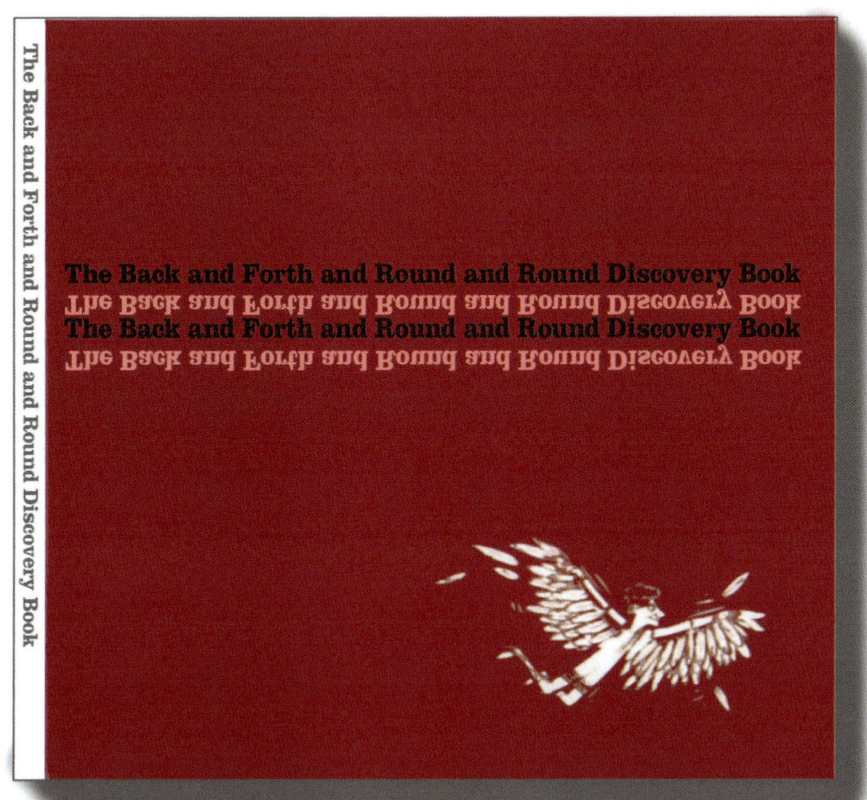

"The Back and Forth and Round and Round Discovery Book"
©1968 Curtiss-Wright Corp., Wood Ridge, NJ.
Illustrated by Donald Silverstein;
Partially introduced in Chapter II, and VIII.
(Some pages are shown on page 82~83)

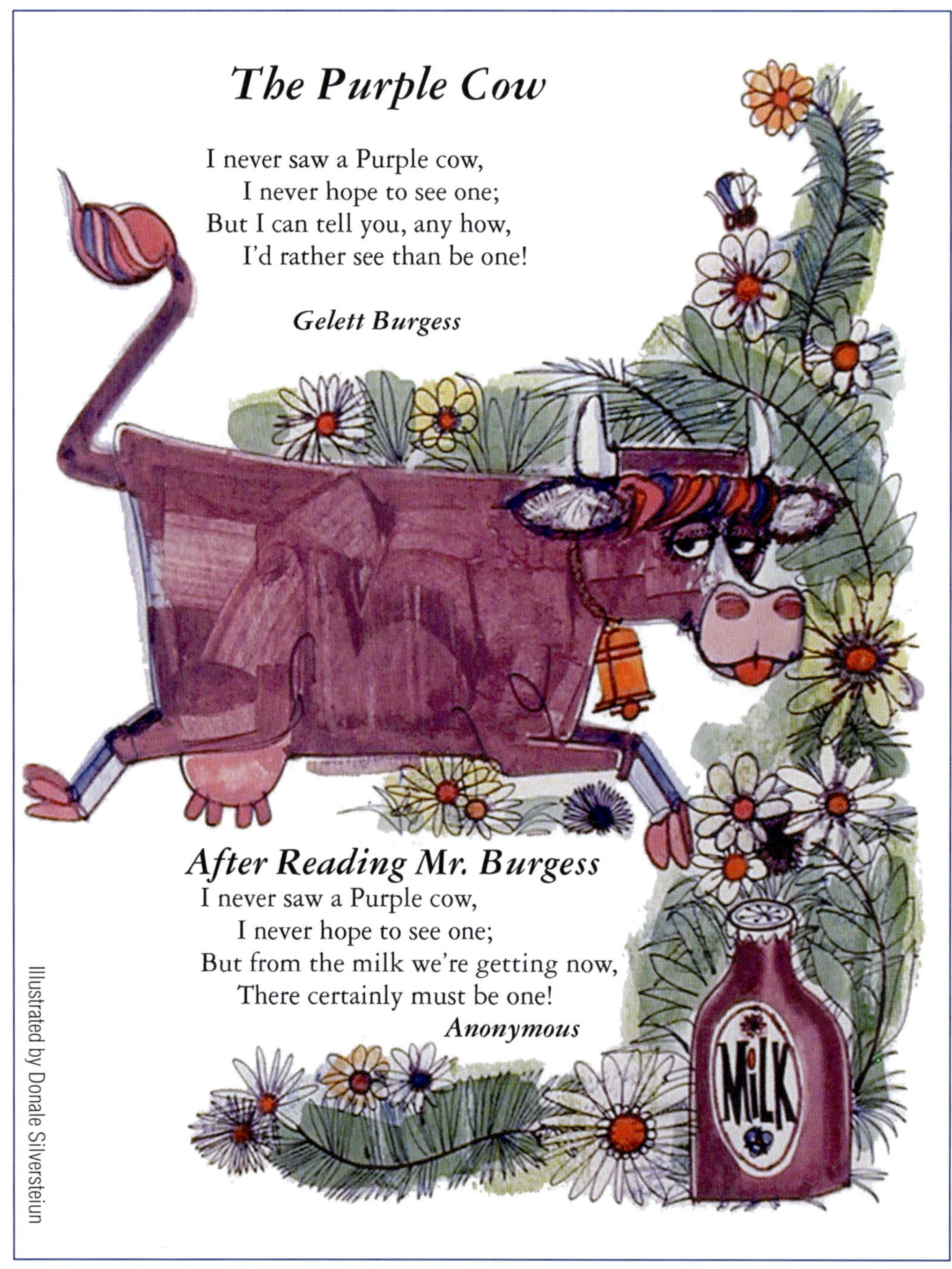

The Purple Cow

I never saw a Purple cow,
    I never hope to see one;
But I can tell you, any how,
    I'd rather see than be one!

Gelett Burgess

After Reading Mr. Burgess
I never saw a Purple cow,
    I never hope to see one;
But from the milk we're getting now,
    There certainly must be one!
Anonymous

MiLK

Illustrated by Donale Silversteiun

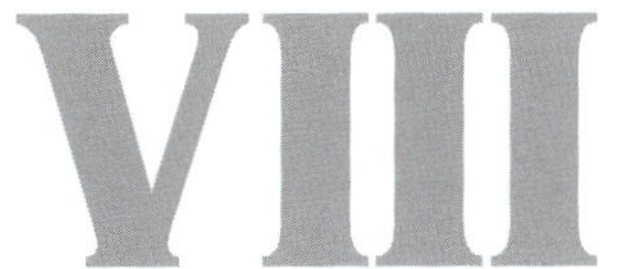

Cars,
Hi-Tech,
&
Slowboats to Nowhere.

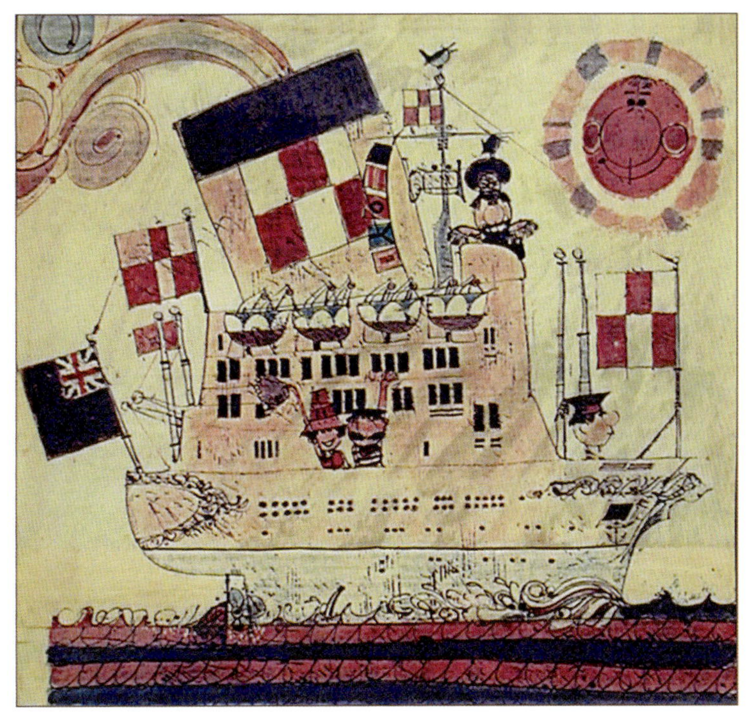

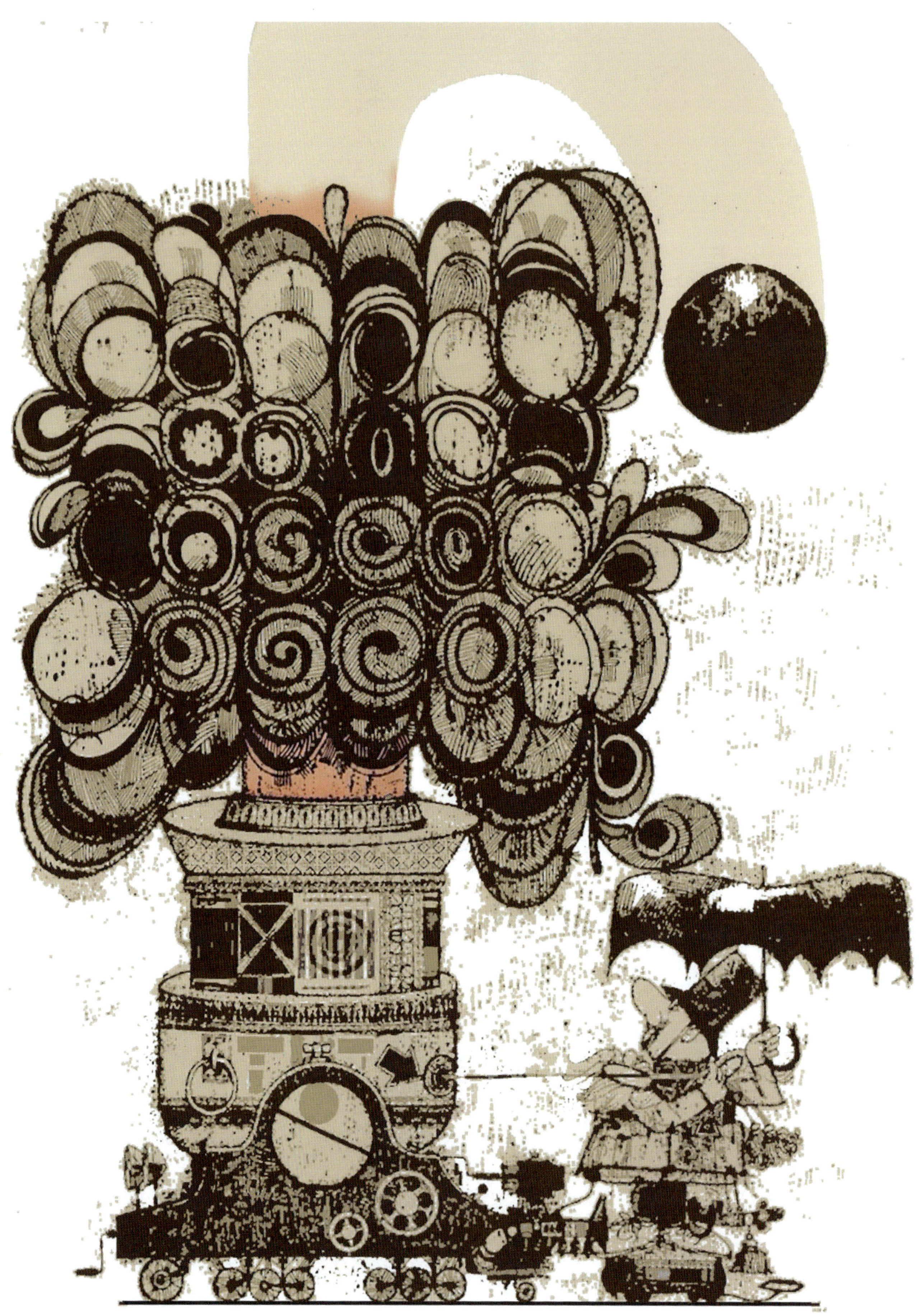

This is a page ripped out of "Brief Portraits Of Less Known Lunatics" by Fritz Bockelmann engraved six times. Shown in this beautiful twelve-color, rubber engraving is the gold plated medal winning sensation of the 1902 Berlin National Crossbow, Mortar and Cannon Ball Shooting Competition, Helmutt R. Fuzzheimer, wearing a stove pipe hat with a concealed cheese and rubber band sandwich inside, frosted monocle, elastic chin strap, engraved sword and borrowed under-wear — pulling the black and white velvet sash. As you can see by this magnificent illustration, the elevation control was set incorrectly, which resulted in the 500 pound projectile returning prematurely to earth passing through Fuzzheimer's umbrella, hat, sandwich, skull, monocle, teeth, beard, ribs, belt, knees, shins and feet, bending his sword, and scorching his left sock. He made a remarkable recovery in the unbelievable period of seven years, in time to enter the 1909 competition and blow his left thumb off.

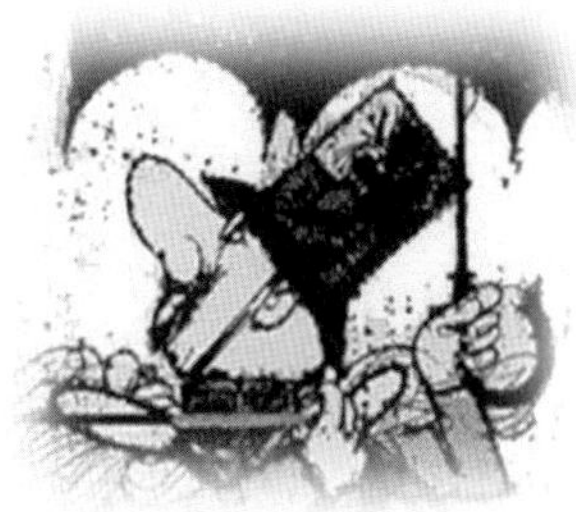

In 1910, he set two outstanding records; first, he shot a 500 pound brass ball a total distance of 4 miles, 16 feet, 2 3/4 inches, and second, he was arrested six times by the Bremen Police in Hamburg, for pinching Freda Brautenburger in the Frankfurt City Zoo, in one afternoon. A year later, he married Freda, who obvious-ly didn't mind being pinched six times in the zoo. Fuzzheimer survived the First World War by volunteering Freda for the Front Lines as ammunition carrier and bugler. In 1925, he retired from active sports competition after a cannon cleaning accident, which tore the end off his sword and removed one of his shins.

He became Fuhrer of The Futzler Stove And Cannon Works manufacturing trench mortars and chin straps. In 1937, after twelve years of devotion, long hours, hard work and embezzling 6,000,000 Marks, he retired from the company and re-ceived a gold plated chin strap as a token of gratitude from the stupid stock holders.

The end of Fuzzheimer's life came in 1938, when he was trying to snap some long range portraits of 16-year old Binnie Grossbumm in the bath, floating her toy submarine. The drain pipe from which he was hanging, with a portrait camera between his knees, (snapping the shutter with his tongue), collapsed, ending the portraits and his life. Fortunately, the pictures turned out beautifully, with excellent back lighting and every detail of Binnie's submarine in perfect focus. Fuzzheimer was survived by his wife, a bent Navy sword, a smashed portrait camera, Binnie Grosbumm, 10,000 shares of worthless Chinese Rail Road stocks, a 12 by 14 photo of Fanny Blumeburg and her castanets, three rusty World War I trench mortars, and twelve dozen unused, hand polished, brass cannon balls suitable for framing.

Credits for this masterpiece of graphic art (17"w x 23"h):
Artist, Designer, Art Director, Associate Art Director, Creative Director, Reject Director, Funeral Director,
Head Copywriter, Bottom Copywriter, Legal Consultant, and Client: Donald Silverstein
Cleaning Lady: Theda Kowalsky
All Represented by: Joseph T. Mendola, (212) 986-5680
Printing: Turck & Reinfeld, Inc., 207 W. 25th St., New York, NY (212) 924-4636

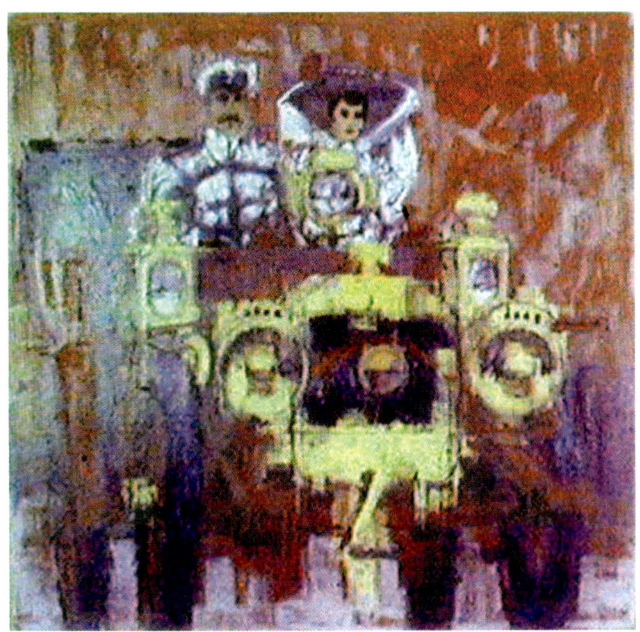

Remembering Donald Silverstein

Harry Borgman*

Don was one of a kind, a really unpredictable character. Those of you who knew him well will say that comment is the understatement of the century. He somehow seemed out of place in the advertising world in spite of the fact that the business was replete with plenty of oddball characters in the fifties and sixties. Essentially he was everything but ordinary, truly an original.

We were very close friends over the years even though we lived continents apart for long periods. In 1952 Don was drafted in the U.. S. Army and stationed in Alaska (I can't imagine a worse situation and location for him to be in!). After working many years in Detroit Don lived and worked in various places including London, New York, Arizona, Connecticut, Japan and oddly enough, Port Said, Egypt. I left Detroit in 1977 and lived and worked in Paris, France for several years, eventually moving to New York City, where we later reconnected.

I first met Don in 1949 while I was working at Allied Artists. Jim Donahue, one of the owners of

the studio who had a real eye for potential talent, hired Don right out of art school. I came in one morning and here was this new guy sitting at a drawing board doing all these great things, everyone was quite impressed with his work. Don was just amazing. He did some wonderful work for Ford Times magazine. Don, Cliff Roberts and myself were all doing a lot of art for the magazine and having a great time. It was more fun than most of the advertising assignments. I guess those were "the good old days."

I left Allied Artists in 1952 and started working at Grey Garfield Lang Studios. Don was drafted and sent to Alaska. I left GGL in 1953 and worked at Jose Cavillo Studios for a few months with Cliff Roberts, then we both moved on to McNamara Brothers. Don was back from his military tour of duty and began working at New Center Studios at that time. It probably was in 1954.

Here is a typical Don Silverstein story. Dave Lindsay and I were working at McNamara Brothers and Don was working at New Center Studios in the Penobscot Building in Detroit. We met Don to have a couple of drinks at the Caucus Club, an upscale bar in the building. They refused to let us in because Don did not have a tie on. So we went back up to Don's office where he found an old burlap bag and he just ripped off a long piece and quickly painted some bold colors on it. He then put in on as a tie. It was almost dragging to the floor. It was hilarious. We went back to the Caucus Club, and yes, they did let us in.

In 1955 Dave Lindsay and I left McNamara Brothers Studios and joined MDM Studios as partners. The other partners were Gordon McGowan, Mike Doyle, and Len McCullough. We had a great studio that was loaded with prime talent, including Don who joined MDM shortly after we arrived. He worked there for a couple of years. I left after one year, I had been working day and night and I was burned out as well as fed up with the studio end of the advertising business. I was determined to switch fields and work as an art director. Campbell- Ewald hired me as head art director on the Chevrolet account to design catalogs and other sales promotion material.

In 1958, Don and I decided to take a painting trip out west. We drove my Volkswagen out to Utah and Arizona. Everyone in those desert towns

* Harry Borgman was an art director at Campbell-Ewald; chairman of the Advertising Dept., at the Society of Arts and Crafts *(now the College for Creative Studies)*. His artistic talent has spanned from graphic design to illustration, painting, and computer graphics. He has written several art technique books including "Pen and Pencil Drawing Techniques."

thought we were government agents looking for sites that might be uranium-rich. Apparently these agents always drove Volkswagens as they were perfect vehicles to drive through the rugged desert. We had a great time out west and both did a lot of painting. However, Don never painted scenes outside, he always painted abstractions in the motel room. He might as well have stayed back in Detroit.

Another typical Donald incident that I recall was when I met him for a drink in the New Center area. I was working at Campbell-Ewald at the time. In the bar were many of the young women that worked for the agency. This particular bar had a bowling alley and Friday night was their night for bowling. We were the only guys sitting at the bar. It was occupied by the gals from CE, some had placed their bowling balls on the bar. Don spotted a real beauty that he wanted to meet. I told him I knew her and could introduce him, but she really was quite aloof and he would have had better luck with her bowling ball. Of course, that remark triggered Don's wild imagination. He immediately went over to the lovely lady and said, "Can I buy your bowling ball a drink?"

Don moved to London for a couple of years, then back to New York where I saw him whenever I came to the city to deliver or pick up assignments. I lost touch with him during the years he was in Arizona, Connecticut and Japan. When I left Paris in 1983, I moved to New York and was still living there when Sakiko and Don came back to the States. We saw a great deal of each other until my move to Sawyer, Michigan.

Fifty-five years have passed since I first met Don. Much of the mirth I have experienced during those years was due to Don's sharp wit. Life was never dull when he was present. He was an extremely talented, eccentric, complex person with a very unusual sense of humor. He was a wonderful painter and his humorous illustrations were done with great flair and ingenuity. I often chuckle as I remember my good friend and his legendary antics.

There will never be another Don Silverstein.

H. B., 2005

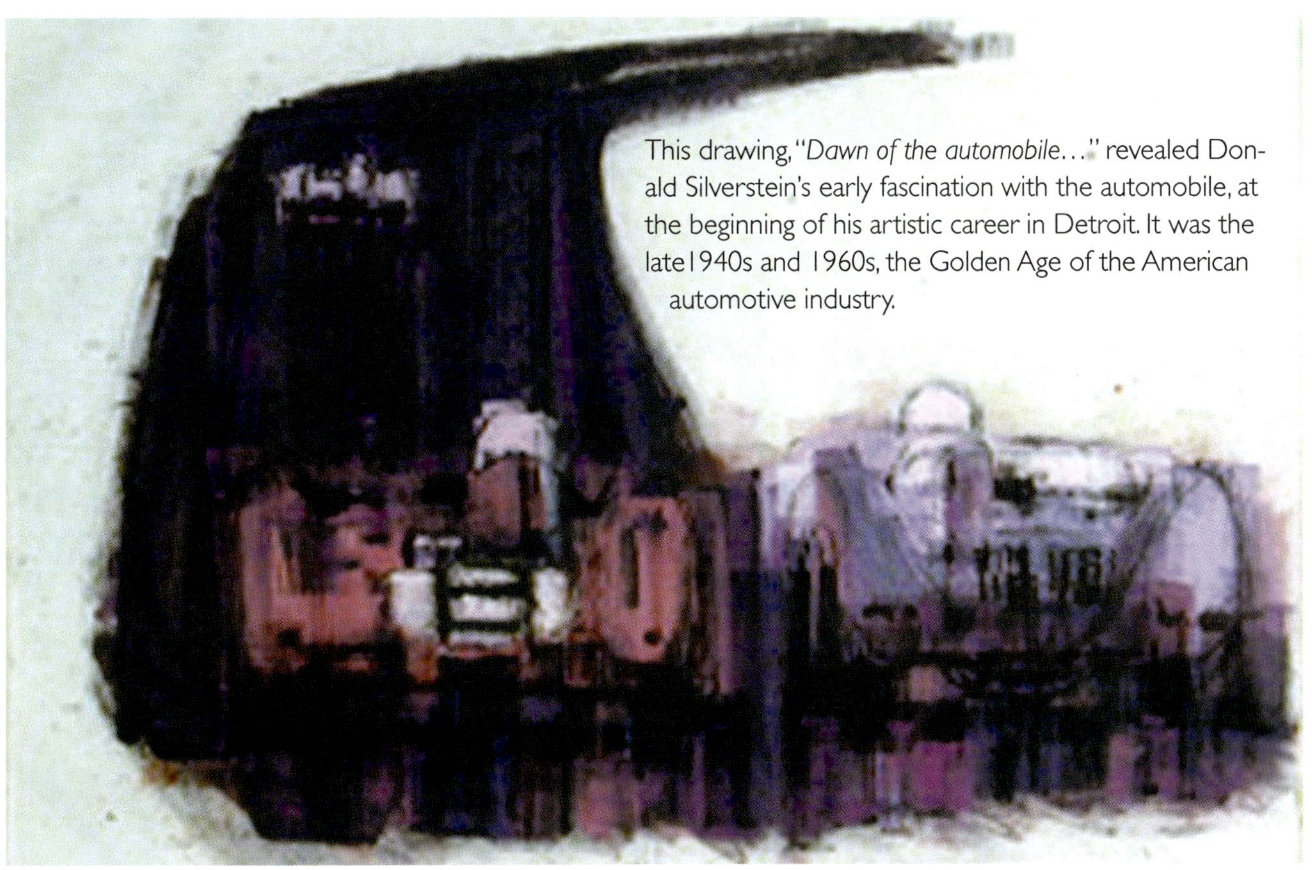

This drawing, "*Dawn of the automobile…*" revealed Donald Silverstein's early fascination with the automobile, at the beginning of his artistic career in Detroit. It was the late 1940s and 1960s, the Golden Age of the American automotive industry.

"Gentlemen, start your engines!" ...Bang!

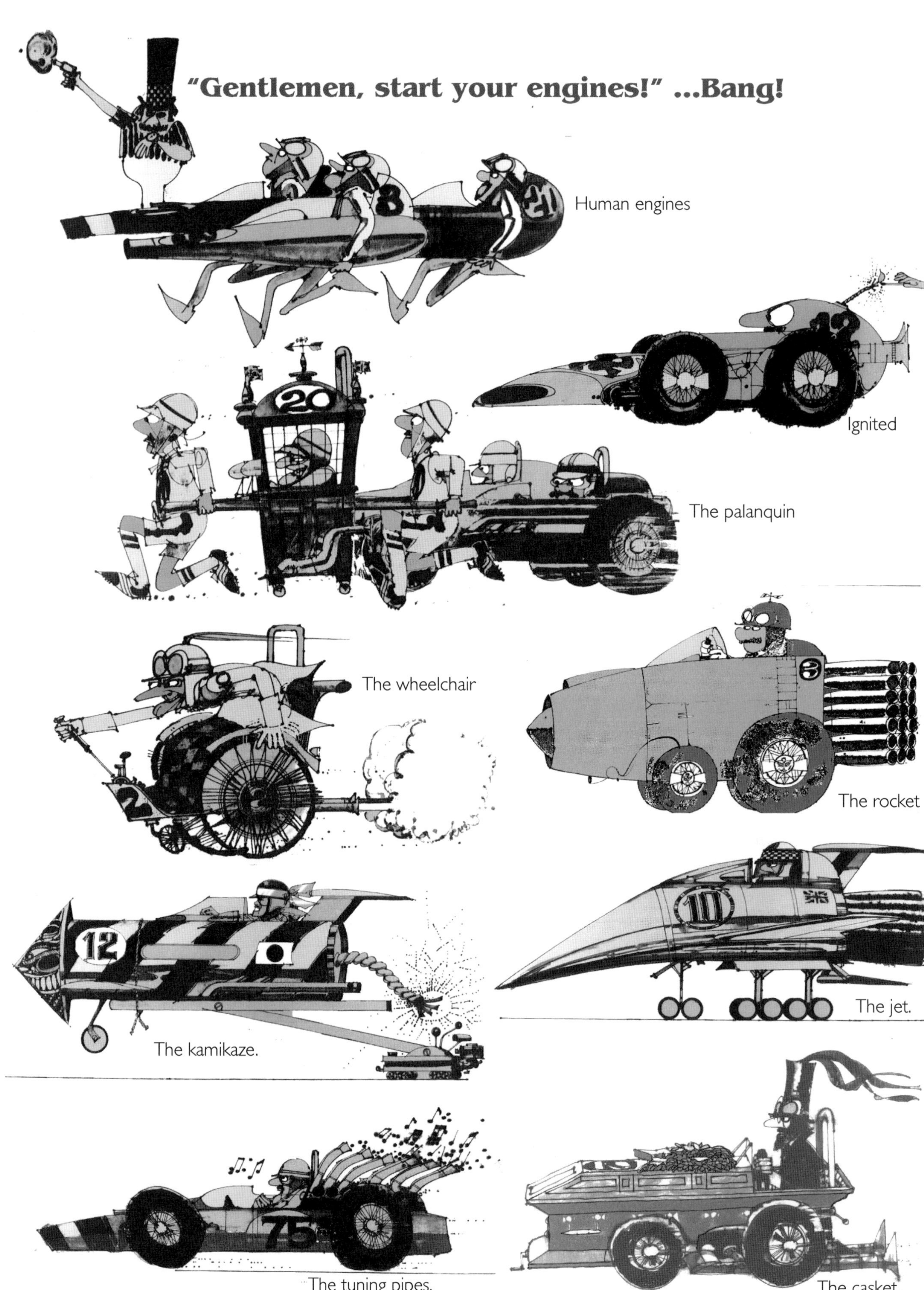

Flash messages to the driver...

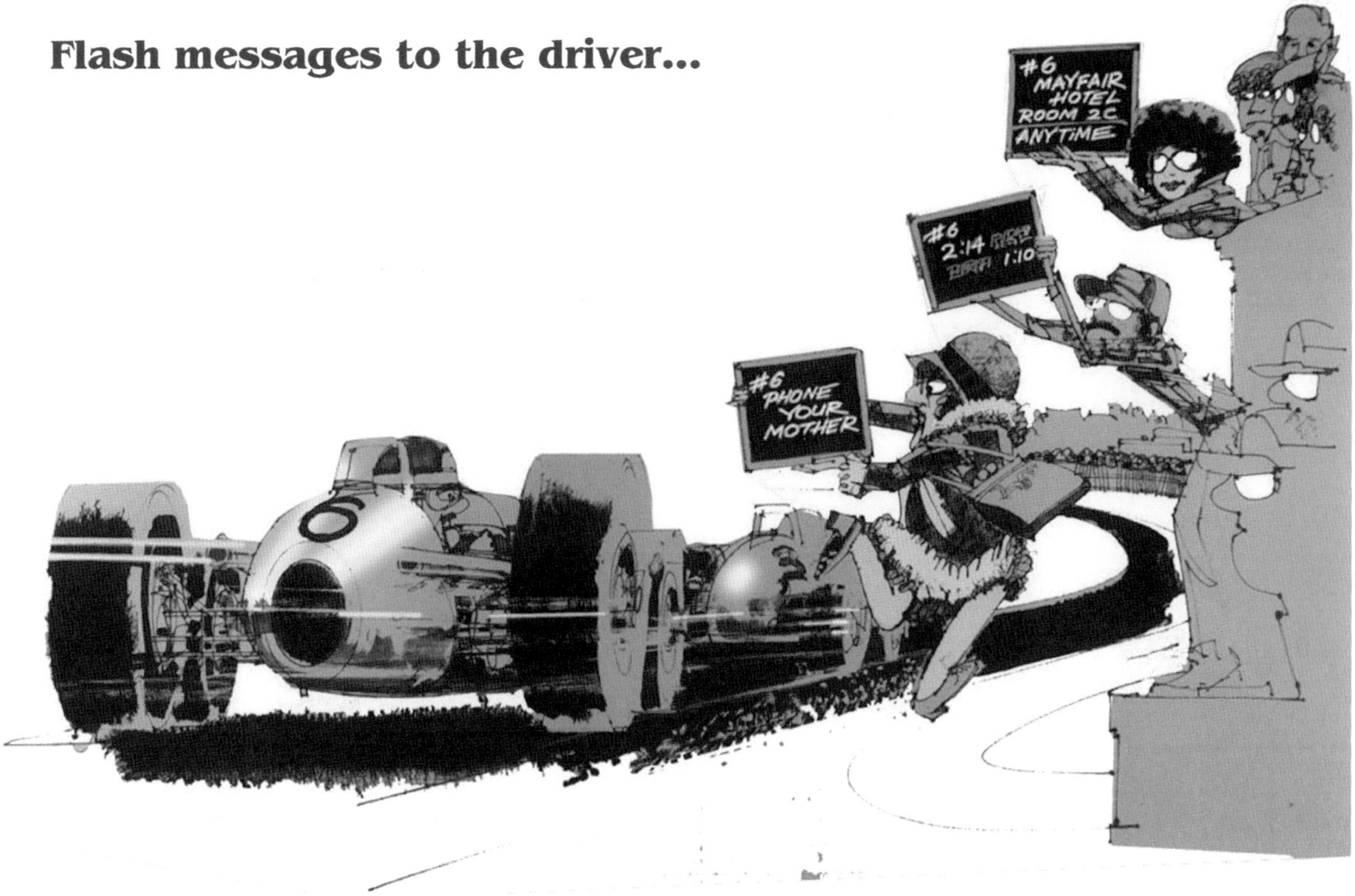

Disappointments

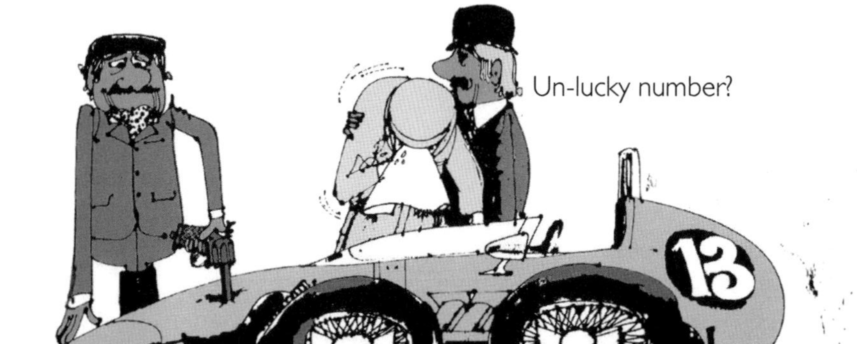

Un-lucky number?

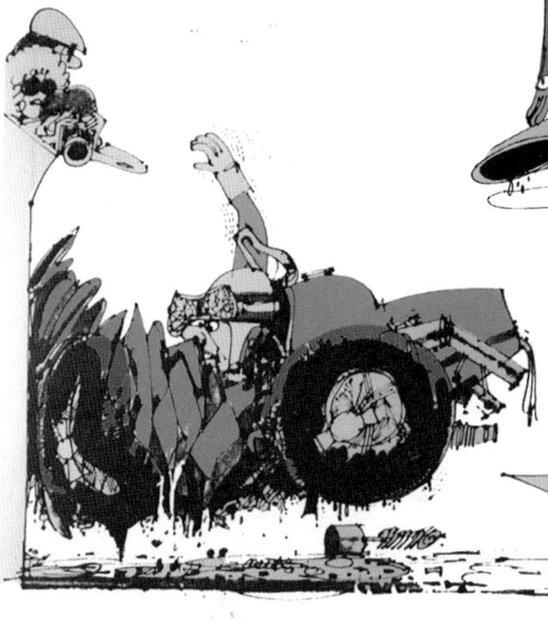

Rescue operation "Can-Opener."

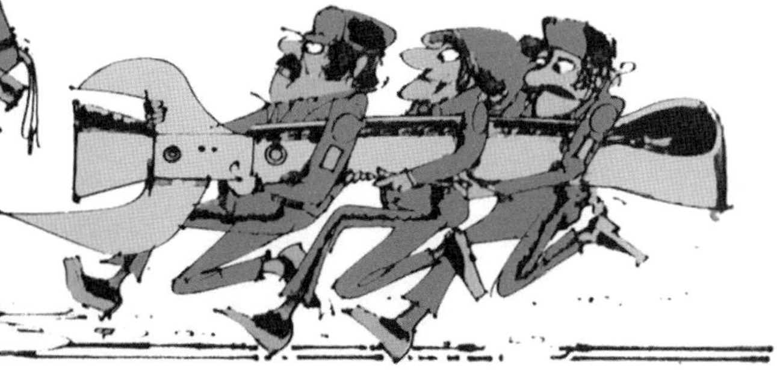

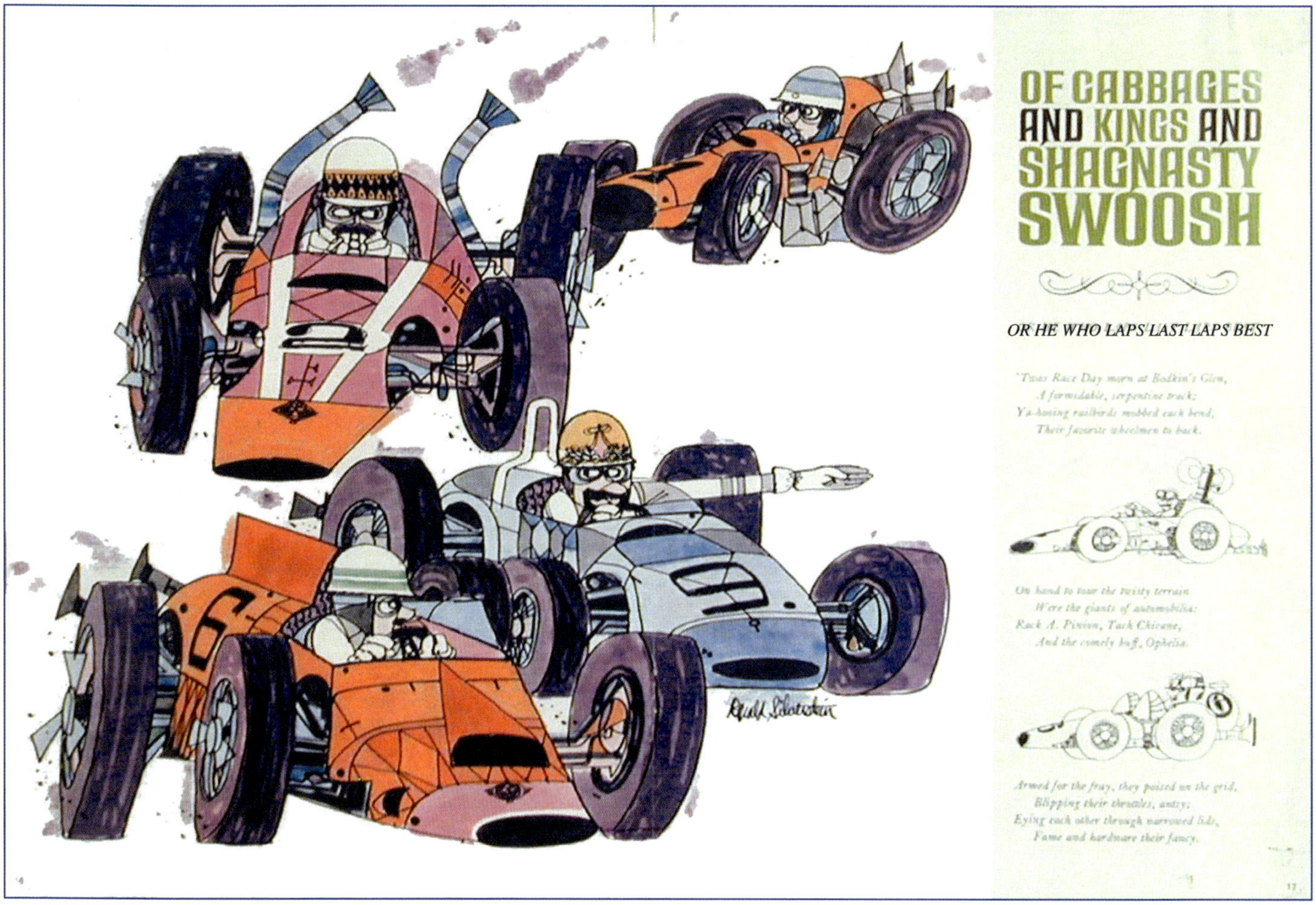

...he who laps last laps best

'Twas Race Day morn at Bodkin's Glen,
A formidable, serpentine track;
Ya-hooing railbirds mobbed each bend,
Their favorite wheelmen to back.

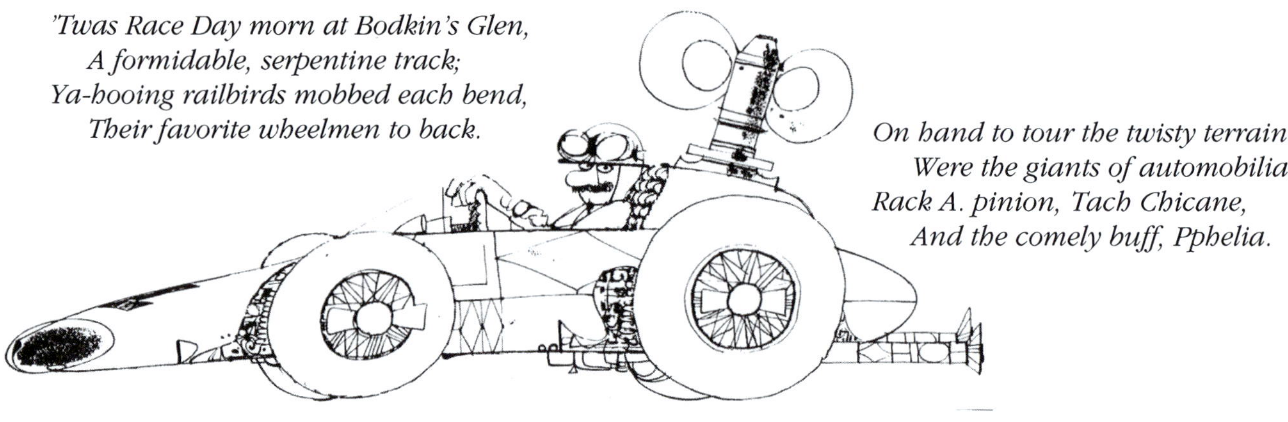

On hand to tour the twisty terrain.
Were the giants of automobilia:
Rack A. pinion, Tach Chicane,
And the comely buff, Pphelia.

Armed for the fray, they poised on the grid,
Blipping their throttles, antsy;
Eying each other through narrowed lids,
Fame and hardware their fancy.

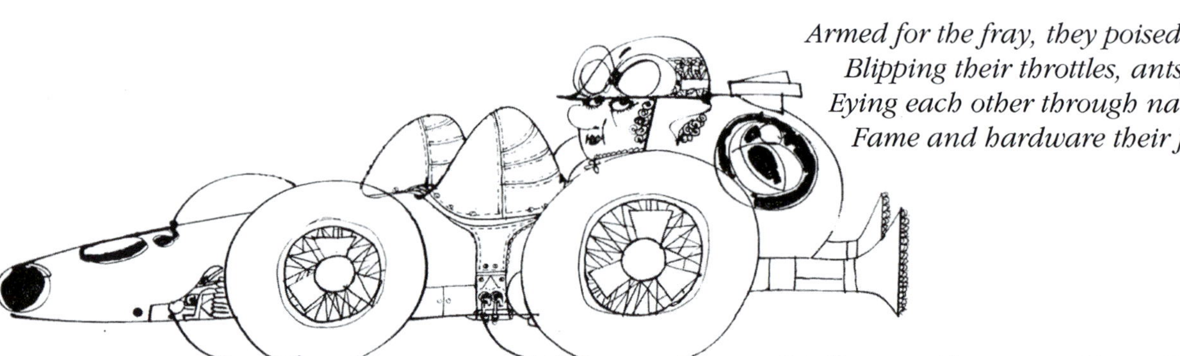

Note: The creator of these poems on this spread is unknown.

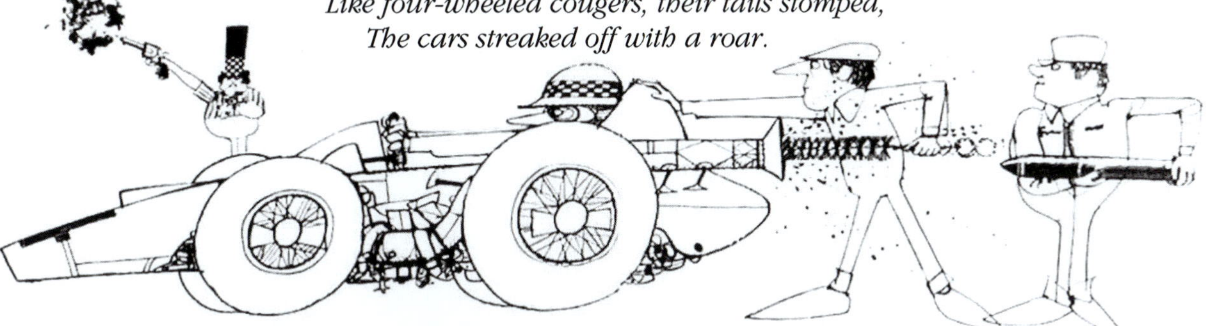

The starter stepped up with pistol and pomp.
And performed his noisy chort.
Like four-wheeled cougers, their tails stomped,
The cars streaked off with a roar.

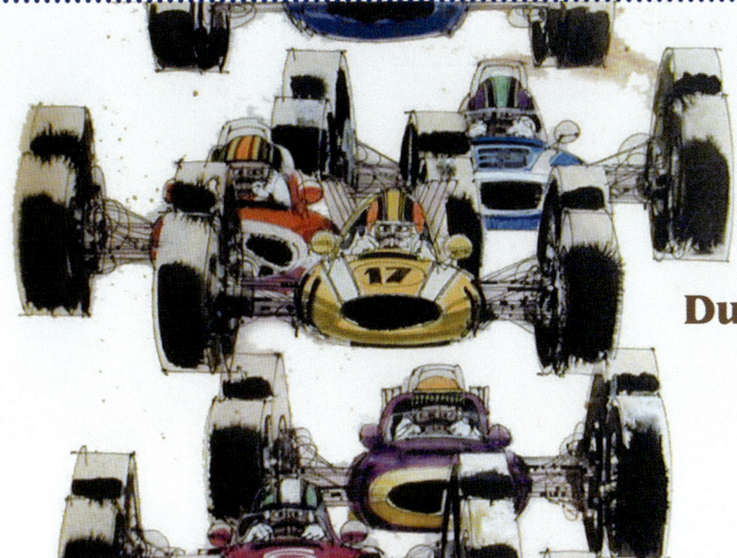

Duel on the Track

Rack grabbed the lead in the throat of a turn.
But Tack gained ground in the straight;
Ophelia ran third with little concern
In her twin-turret Belchfire Eight.

Soon Rack and Tack was dueling for first,
Shades of Clay and Liston,
'Til Tack's car developed an oil thirst,
And died of an airborne piston.

It looked like Rack was a shoe-in to win.
So he slacked a tad on his go.
But he forgot a mirror is for looking in,
And it soon framed a charging foe.

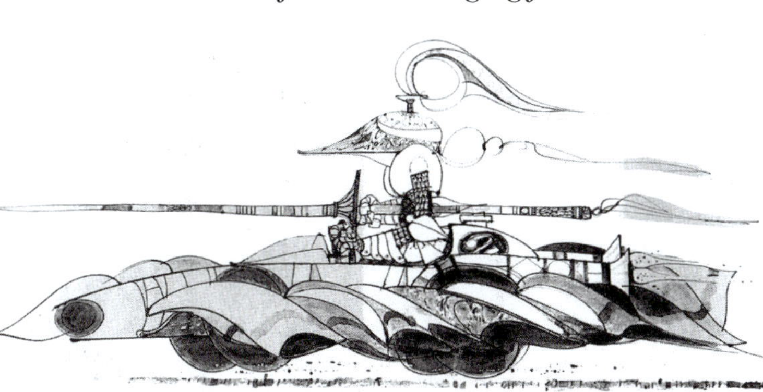

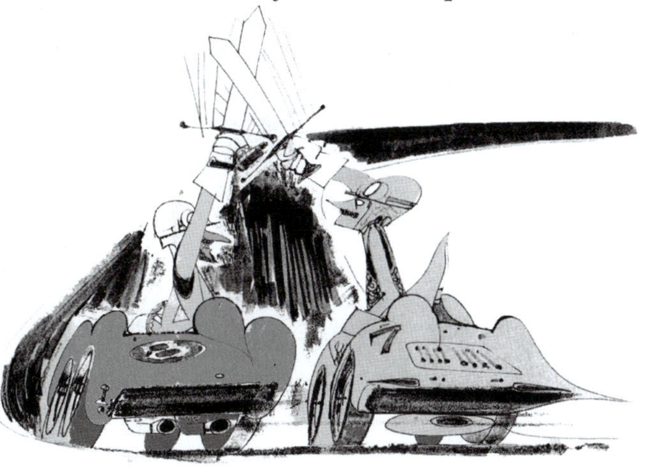

The Steam Engine

Well, like schoolboys, men fell in love with
James Watt's little toy and pretty soon
back-and-forth steam engines
were squeakily turning wheels in mines,
factories, steamboats, and
railroad trains all over the world.

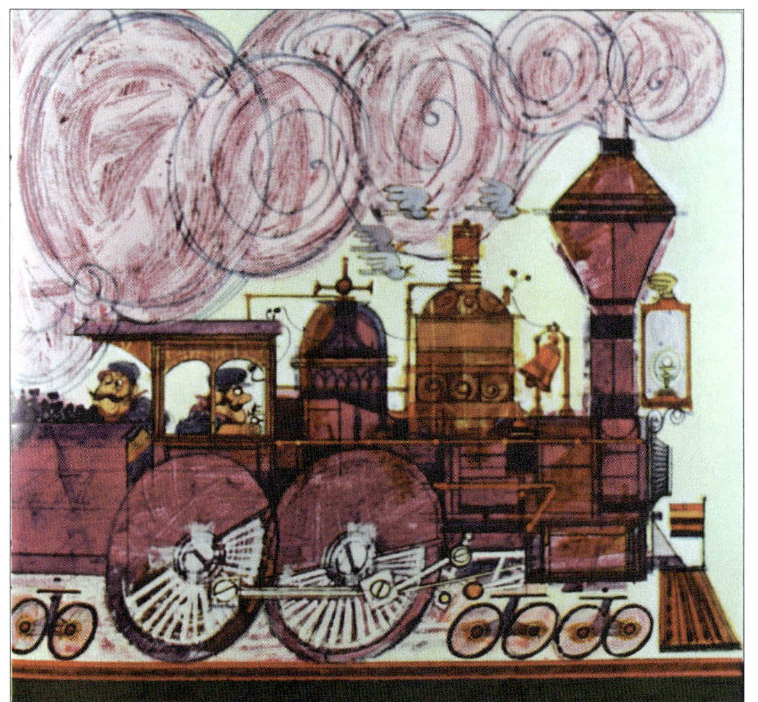

The Industrial Revolution

We now jump ahead about a century
and find great progress had been made
in the Industrial Revolution.

In fact, they didn't even call it that
any more; it was called Capitalism.

Hi-Tech; Low-Tech

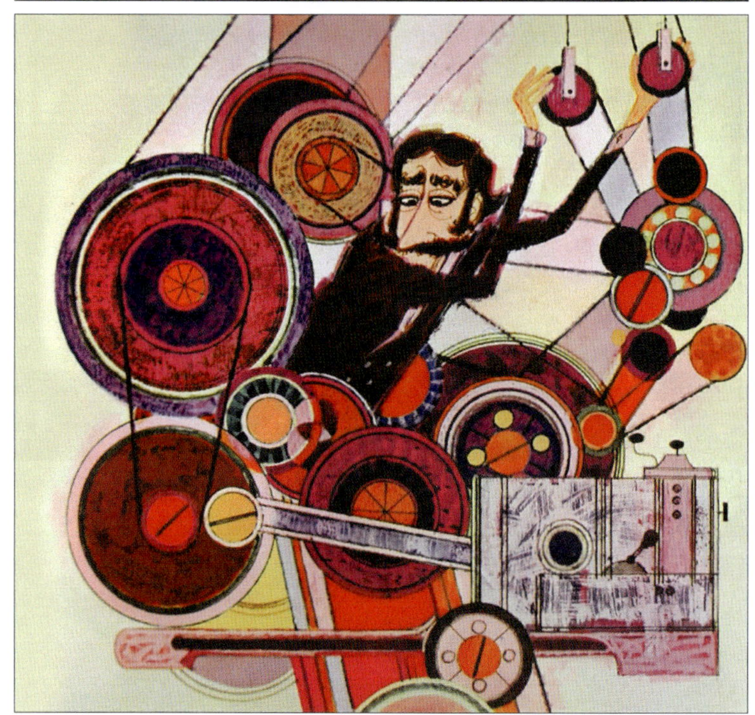

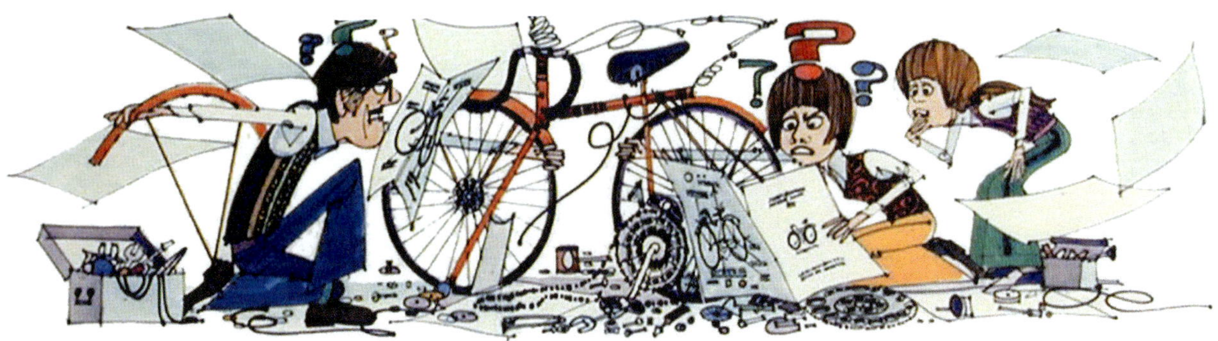

Learning the basics of low technology is the foundation of high technology. (from "Efffective English")

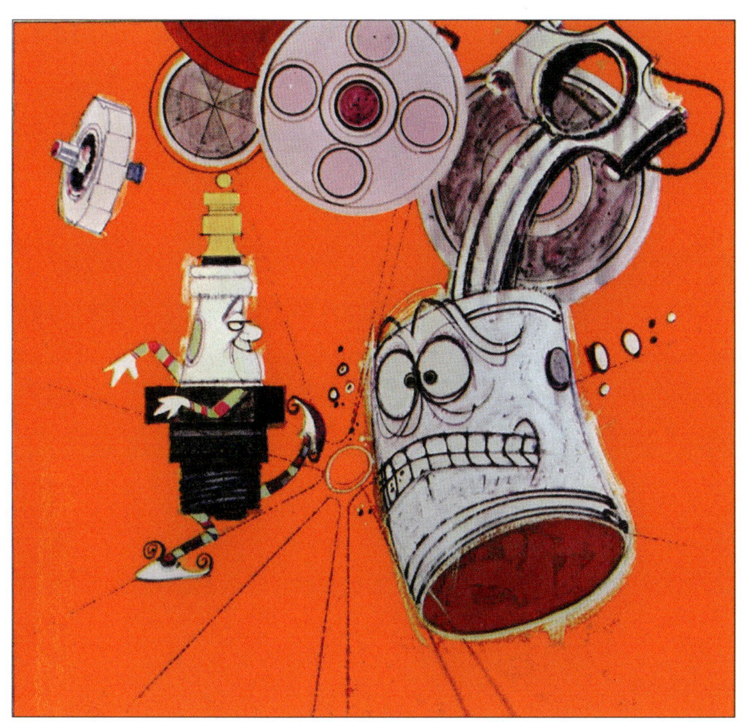

The Piston

Enter now Gottlieb Daimler, an ingenious German, who in 1885 figured out a way to explode gasoline in a cylinder and make it push pistons.

This brilliant innovation had only one serious flaw. Same old back-and-forth movement. Same old connecting rods and crankshafts straining to make back-and-forth come out round-and-round.

Same old waste of motion.

"The Steam Engines," "The Industrial Revolution," "The Piston," and "The Motorboat" are from Curtis-Wright Book of "The Discovery Book." *(See page 71)*

Slowboat, Fastboat

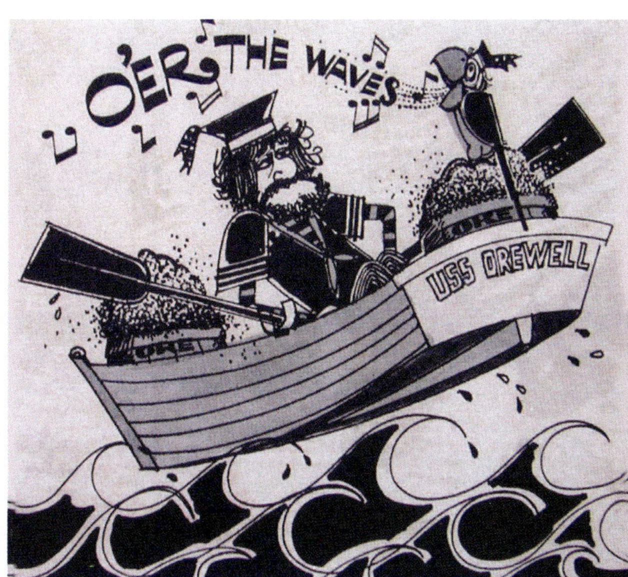

Simplicity or Velocity.

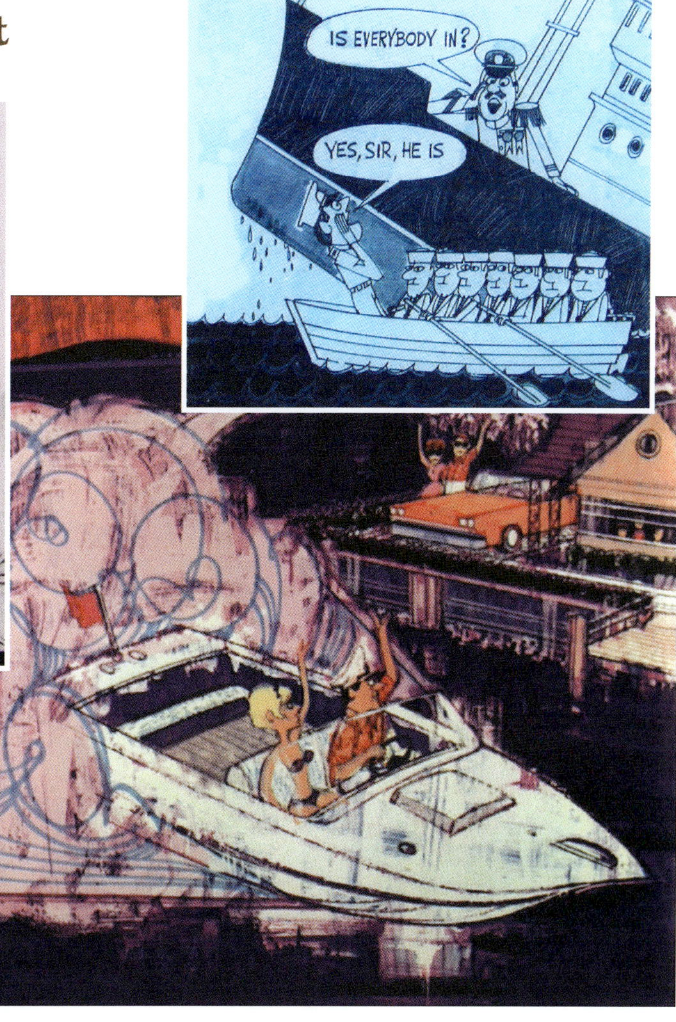

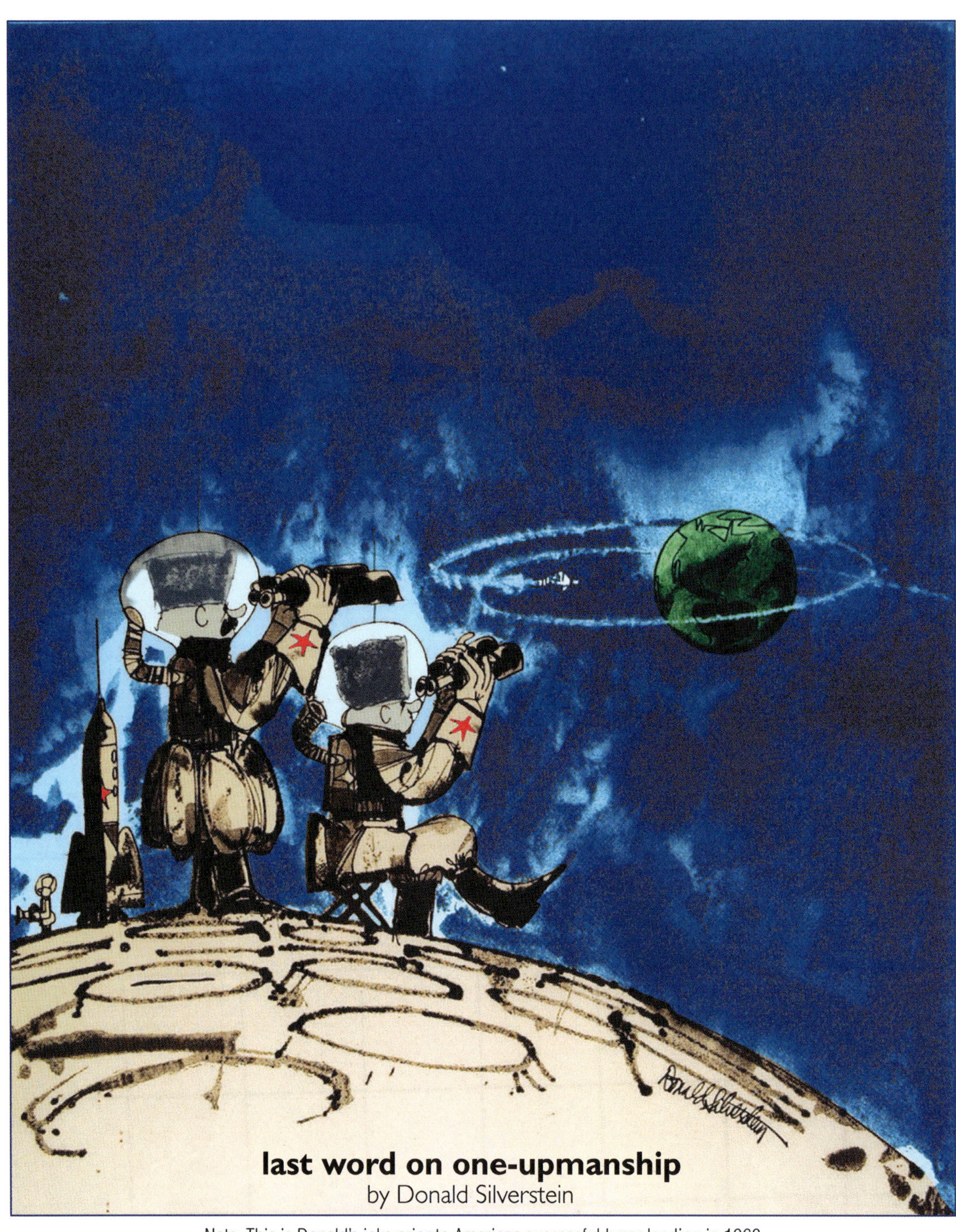

Note: This is Donald's joke prior to American successful luner landing in 1969.
He was not necessarily pro-Russia, despite his some Russian heritage.

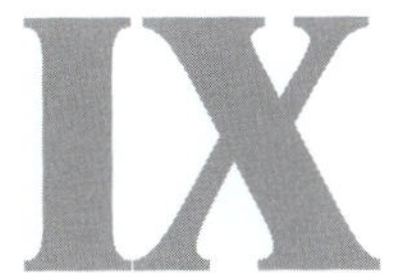

IX

Sex, Violence, & Wicked Ones.

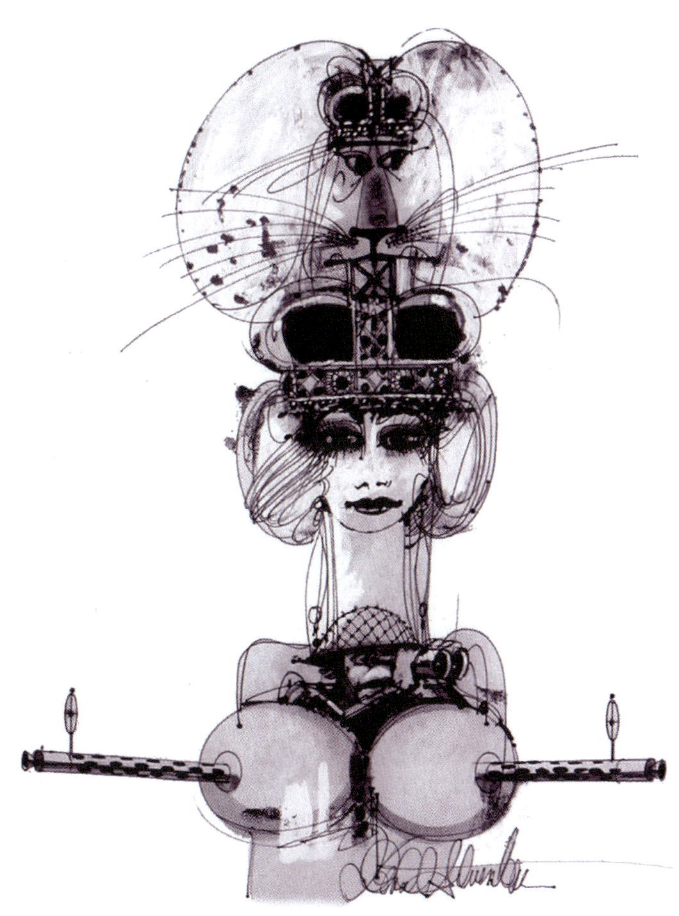

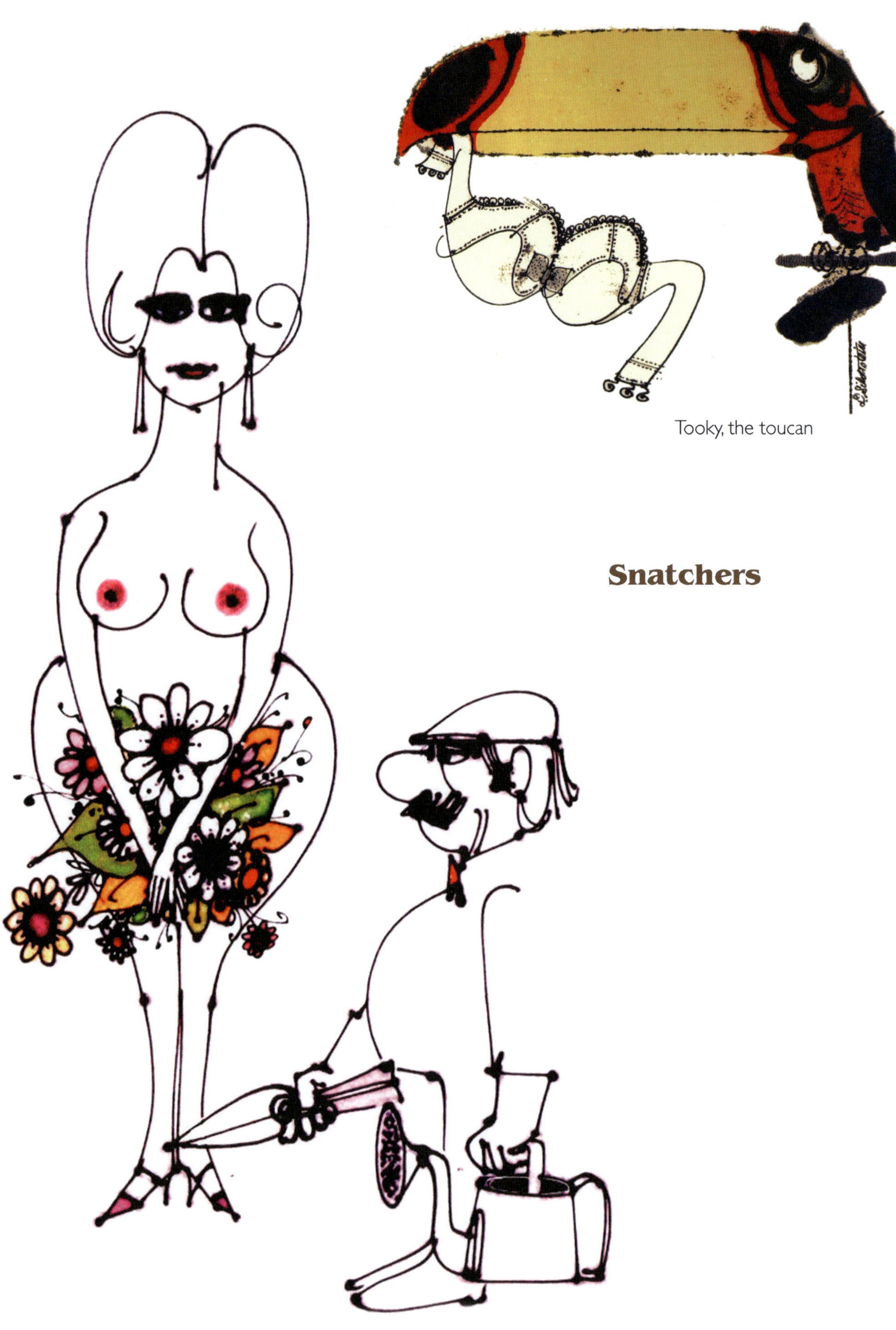

Tooky, the toucan

Snatchers

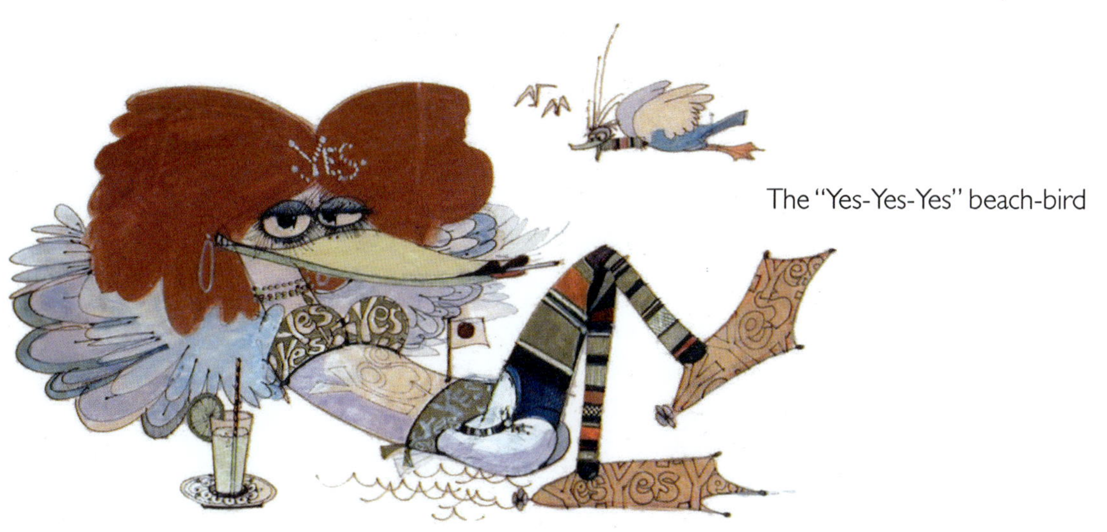

The "Yes-Yes-Yes" beach-bird

Lazy Girls & Lazy Boys

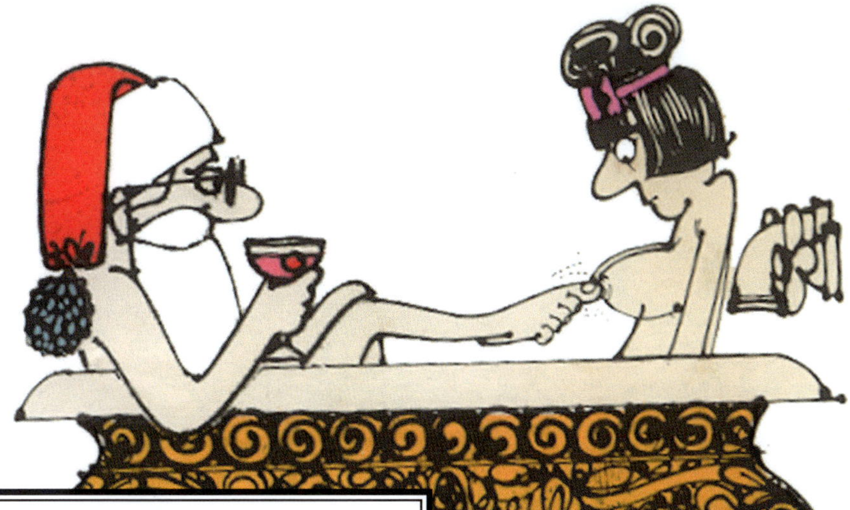

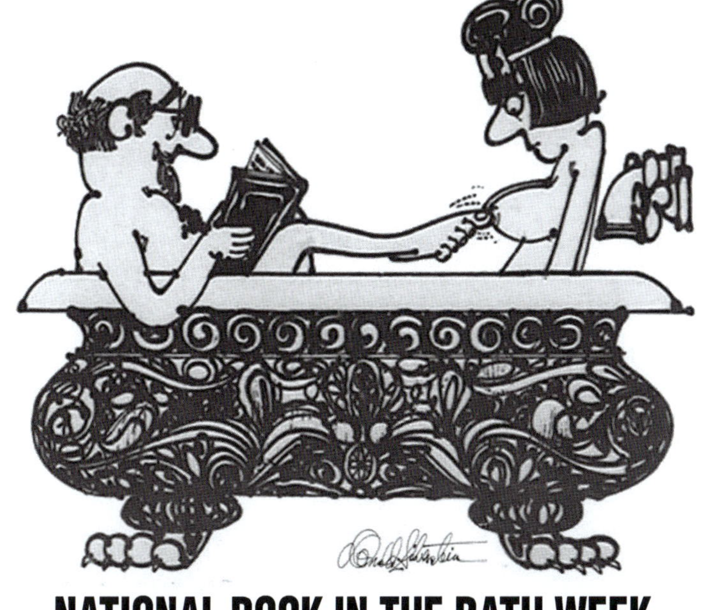

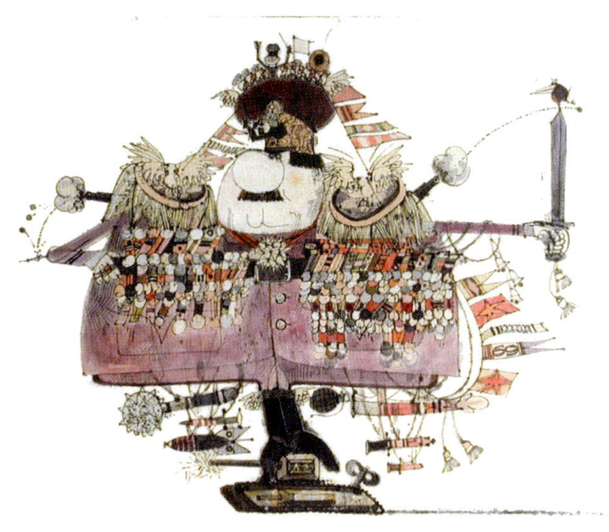

"Oh, what a lovely war! Oh, what a bloody mess!"

"Untitled" *(Adding captions is your option.)*

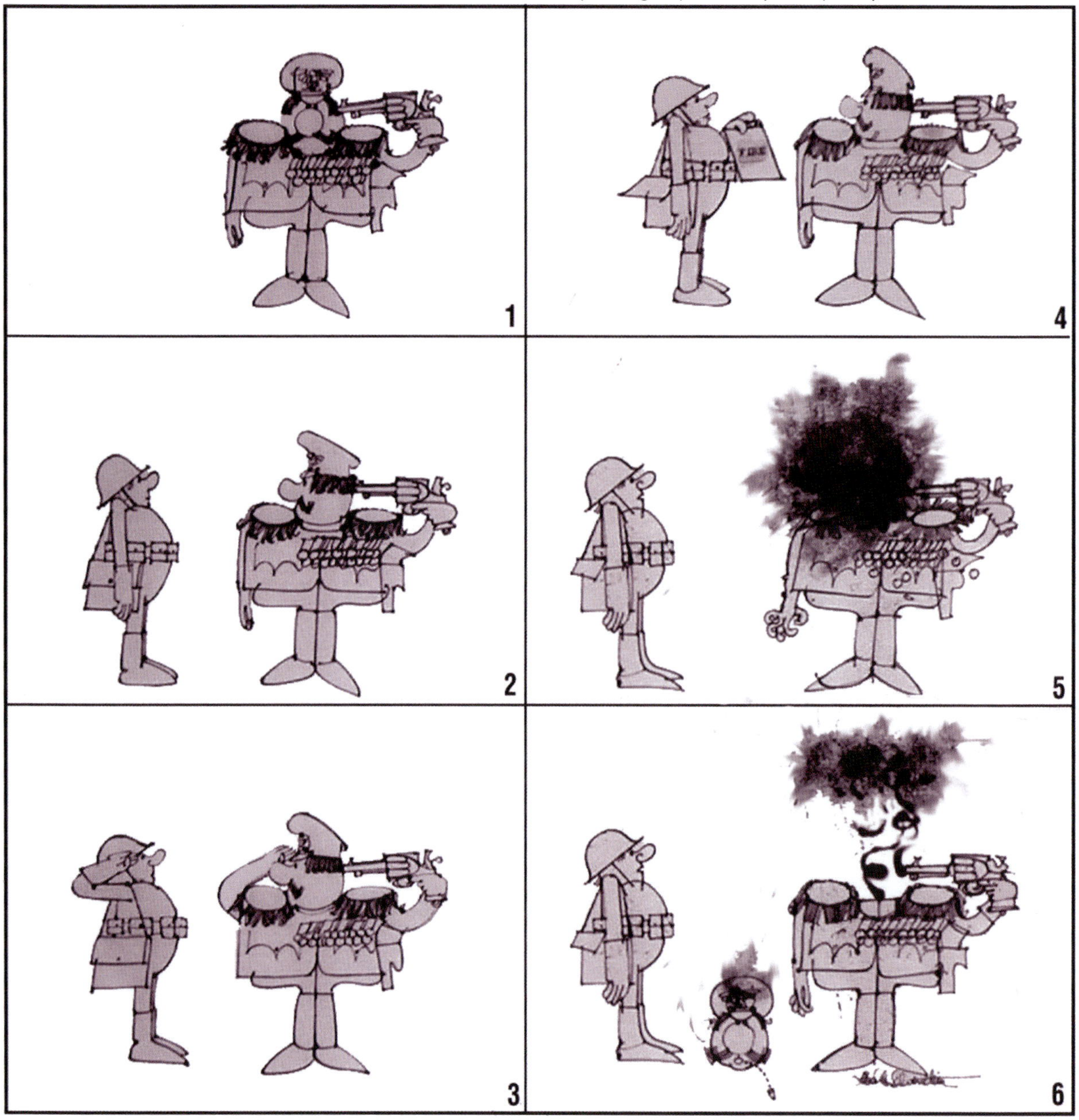

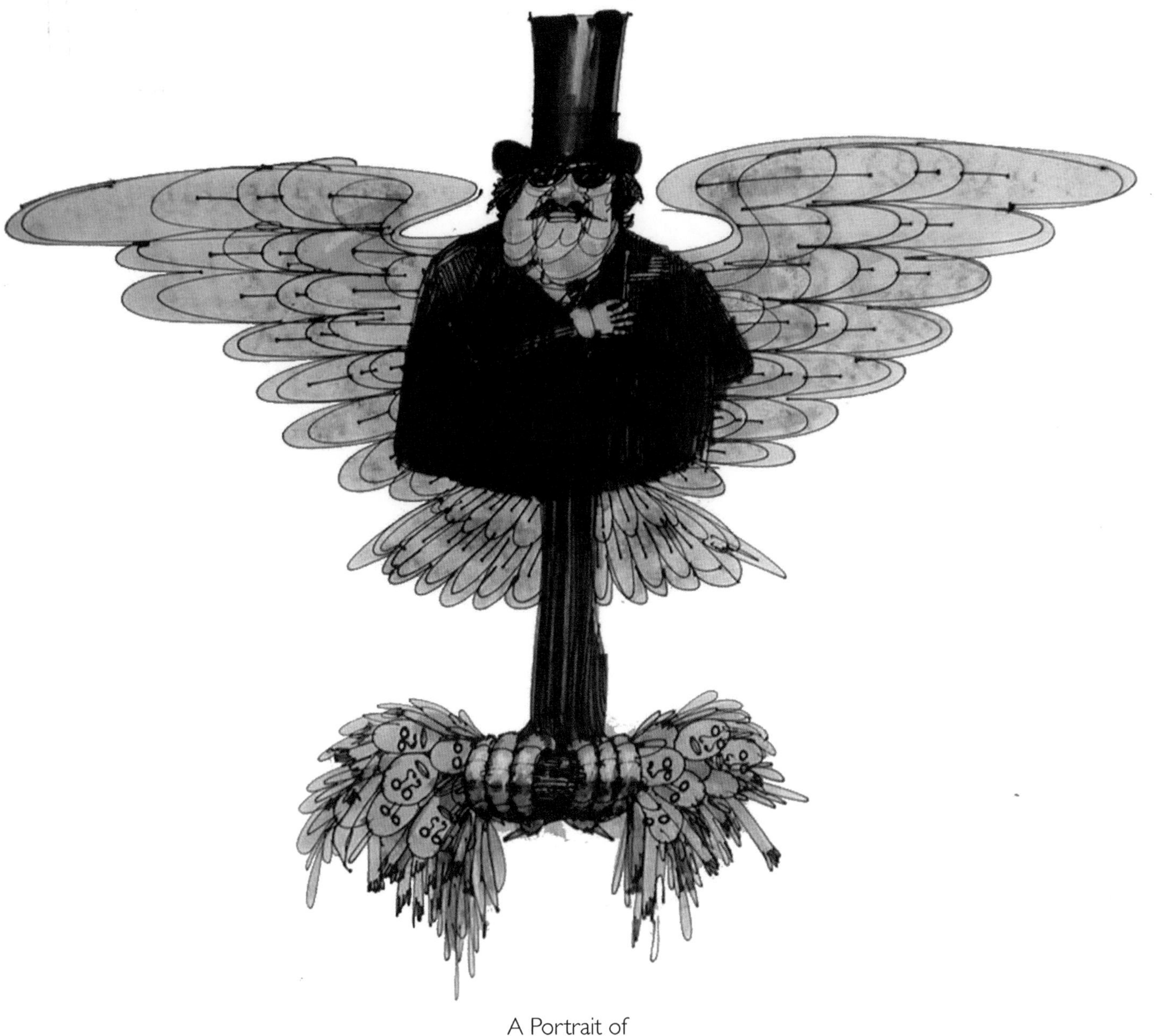

A Portrait of
The Power-Hungry Man

Matter of fact is,
Donald Silverstein was gentle and shy,
yet naughty and tricky.
He loved practical jokes.
When Donald took "sex and violence"
as his subject matter,
he treated them with mild cynicism,
and expressed a unique and extreme touch.

This was Donald's way
of observing and criticizing
sex, violence, and war.

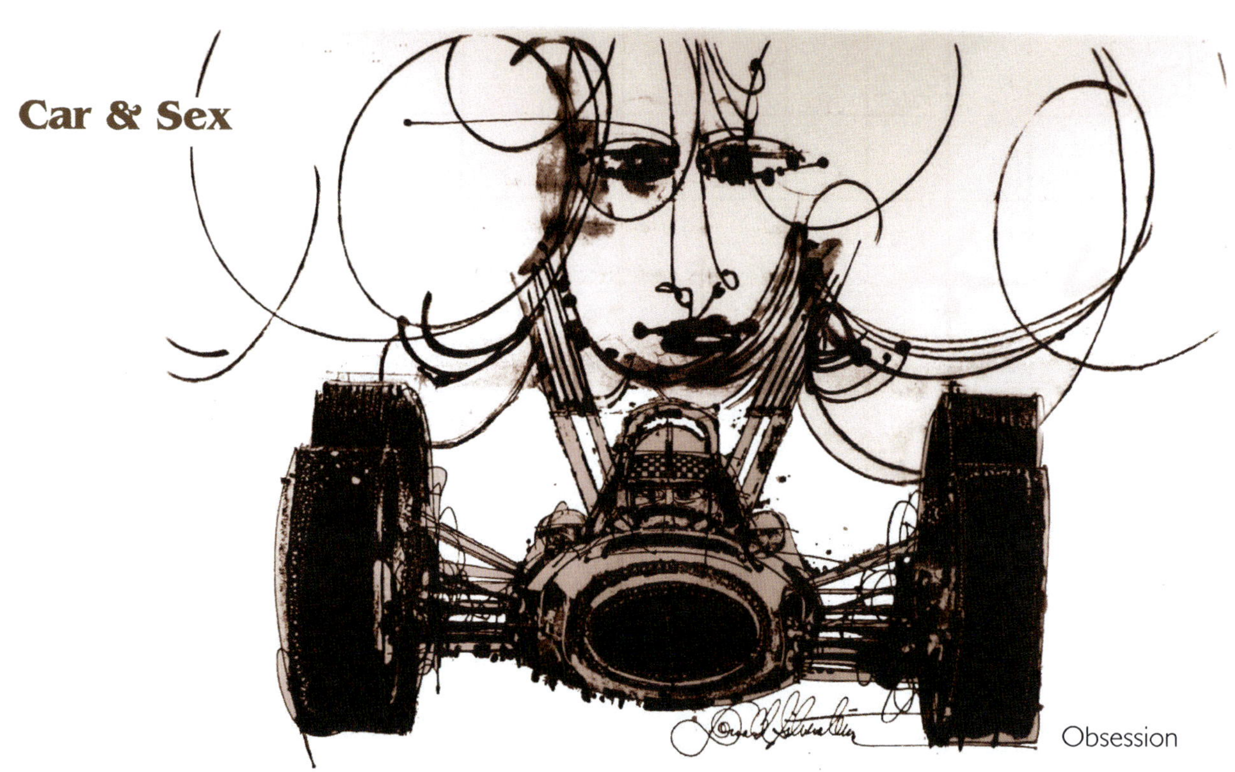

Obsession

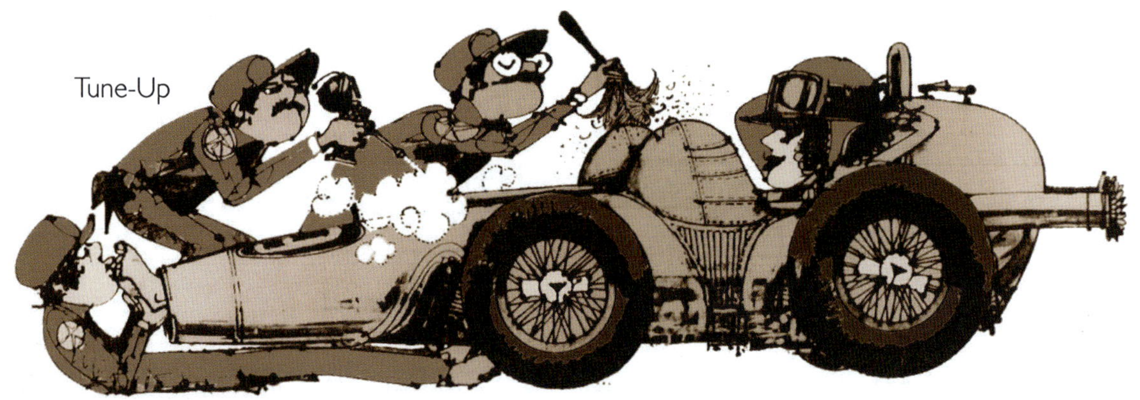

Tune-Up

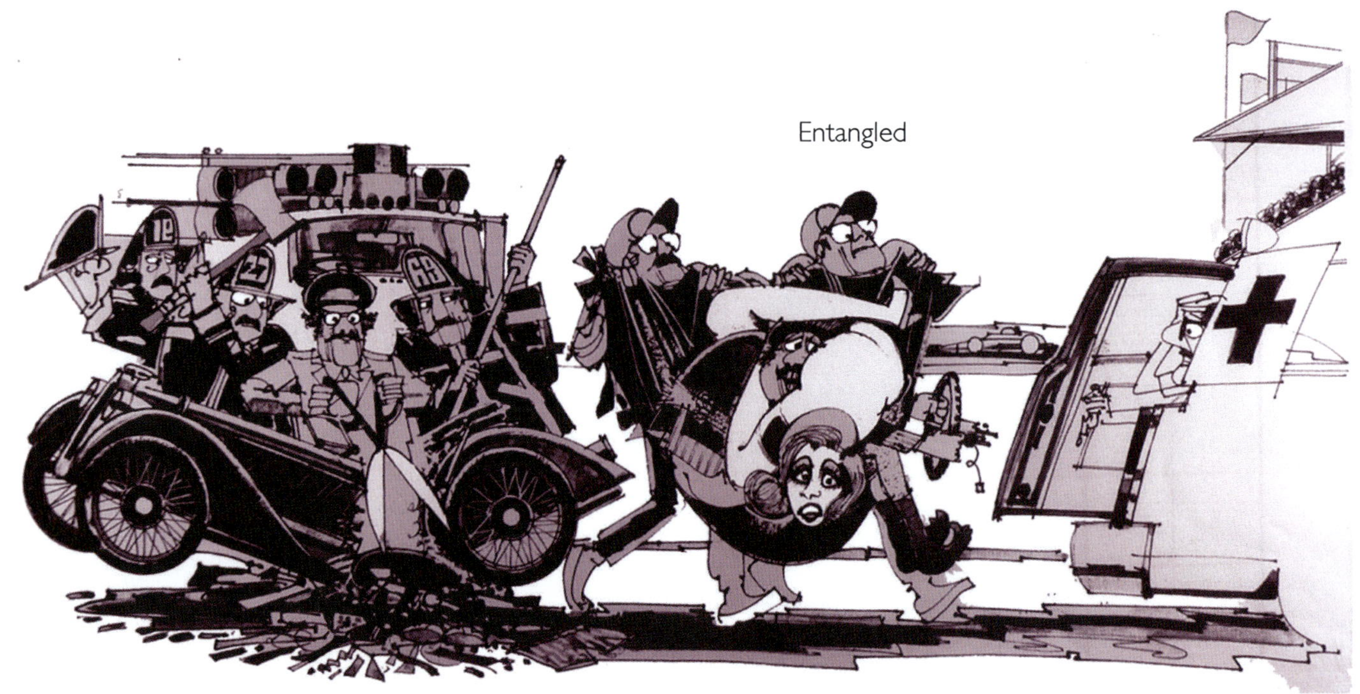

Entangled

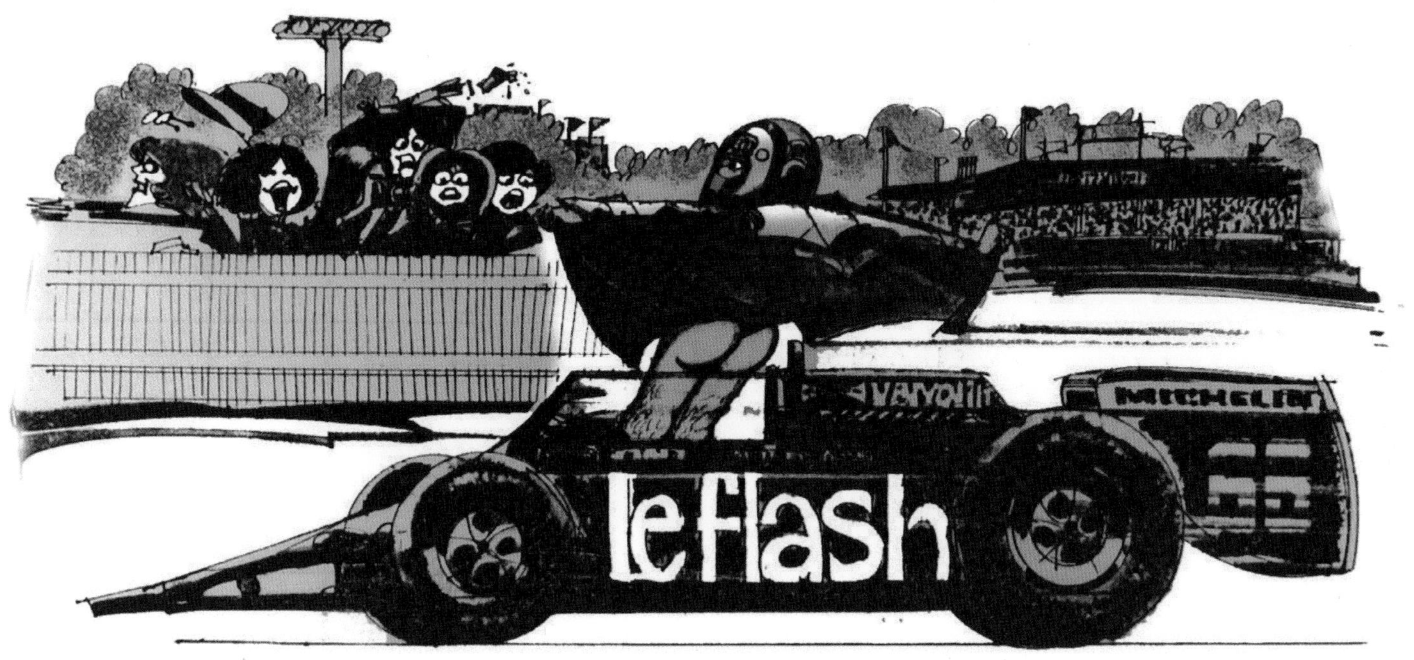

Side Show

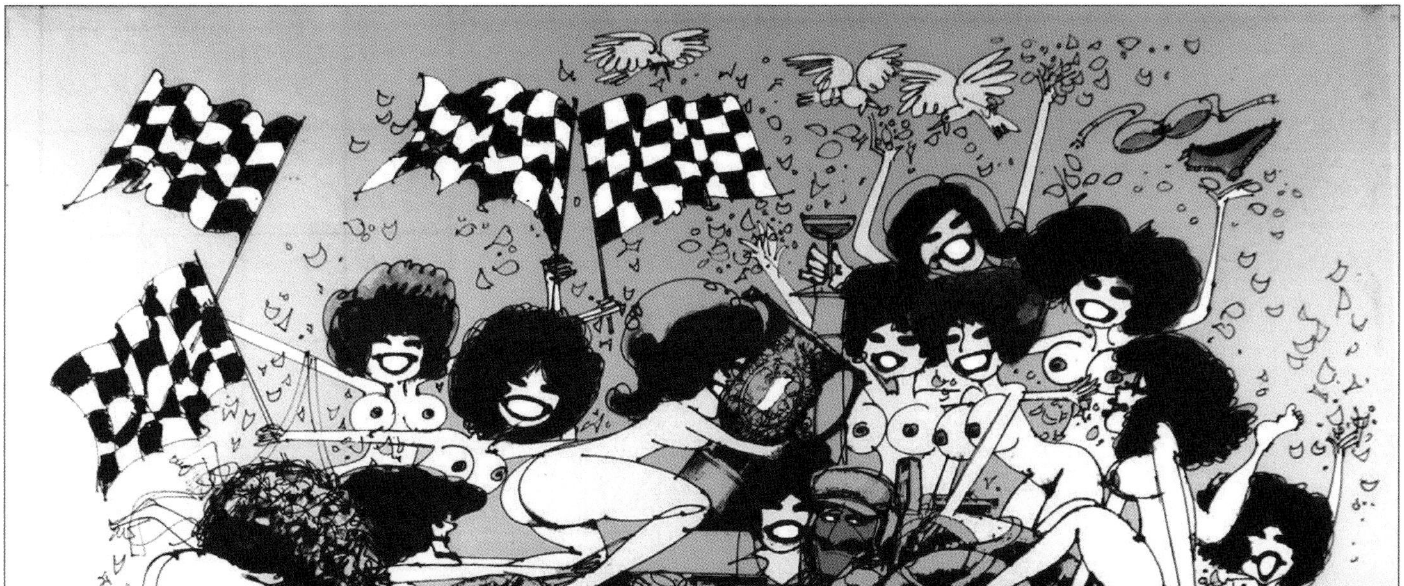

The Winner's Circle

Uncontrollable Guns

The Lady-Killer

Domestic violence I

Predators

"Mirror, mirror…who is the wickest…"

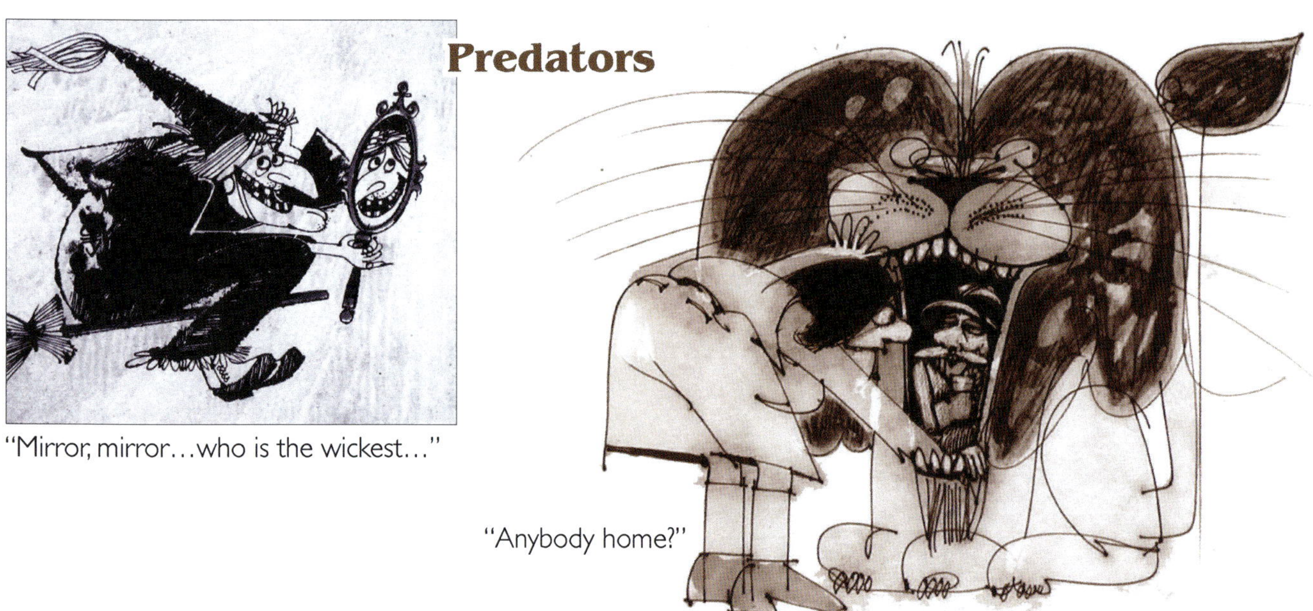

"Anybody home?"

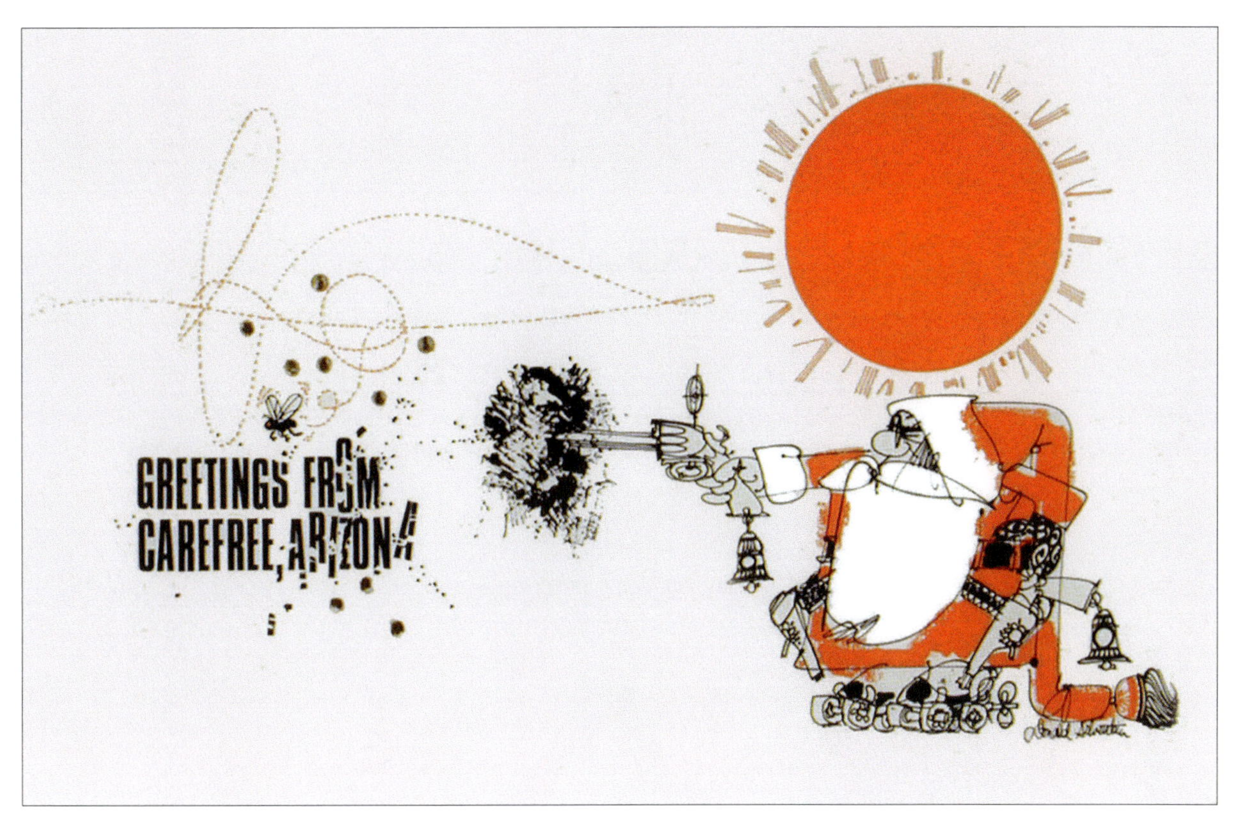

Woman-Power

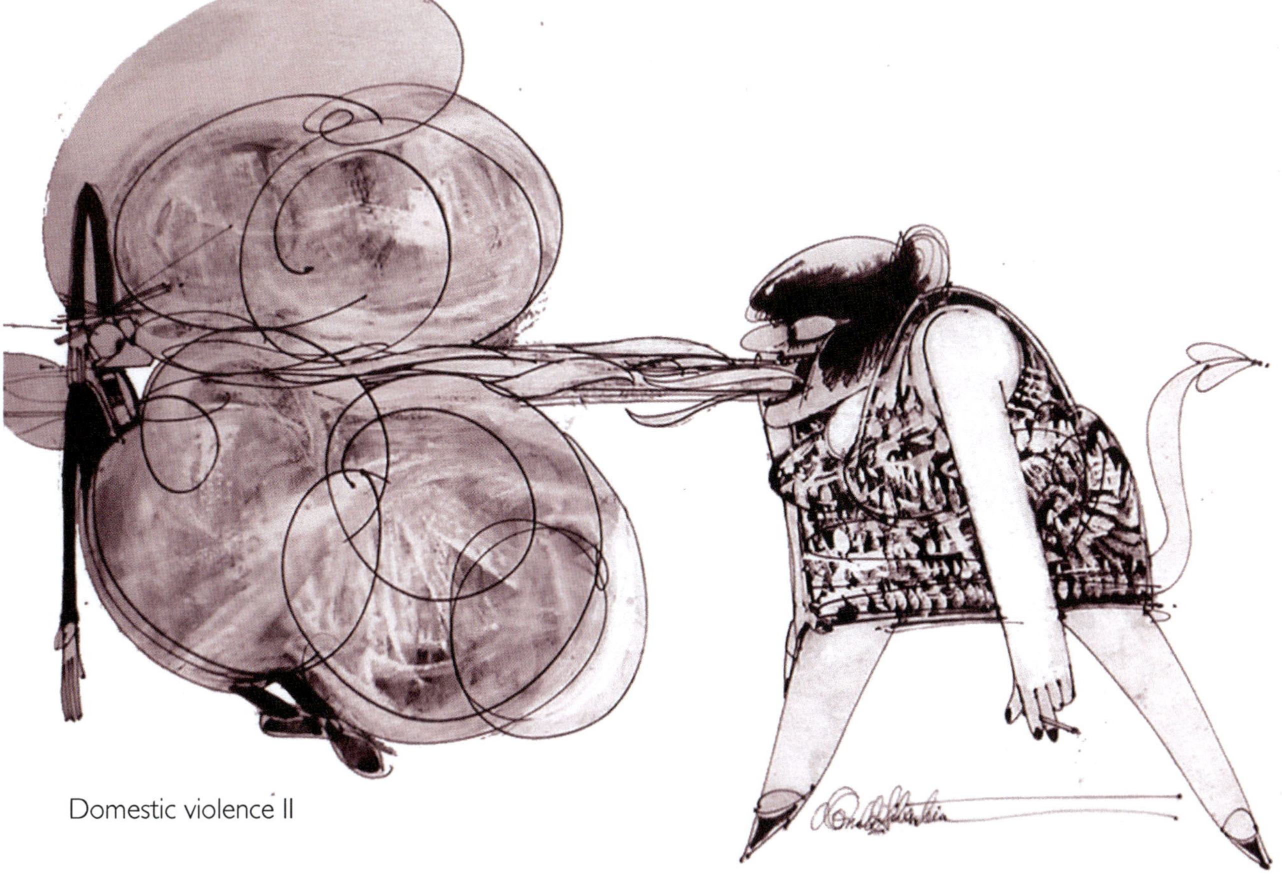

Domestic violence II

P.S. IX

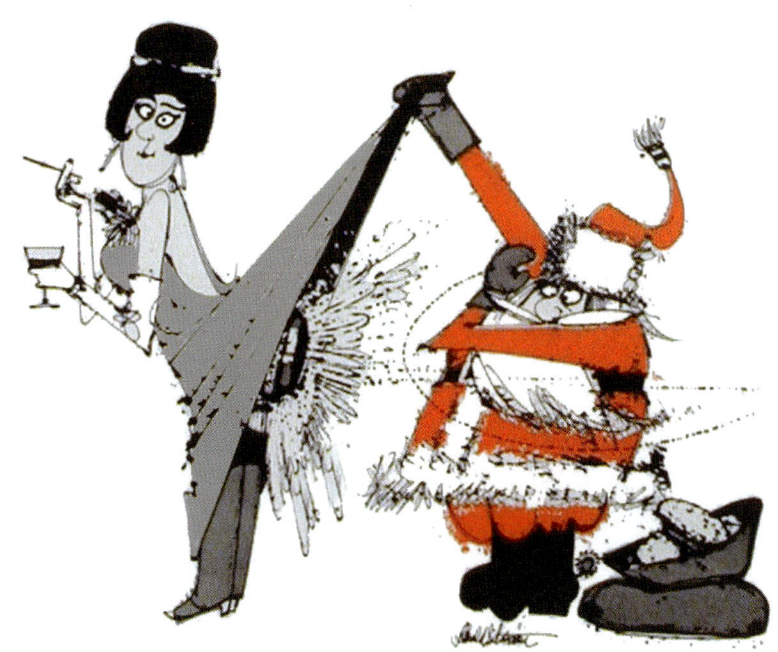

X

"The Urban World of Donald Silverstein"

by
Donald Silverstein

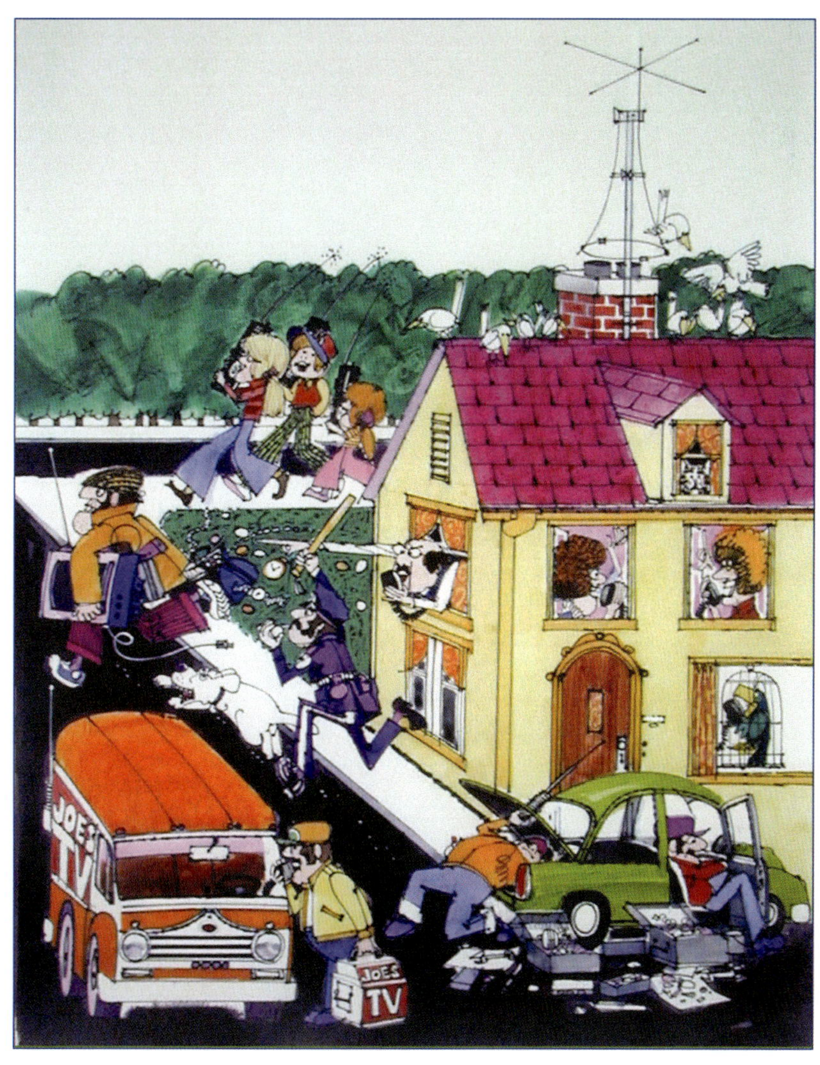

Exodus and Returning

Up to the late 1960s, Donald Silverstein lived alone in the brown stone town house in Greenwich Village, New York City. As a freelance illustrator, he was working mostly for publishers and ad agencies. He received some awards from the Society of Illustrators, for his artwork of children's books. His fifth floor studio was cozy and well illuminated by a skylight — ideal quarters for an artist.

Donald was popular among art directors in the field. He was comfortable as far as his daily life was concerned. Nevertheless, Donald started complaining about New York City's rat-race living environment. Blaming and cursing, saying, "I don't have to be in New York. I can do my work anywhere in the world." In fact, he moved out to Carefree, Arizona. Why there? Everyone was puzzled.

Shortly before his departure, he gave a bunch of keys to one of his friends, telling him "I'm keeping my studio while I'm away. You can use the space anytime you want." Imagine his friend's and his wife's excitement.

Mrs. Friend could hardly wait for Donald's departure. One weekend, Mr. and Mrs. Friend went to the studio, eager to open the door and nervously juggling the keys that Donald gave them. Alas, none of them worked. The superintendent of the building heard suspicious noises and came upstairs to see a couple of strangers. He accused them of a break-in. The couple explained why they were there. The superintendent sternly declared, "Silverstein doesn't live here." Needless to say, the couple realized they were fooled, and shamefully embarrassed. Evidently, Mrs. Friend didn't hate Donald. She recognized their own stupidity.

A year or so later, Mrs. Friend became a matchmaker for Donald and Sakiko.

Donald and Sakiko lived in Arizona until…

The address change notice distributed to their friends; — late 1972.

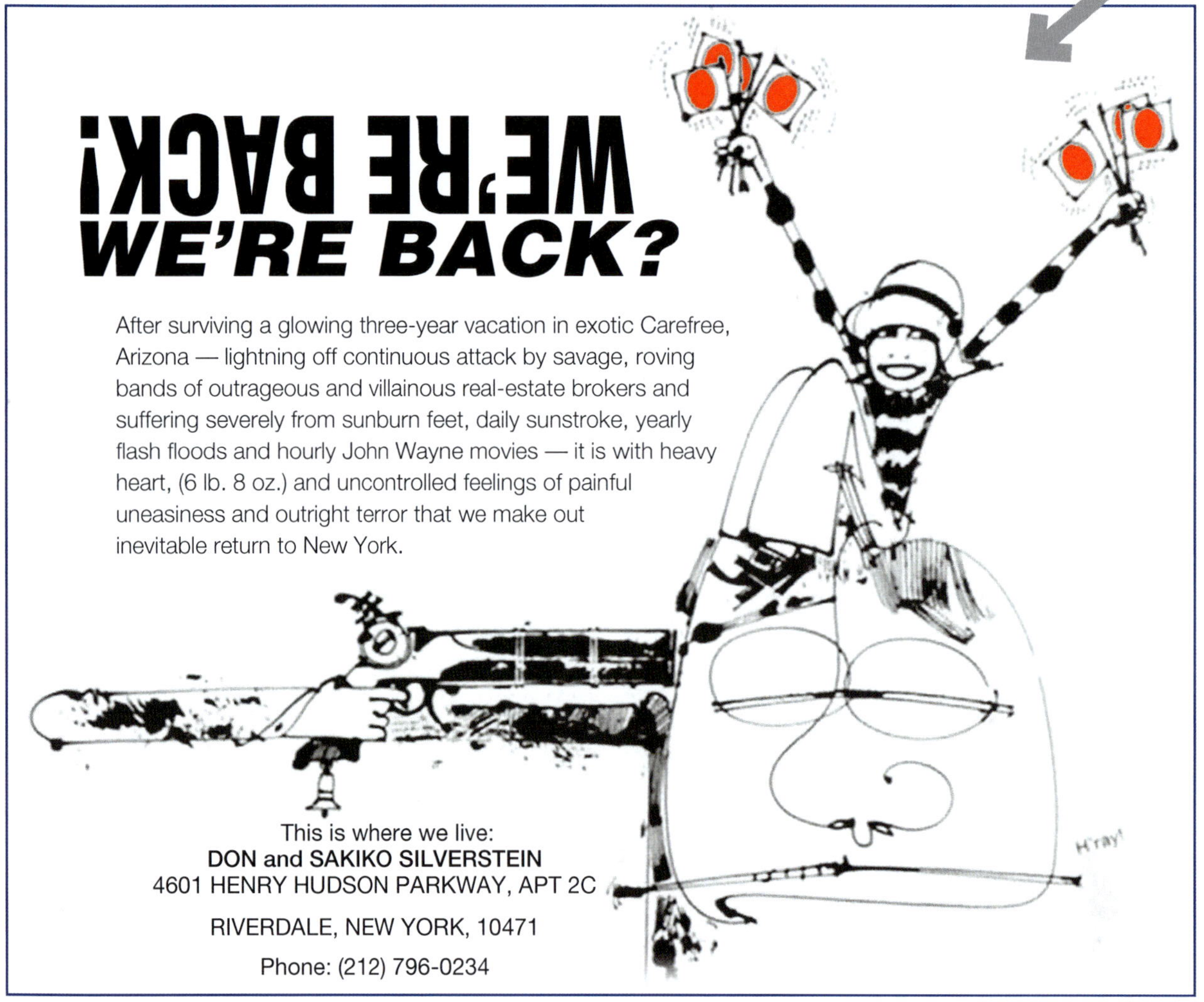

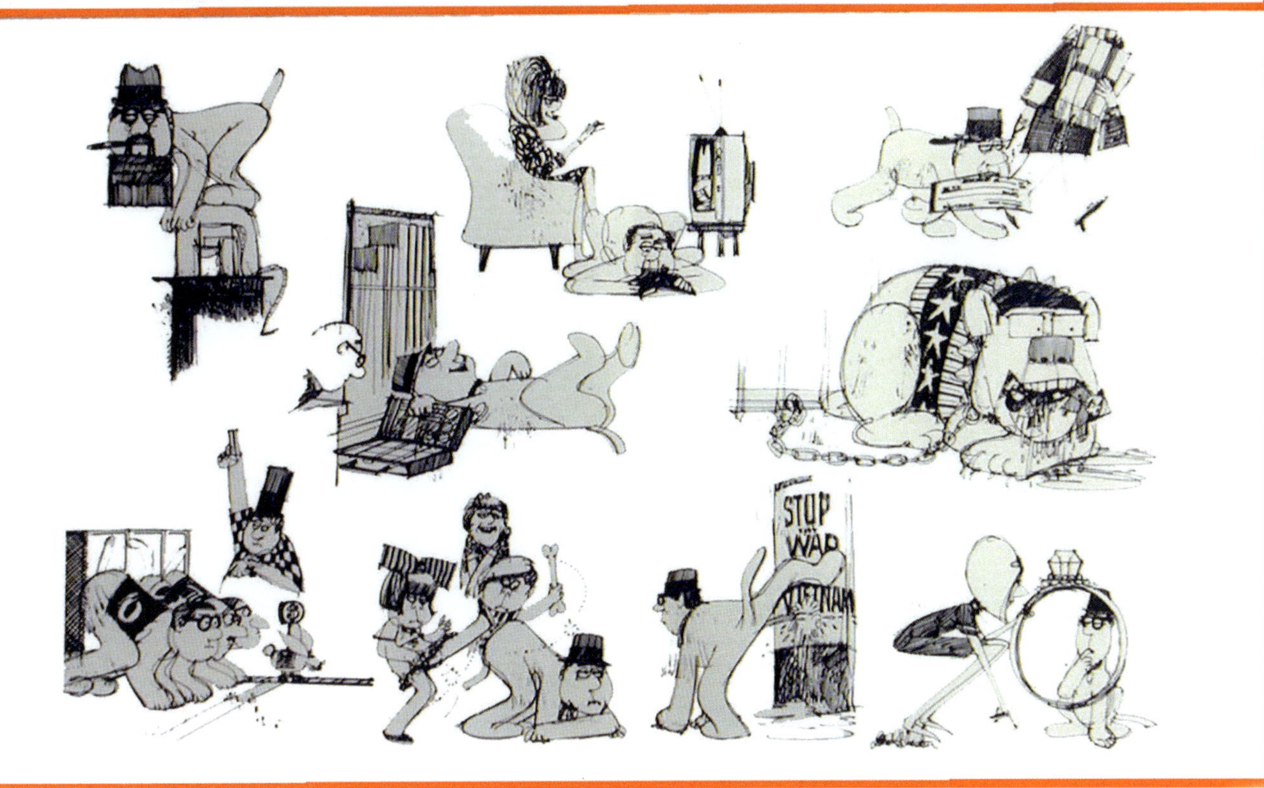

"The Dog Men"

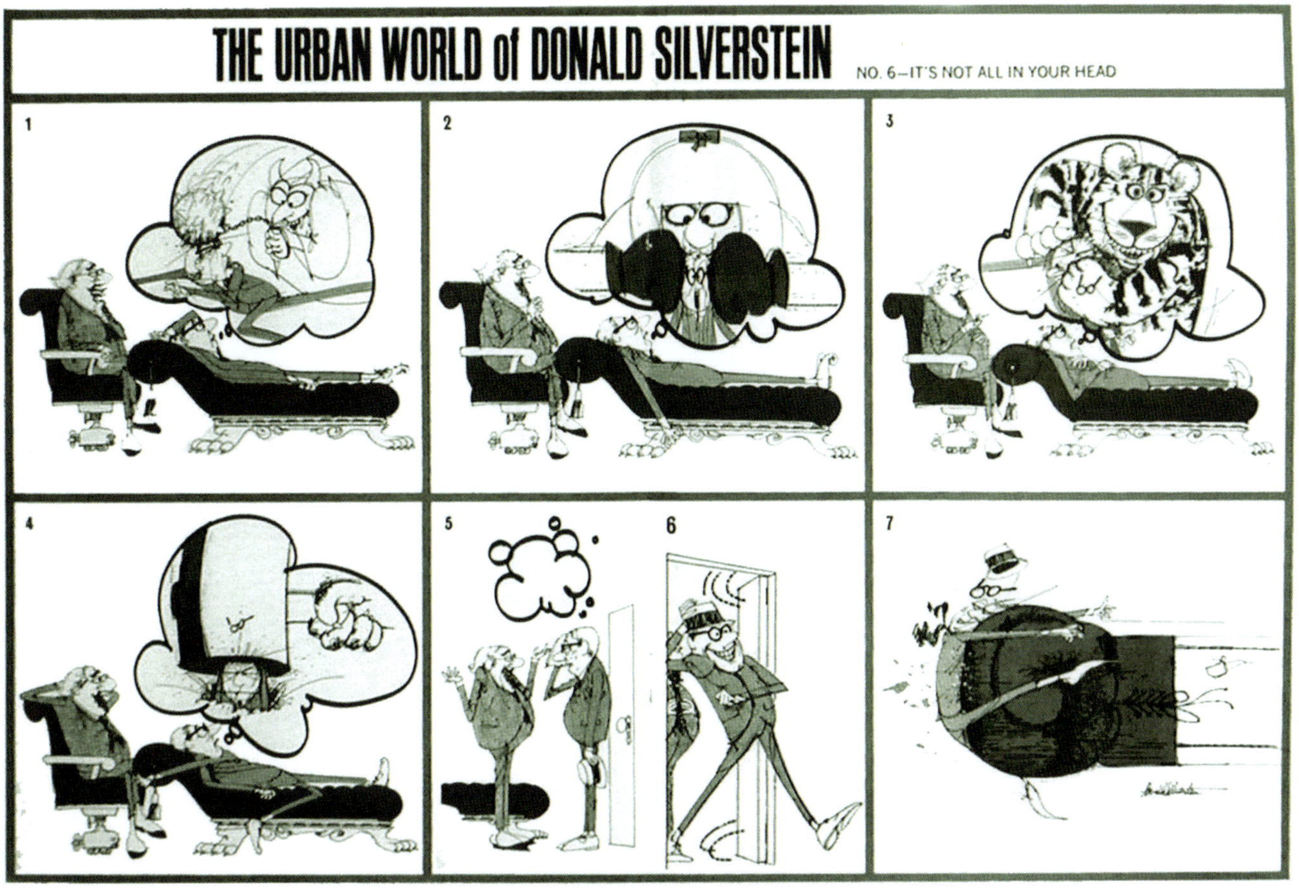

"It's Not All In Your Head"

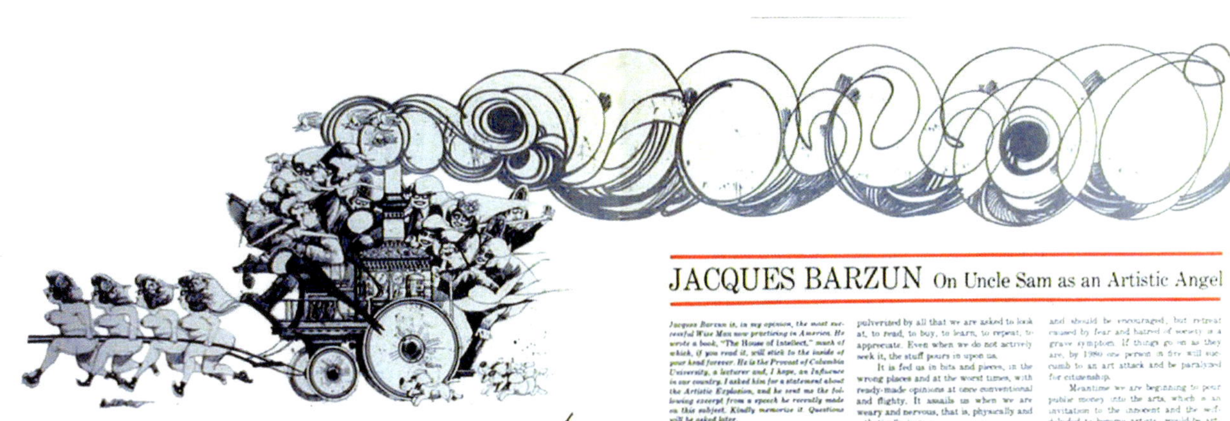

"(Naked) Firewomen"

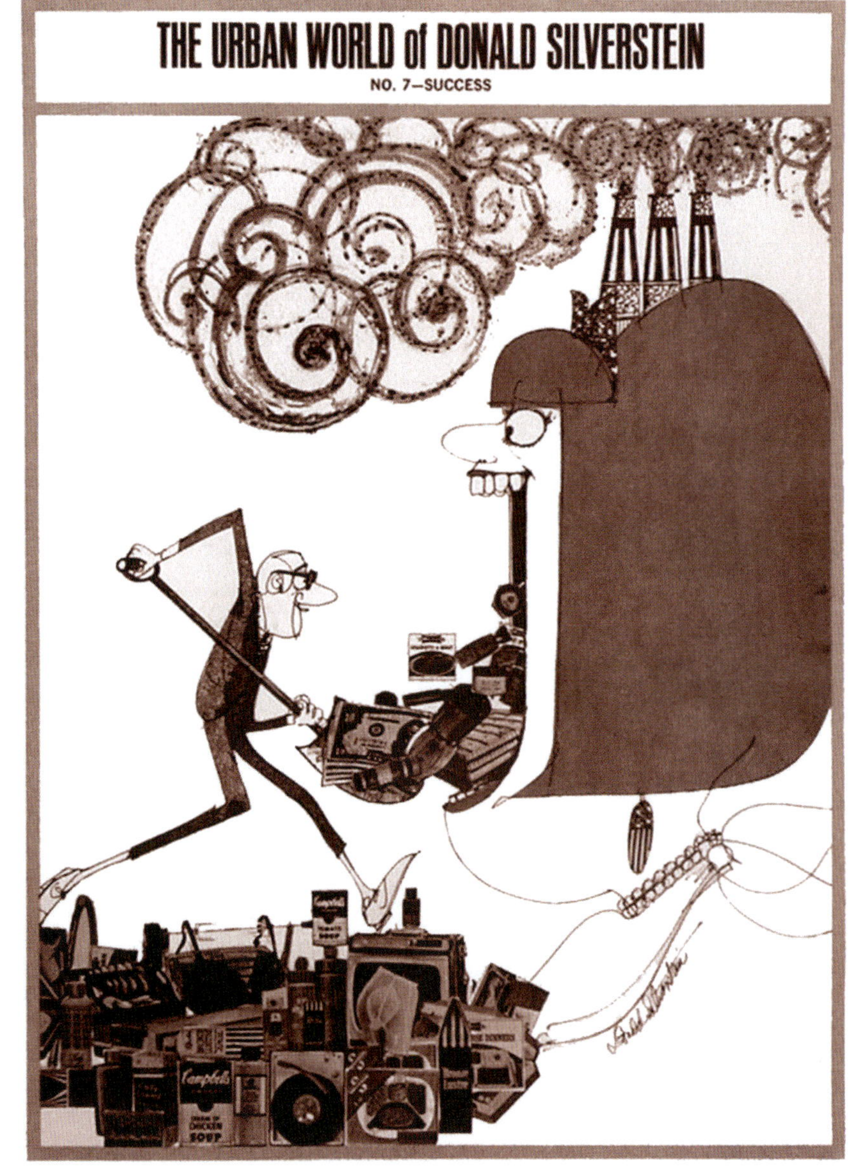

"Success"

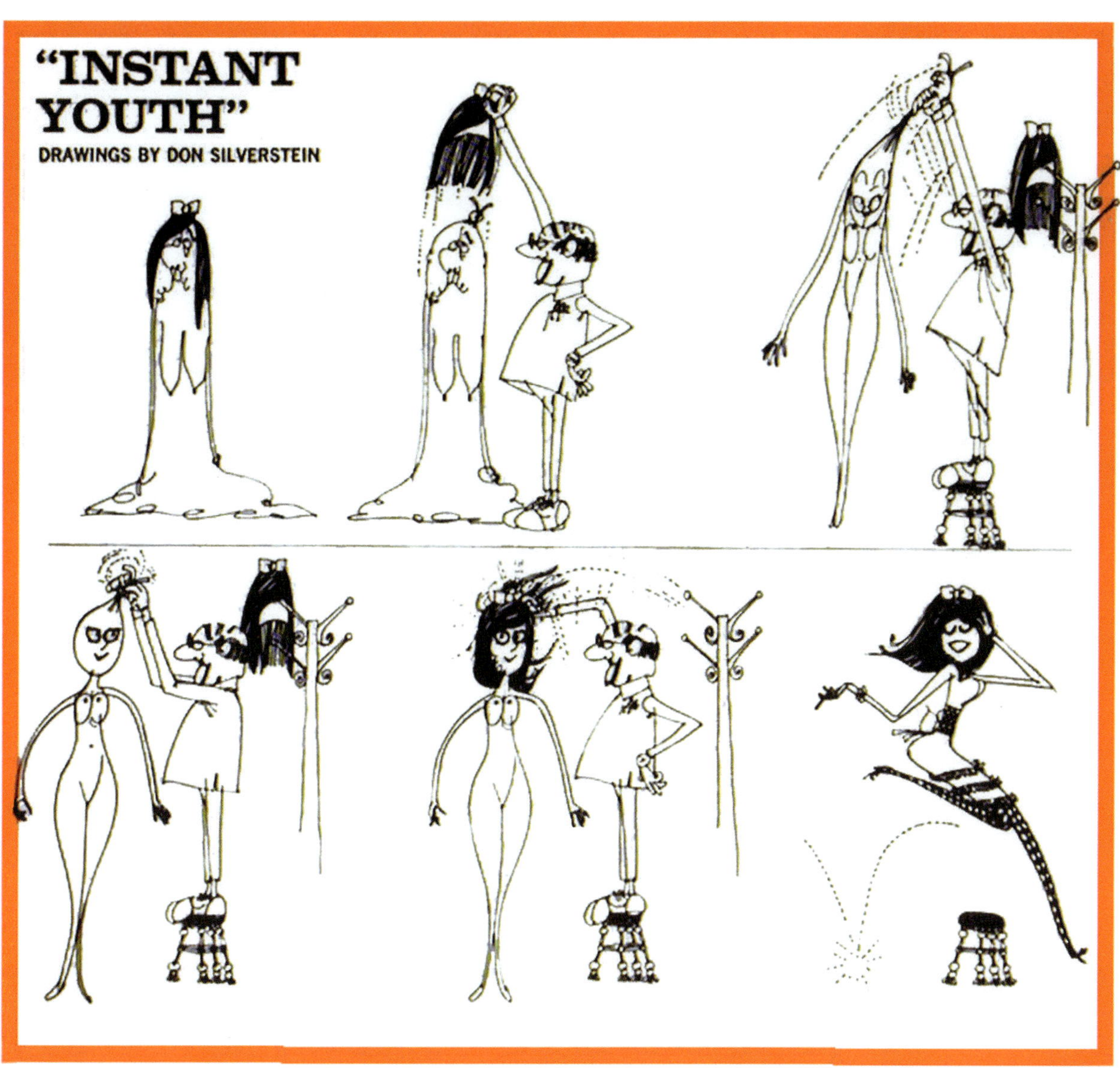

"Instant Youth"

P.S. X

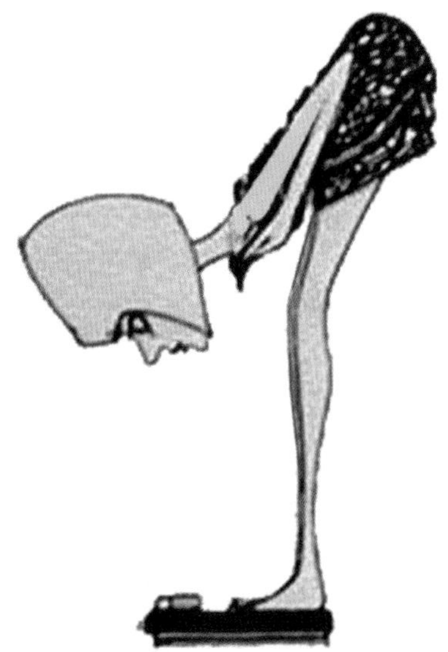

The Weight Watcher

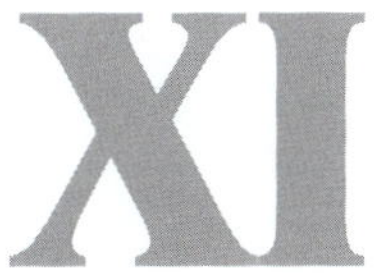

XI

Donald's Almanac

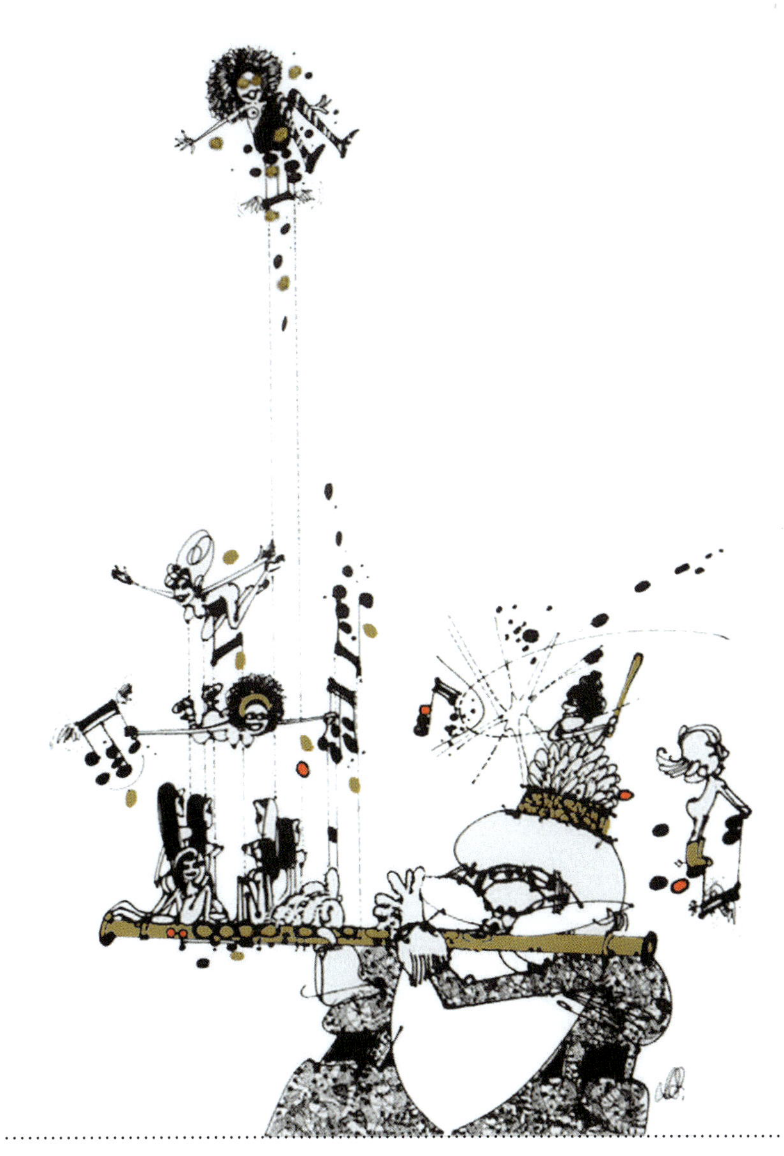

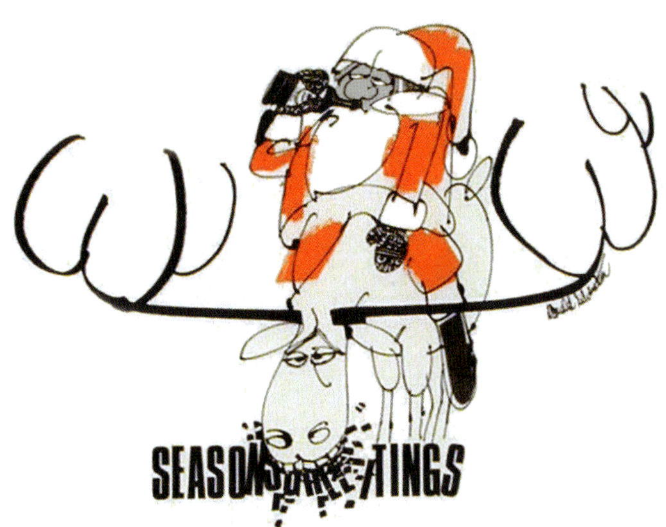

Donald Silverstein and Sakiko moved to Tokyo, Japan, in late 1982. Soon, they moved again to Funabashi, Chiba, not far from Tokyo, where they stayed for the next ten years.

Donald never learned Japanese, but he made many Japanese friends, including celebrities. One of them was Miss Tetsuko Kuroyanagi (*photo in page 106*), a popular TV personality who had her own talk show that broke the record-run of the Johnny Carson's "Tonight" Show.

Even though Donald couldn't read or speak Japanese, he pretended reading newspapers on the train; the major mean of Japanese transportation. Other passengers thought he could be one of those "know-Japan-well" foreigners… *gaijin*. Donald liked to wear sweat shirt marked "*gaijin*" (*see this picture and page 105*).

Donald was working illustrating for the articles and text books for the publishers in Tokyo. At the same time, he was painting semi-abstract landscape of local scenes.

His sensitive artistic skill had already developed prior to coming to Japan, when he lived in Connecticut (*refer to "Dynamically Sensitive Art" book: p.109*). However, he was fascinated by traditional Japanese culture… calligraphy, clothing and its fabric, temples, shrines, castles, unreadable newspapers, symbols, and picture framing format.

Donald's creativity bloomed during his res-

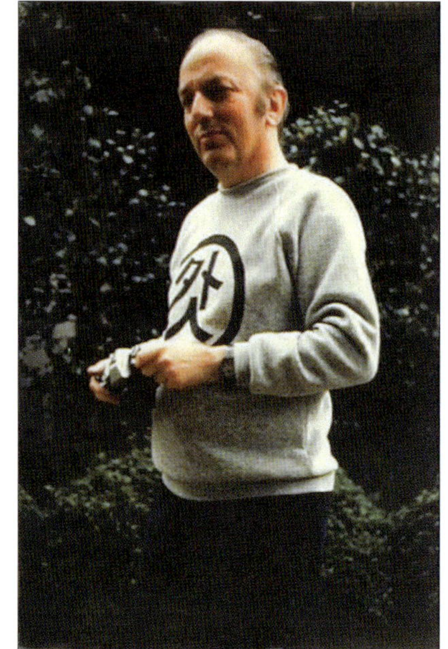

idency in Japan. His sensitivity allowed him to absorb Japan's beauty and skills, and anything he could utilize and applied to his own paintings.

His wife Sakiko believes it was the peak of Donald's entire career. He was so enthusiastically focused on his creation. The best of all, Donald was filled with joy.

Evidently, Donald had many opportunities to exhibit and show his paintings at various galleries. Meanwhile, he was still working on illustrations for commercial and editorial purposes.

Donald blended in the Japanese society even though he had a language handicap. The fact of the matter was, in most cases, he didn't have to speak Japanese. Many Japanese understood Donald's English, and were able to communicate with him in either broken or fluent English. They even understood Donald's naughty jokes.

Donald acquired some Japanese customs. He especially liked exchanging seasons greeting cards in the traditional Japanese way. Japanese celebrate Christmas. However, the significant event to them is not a year-end celebration, but the new year holiday festivity both spiritually and for entertainment.

As you will see on the following pages, Donald mailed out his own New Year's greeting cards, instead of Christmas card. Each year representing particular animal. He enjoyed doing this as well as the recipients enjoyed getting them.

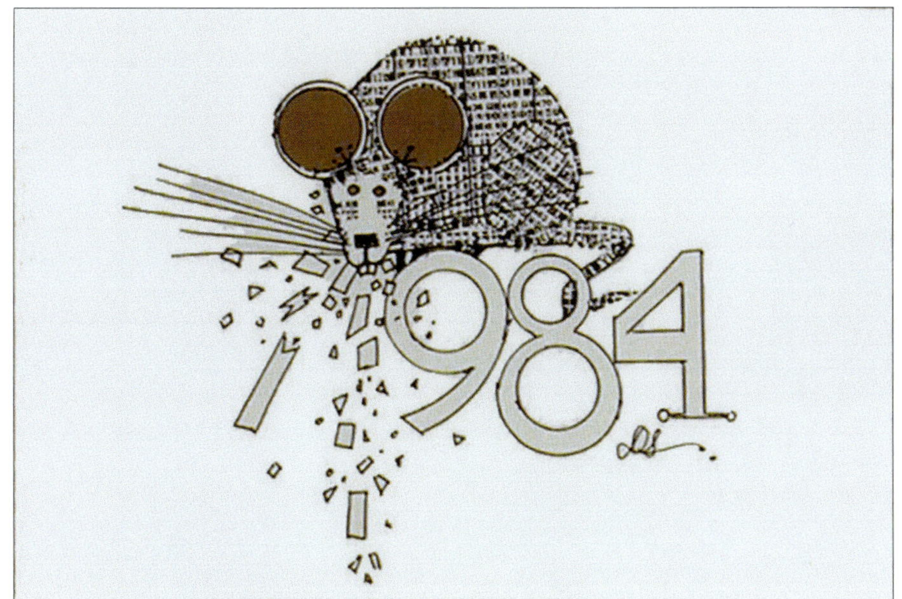

1984;
The year of the Mouse

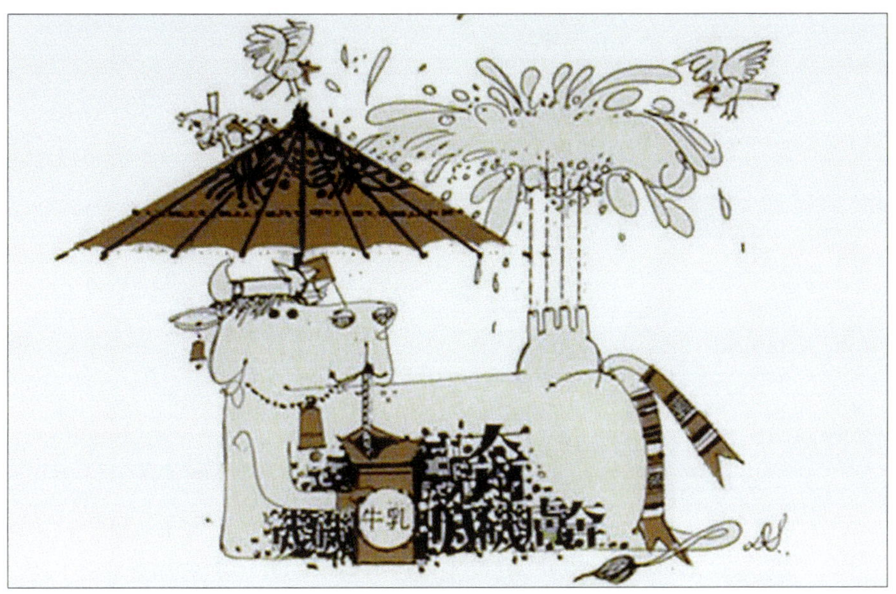

1985;
The year of the Cow

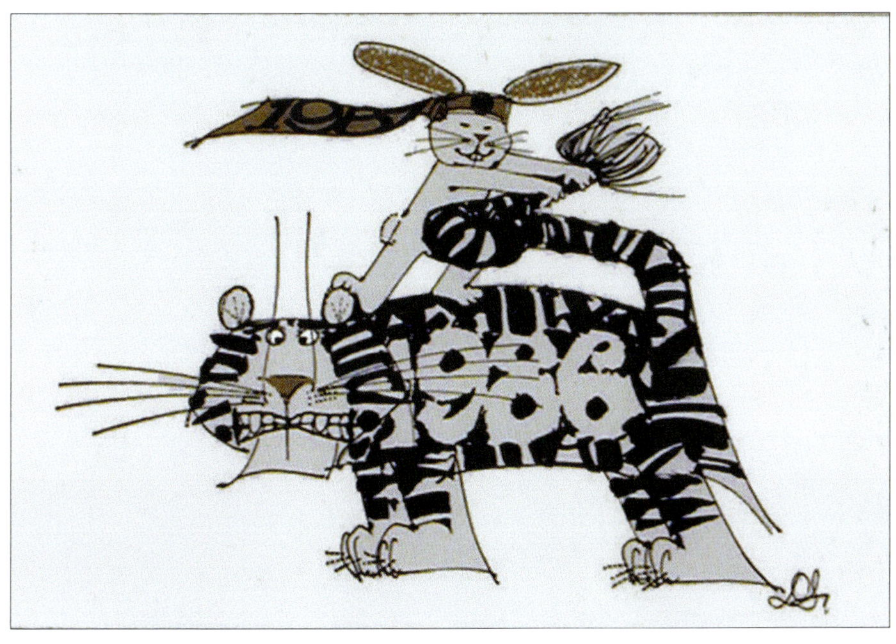

1986 to 1987;
The year of the Tiger to
the year of the Rabbit

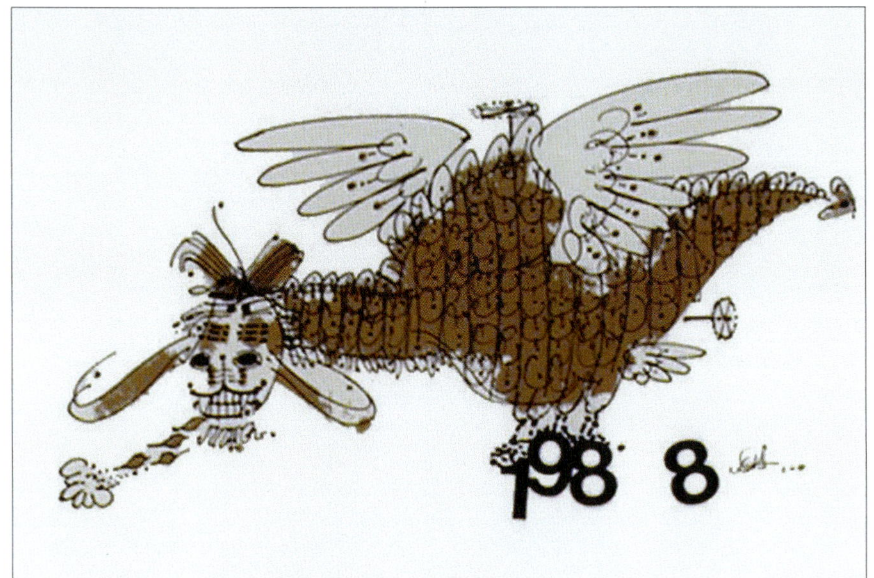

1988;
The year of the Dragon

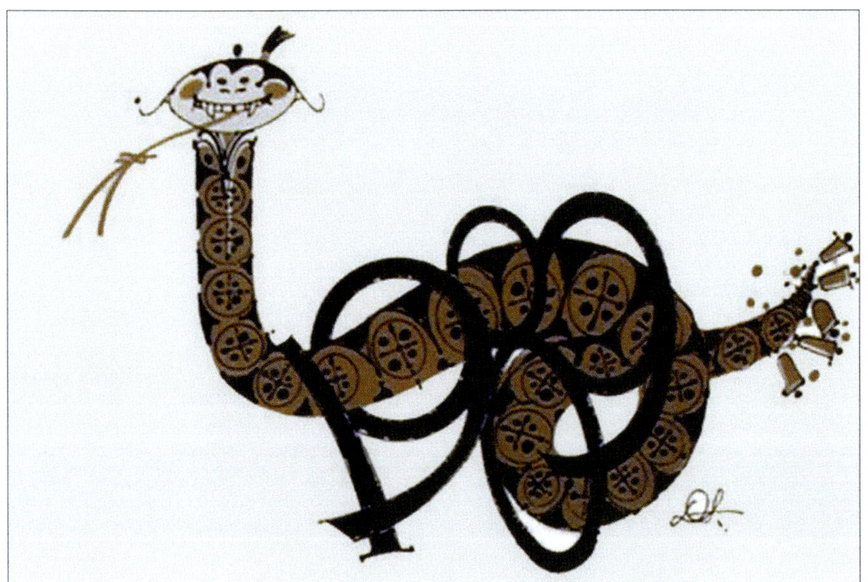

1989;
The year of the Serpent

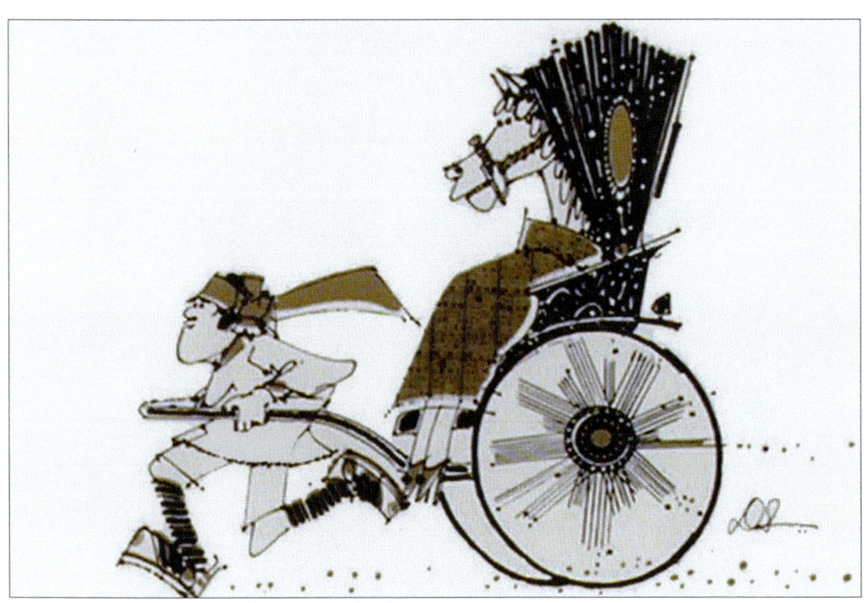

1990;
The year of the Horse

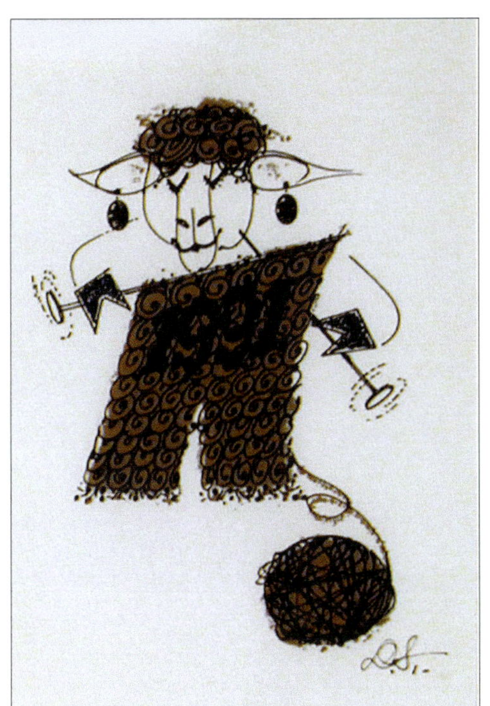

1991;
The year of the Sheep

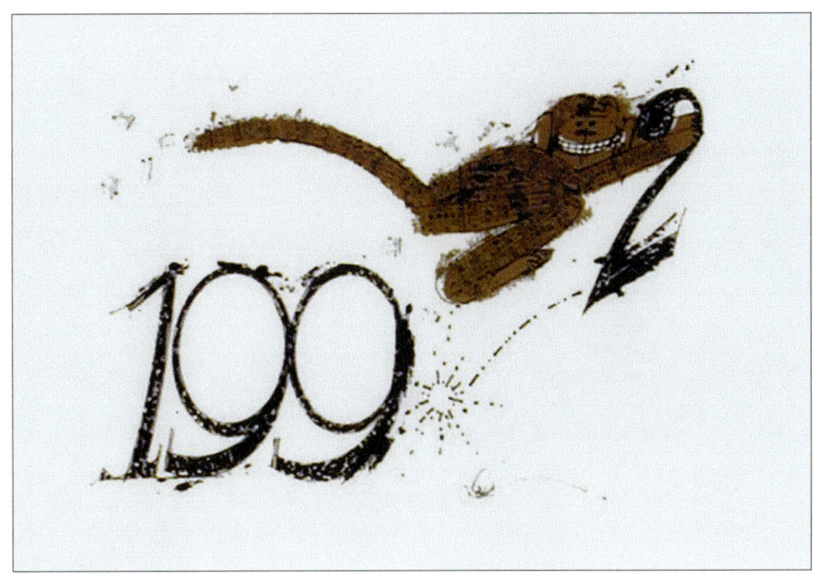

1992;
The year of the Monkey

1994;
The year of the Dog

"Gaijin" artist

During Donald Silverstein's 10-year residency in Japan, he had participated to show his works, including one-man shows.

- 1983: International Artist Exhibition, at
  Mitsubishi Gallery, Tokyo.
- 1984: Tokyo Metropolitan Museum of Art.
- 1989: One-man show; Aki-Ex Gallery, Tokyo.
- 1992: One-man show; Shirota Gallery, Tokyo
  and several more.

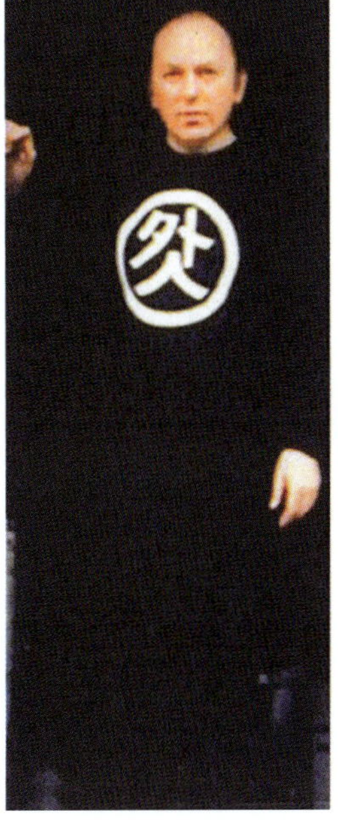

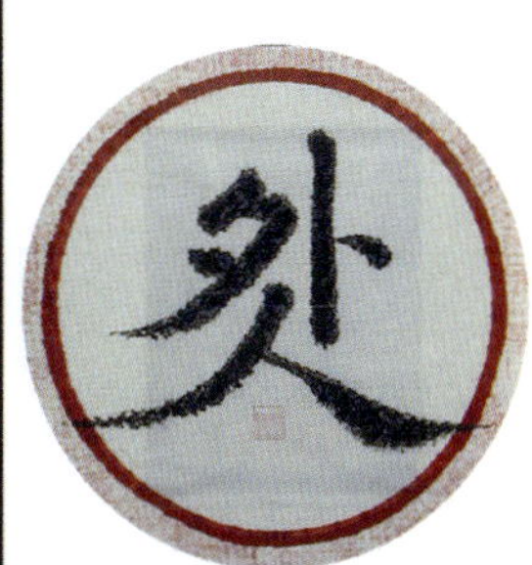

"Gaijin, the foreigner"
Donald's recreation from
Japanese calligraphy:
stamped ink on fabric.
12" diameter.

P.S. XI

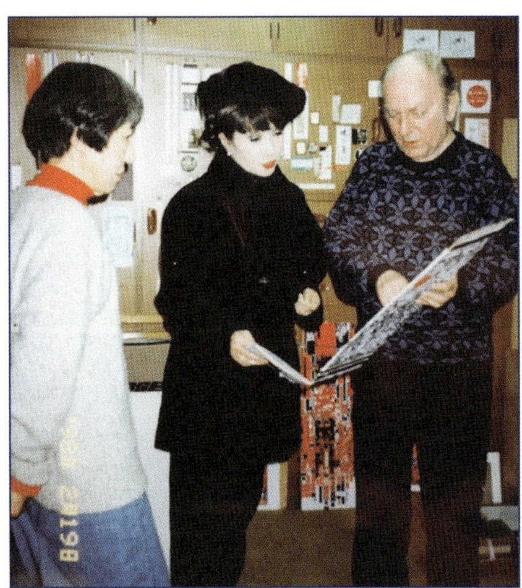

Sakiko, Ms. Tetsuko Kuroyanagi, & Donald.

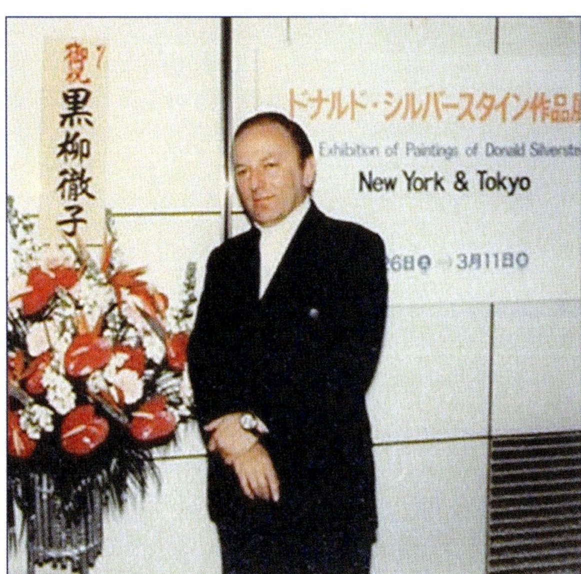

Donald, being allergic to flowers, is about to sneeze.

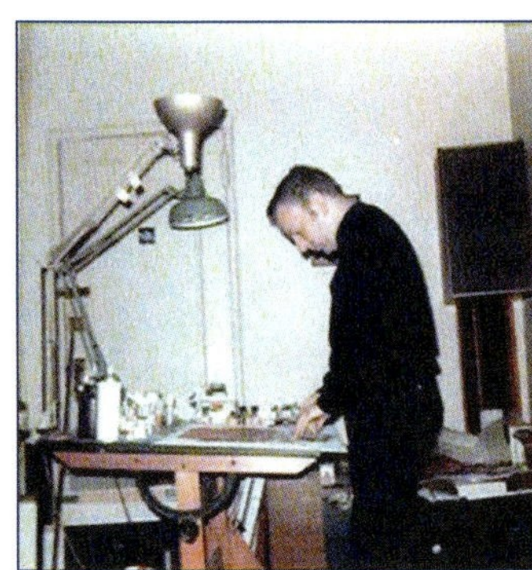

Don discusses his work with his lamp.

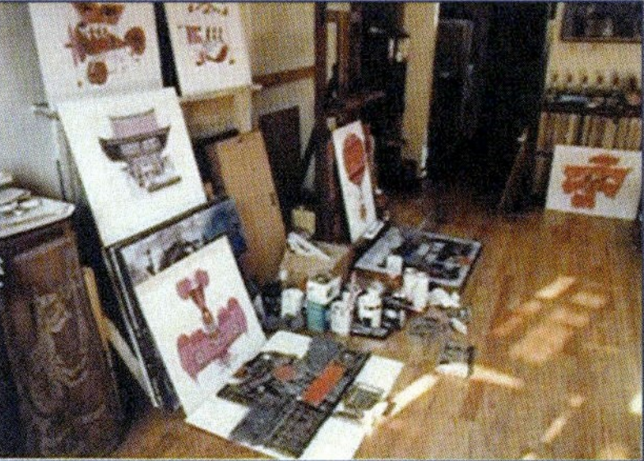

During the night, someone (probably Donald), is sure to trip over all of this stuff!

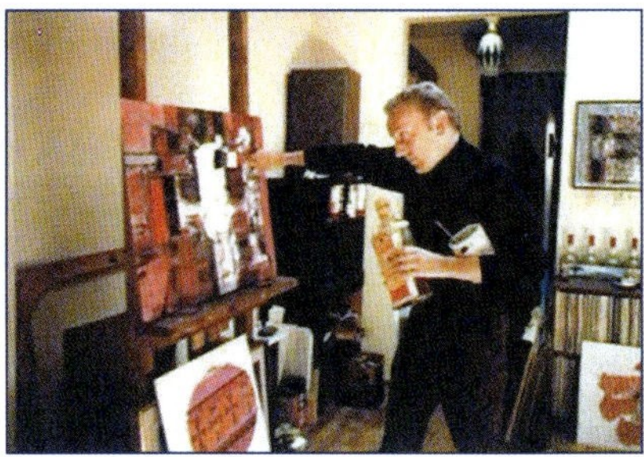

Oil and water may not mix, but acrylics and alcohol do!!!

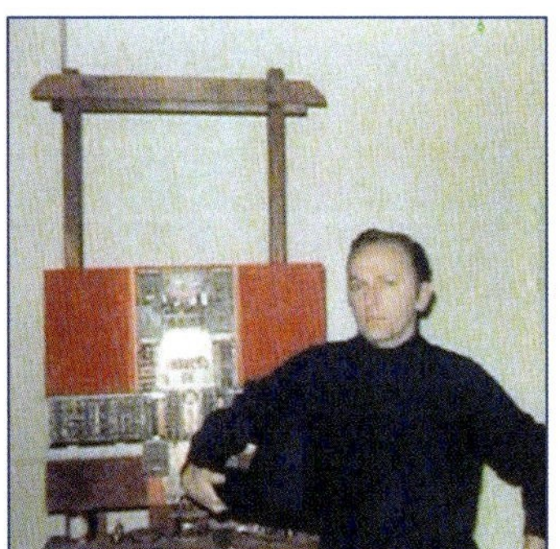

I'd much rather be a cowboy!

Note: Above captions were written by Harry Borgman.

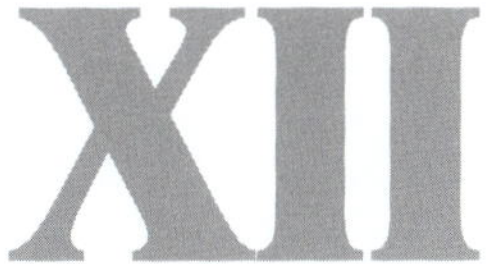

XII

R.I.P.

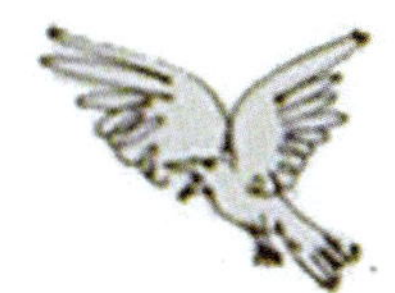

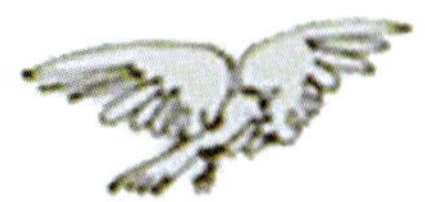

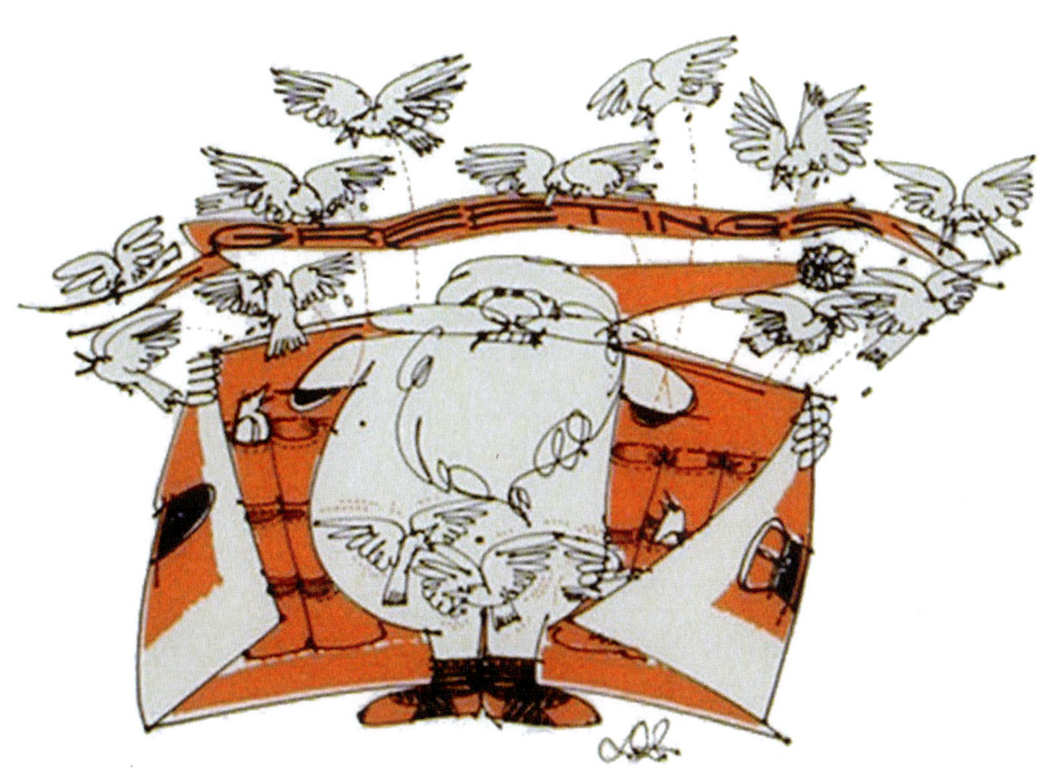

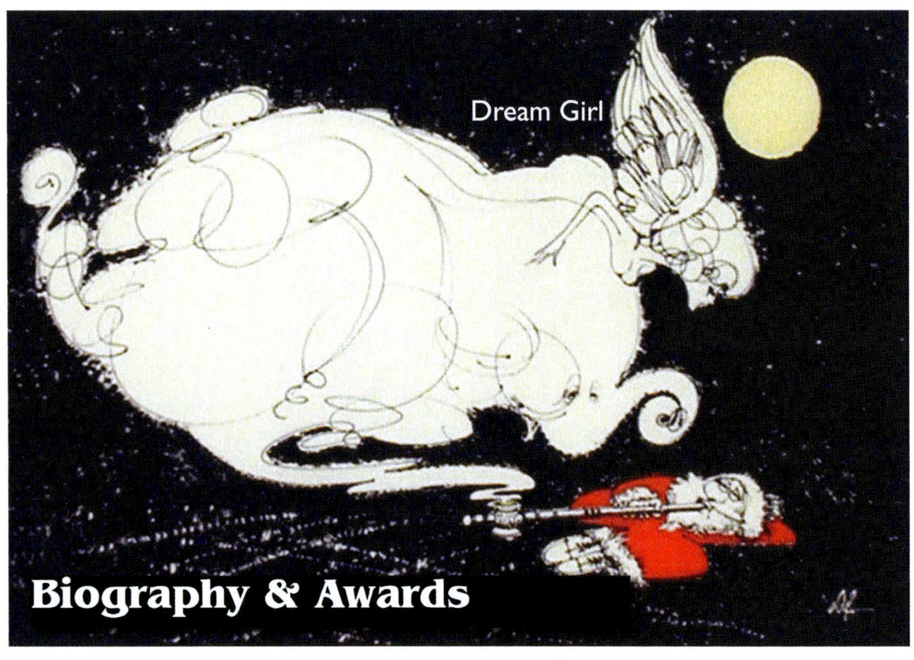

1932: Donald Silverstein was born in Wilkes-Barre, Pennsylvania.

1938: The Silversteins move to Detroit, Michigan.

1949: Upon graduation from the Society of Arts and Crafts in Detroit, Donald started to work at Allied Artists art studio as an illustrator. Does work for Ford Times Magazine.

1950: Donald wins the "Michigan State Award."

1951: Donald again wins the "Michigan State Award."

1952: Donald is drafted into the U.S. Army, and is stationed in Alaska during the Korean War.

1954: After his discharge, Donald begins to work at New Center Studios in Detroit.

1955: Donald leaves New Center Studio and joins MDM Studios in Detroit.

1955~1961: Works as illustrator at New Center Studios.

1960: Receives award "Exhibition for Michigan Artists" by the Detroit Institute of Arts.

1962: Moves to London, England, for two years. Works for various publishers and advertising agencies as an illustrator.

1964: Moves to New York working various publishers and advertising agencies as an illustrator.

1967: Donald's illustrated poster "The Viking" wins the "Award of Excellence" by the Society of Illustrators, New York.

1968: Travels from New York to the Pacific Rim — Japan, Hong Kong, Thai, Singapore, Vietnam, Borneo, Australia, and Fiji Island.

1969: Moves to Carefree, Arizona.

1970: Marrys to Sakiko, a fashion designer.

1972: Lives in Los Angeles for 6 months. Donald's illustration of "The ABC Dog Show," published by Bowma, California, wins "the Best Children's Illustration of the Year (1974)" of West Coast Illustration Award. Later that year, he and Sakiko moved back to New York.

1973: Moves to West Redding, Connecticut, where Donald works on his own paintings.

1982: Moves to Chiba, Japan. Donald works for publishers in Tokyo, as an illustrator. Meanwhile, he develops his own fine art paintings, and holds several one-man art shows.

1992: Donald and Sakiko lived in Port Said, Egypt for 6 months.

1993: Moves to Riverdale, New York.

1994: Donald has health problems, has surgery, is hospitalized, and has rehabilitation for six months.

1998: Donald and Sakiko move to the Midtown Manhattan.

2004: On January 30, Donald Silverstein dies. He was almost 72.

P.S. XII:

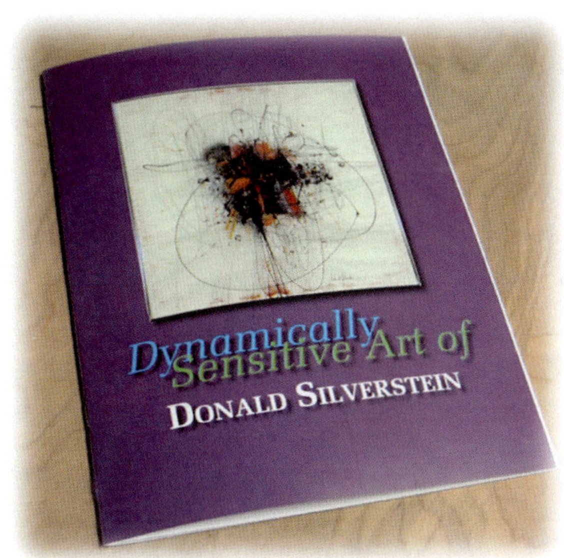

Donald Silverstein
had been an unique illustrator.

He had another impressive talent.
As a fine artist,
Donald Silverstein
had been
a pure,
dynamic yet sensitive
fine artist.

You will be convinced
of that when you see his art book:
**"Dynamically Sensitive Art of
Donald Silverstein"**
Ask Sakiko to obtain a copy;
sakiko@gallerySakiko.com

Printed in Great Britain
by Amazon

81783152R00067